1/12

PRAISE FOR
THE SELF-EMPLOYED WOMAN'S GUIDE TO LAUNCHING A HOME-BASED BUSINESS

"Priscilla Huff is the authority for the self-employed woman. Buy this book, it's a gold mine of valuable information!"

—Rosalie Marcus, women's business success coach,
www.bestbiztips.com

"There are few people who know more about home-based businesses for women than Priscilla Huff. Her insights, experiences, and advice are an invaluable resource for even seasoned business professionals. I wish I had had her how-tos when I started my first company. I would have saved years of mistakes and thousands of dollars."

—Maria T. Bailey, founder, BlueSuitMom.com
and author of *The Women's Home-Based Business Book of Answers*

"Plenty of resources and practical tips to help you fulfill your dream of owning a successful home business."

—Patricia C. Gallagher, author and creator of the
"Send a Team of Angels" movement,
www.teamofangelshelpme.com

"Priscilla Huff has taken the guesswork out of home business start-ups. This comprehensive book is destined to become the preferred resource of entrepreneurial women everywhere. Thanks for paving the way, Priscilla."

—Kim Lisi, managing editor,
HOMEBusiness Journal

W9-CEK-052

Also by Priscilla Y. Huff

101 Best Home-Based Businesses for Women, 3rd Edition

101 Best Home-Business Success Secrets for Women

101 Best Small Businesses for Women

HerVenture.com

More 101 Best Home-Based Businesses for Women

PRISCILLA Y. HUFF

The
Self-Employed Woman's
Guide to
Launching a
Home-Based Business

 THREE RIVERS PRESS · NEW YORK

Published by Three Rivers Press, New York, New York.
Member of the Crown Publishing Group, a division of Random House, Inc.
www.crownpublishing.com

THREE RIVERS PRESS and the Tugboat design are registered trademarks of Random House, Inc.

Originally published by Prima Publishing, Roseville, California, in 2002.

Disclaimer:
This book contains information of a general nature regarding starting and operating a business. It is not intended as a substitute for professional, legal, or financial advice. As many laws may vary from state to state (or province and territories), readers should consult a competent legal or financial professional regarding their own particular business. In addition, readers should understand that the business world is highly dynamic and contains certain risks. Therefore, the author and publisher cannot warrant or guarantee that the use of any information contained in this book will work in any given situation.

Printed in the United States of America

Library of Congress Cataloging-in-Publication Data
Huff, Priscilla Y.
    The self-employed woman's guide to launching a home-based business/ author, Priscilla Y. Huff
      p.   cm.
    Includes index.
      1. Home-based businesses. 2. Women-owned business enterprises-Management. 3. New business enterprises-Management. 4. Self-employed. I. Title.
    HD62.38 .H844 2002
    658.1'141-dc21   2002066277
    ISBN 0-7615-6350-4

10 9 8 7 6 5 4 3 2

First Edition

*To self-employed women everywhere
who embody the entrepreneurial spirit—
their way!!*

*And to the memory of my best friend,
the Reverend Pamela Chomitzky,
who pursued her own dream and achieved it—
even if only for that one short, but glorious year!!*

CONTENTS

PREFACE:
A HOME BUSINESS
AND *YOU!*

When I first began writing about self-employed women back in the eighties, it was primarily about women who were "pioneers" in the burgeoning home business movement. Though they really were not aware they were at the forefront of a new entrepreneurial trend, they had begun to question our society's expectations of the new twentieth-century woman (dare I say "liberated" woman?) having a full-time career, a family, and at the same time, a meaningful relationship with a significant "other." As one woman told me, "I believe what my T-shirt says: 'I am woman, I am invincible, and I am tired!!' "

Some were becoming frustrated in their workplaces with the empty promises of advancement and angered that their opinions did not always carry the same weight as those of their male counterparts or that they did not receive the same pay rate or salary in a comparable job. Others were finding it difficult to work full time and balance the needs of their families, especially when an unexpected family "crisis" or illness occurred. While various employers were sympathetic, many were not, resulting in women being laid off or fired because of time lost. Still other women were less than pleased at their career choices and desired to work at something they enjoyed doing, such as an outgrowth from a hobby or a previous volunteer experience.

Having more flexibility and control in their work lives was, and continues to be, a motivating factor in starting not just a home business, but in owning any type of business. As one woman, a certified counselor specializing in counseling women and girls, states on her business card: "Destiny is shaped by our choices." Basically, women (and men!) want that freedom to choose what they do in their lives.

This new twenty-first century will hopefully offer more work-life opportunities that can be "customized" to fit an individual's needs rather than following corporations' rules of work. Thus the mission of this book is to present to women everywhere practical information to start a successful home business that best suits their lives and their future. The book will not answer all your home business questions, but I have strived to (1) comprehensively cover as many home business basics as possible for your startup; and (2) to provide you with the most helpful resources I could find. If you have questions or comments concerning home businesses or women's self-employment, I invite you to send me an e-mail at pyhuff@ hotmail.com, and write in the subject line, "Home-Based Business Question." I will do my best to find the answer for your question. You can also ask for the latest information about any e-zines and Web sites that I am currently publishing and operating that will provide up-to-date information for a self-employed woman.

I do not promise that by reading this book you will make a million dollars in your venture, but I sincerely hope that it will be a launching pad to your home business success. Please note that there are many other good books, publications, Web sites, and other entrepreneurs who can also assist you in your entrepreneurial quest. Gather as much information as you need, from as many resources as you can. Then, when you feel you are ready, just do it! If the tragic events on September 11, 2001, taught us anything, it is that there are no guarantees for tomorrow, so go forward today and begin to pursue and achieve your dreams!

101 best wishes for entrepreneurial success!!

Introduction

This book includes my basic self-employment overview as the first chapter. It is meant to be an outline of self-employment basics—an introduction to the most important considerations of working for oneself or a quick review to those already familiar with the requirements of running a venture.

In this business starter, look for the following sidebars for tips, ideas, and for some fun, business-related humor:

Smile!	Business anecdotes to make you smile
Get Real!	What *really* works as opposed to what is written in business textbooks
Money$aving Tips	Moneysaving tips
EXTRA!!	News you can use—data on home-based businesses and self-employed women
Profile	Short feature on a successful self-employed woman
WARNING!!	Tips to help prevent business troubles
Related Resources	Books and publications (print and online), associations, and additional helpful sources that will help a self-employed woman in her quest to work for herself
SEW's Suggestions	Self-employed woman's tips

If you are not satisfied with the information in this book, that's good! Especially as an entrepreneur, you should *never* gather your information from just one source. In a quick search on a popular on-line bookstore, I found 309 books listed under women's business; 176 listed for self-employment; and 42 related to self-employed women. Of course, there are also print and online publications, organizations, and many, many Web sites that will provide you with all the answers (and more!) to your self-employment questions.

From all these resources, make a list of your favorites and refer to them frequently as you begin and operate your self-employed venture. As you read this book (and any of the others I've written), please feel free to contact me (see page xii) with your self-employment questions, or let me know your opinions or experiences as a self-employed woman. I will be happy to respond to your comments or assist you as soon as possible.

Self-employment may or may not be the best option for you, but you will never know unless you conduct thorough research of all that is involved and actually try it. If being self-employed does not work out for you, you might try it again during another time of your life—perhaps when you have fewer commitments and more money and time to invest. If self-employment does "agree" with you and your life, know that you are not alone. You have joined the millions of women in the U.S. and around the world who are working for themselves!

CHAPTER ONE

A Woman's Guide to Self-Employment— An Overview

Just who is the self-employed woman? According to the U.S. Census Bureau, approximately 20 million+ people in the U.S. are self-employed (though estimates vary according to which agency or organization has gathered the data). This includes women and men who work for themselves in some capacity, whether as free agents, independent contractors, or owners of part- or full-time businesses. Interestingly, the IRS Statistics of Income in 1998 recorded over 17.4 million sole-proprietorship tax filings. The Census Bureau says that between the years 1988 and 1996, the rate of women who became self-employed grew five times faster than the rate of men.

Then there are the number of women who own businesses and are technically considered self-employed. The Center for Women's Business Research (founded as the National Foundation for Women Business Owners), www.womensbusinessresearch.org, estimated that as of 2002, approximately 6.2 million majority-owned, privately held women-owned firms in the U.S. employed 9.2 million people and generated $1.15 trillion in sales.

We can surmise from this data that the number of self-employed women continues to grow at a fairly rapid rate, and will continue to grow in this new century as women search for a work life that will satisfy their needs. Realize, too, that for one reason or another, many women—including those working "under the table" for friends,

1

families, or as unofficial temporary workers who do not file tax returns or file under other classifications—are not included in these figures. (Unreported self-employment is not legal; nevertheless, it often occurs.)

What do all these self-employed women do? Here are just a few examples of women that I know:

- The technical writer who works on independent projects for companies
- The small business owner of a retail shop that has a thriving mail-order sideline business
- The home baker who makes a variety of cheesecakes from her licensed home kitchen for caterers and special customers
- The woman who helps out in a family member's business during busy times of the year
- The mother of two who works from home for a moving company, making calls across the country to confirm moving dates
- The grandmother who does desktop publishing of promotional materials for local real estate brokers
- The many women doing seasonal work such as landscaping or lawn mowing, summer child care for school-age children, substitute teaching, camp counseling, sports counseling, swim teaching, pet-sitting, and other services to earn income to help support themselves or their families.

Of course, women who work without reporting income are not only doing so illegally, but some face the possible consequences of having no health insurance, no worker's compensation should they be injured while working at these jobs, no legal recourse should they be sexually harassed, and they sometimes risk threats to their safety and overall welfare. So, if you are contemplating self-employment, do it legally for two reasons: (1) it is the law, and (2) you must think of your own welfare first!

Pros and Cons of Self-Employment

Why are so many people, especially women, choosing self-employment options?

Some—especially in today's economy—start because they have been laid off; others are not sure of their job security. Still others choose to work for themselves because they are frustrated by the lack of advancement opportunities and challenges at their present positions, have reached an age that brings a desire for change, know they can do the same (or better) work for themselves, wish to do work they enjoy, or have family-related concerns that make self-employment an attractive option.

If you have always dreamed of working for yourself for any of these reasons (or for your own reasons), now is the time to research the possibilities. Even though you may want to give notice to your present employer and start working for yourself tomorrow, business experts advise that you take your time to research all aspects of self-employment before you write your letter of resignation. To get you thinking, here are some pros and cons of being self-employed:

Con: You are responsible for performing and overseeing all the work and operations.

Pro: You have more control over what types of work you do and for whom you do it. If you should become overwhelmed with operational tasks, you can always outsource some of the duties and/or partner with other self-employed women.

Con: Your self-employment may lead to unresolved conflicts between your work responsibilities and your family.

Pro: You have more independence and flexibility in arranging your schedule around your personal life and/or needs of your family. There are also a number of advantages to involving your family in your self-employment ventures.

Con: Your self-employment option will most likely demand more hours be devoted to it, especially at the startup phase, than a 9-to-5 job.

Pro: You can set your own hours to those times that you work most productively.

Con: It may take six months or longer until you begin earning profits.

Pro: The overall potential for earning more money at your self-employment venture is generally greater than working for someone else.

Con: Self-employed workers face other problems such as isolation, lack of health insurance, and difficulty in getting business.

Pro: You are not alone! By looking in your area (or on the Internet), you can most likely find local business ownership organizations that can offer you affordable health insurance, assist you in finding resources to answer all your questions, and provide contact with other self-employed individuals with whom you can exchange information.

Self-employment is not the best work choice for everyone. Only you can assess whether it's right for you. Should you decide to go for it, you may be making one of the most exciting and challenging decisions of your life!

Self-Employed Women— Common Characteristics

Though each is an individual, successful self-employed women share several characteristics. These women are . . .

- *Persistent:* Self-employed women never stop searching for answers to their questions. They know there is a solution to every problem and they do not give up until they find it!
- *Creative Problem-Solvers:* They definitely "think outside the box" as they meet the everyday challenges of self-employment.
- *Nonstop Learners:* Self-employed women are the first to admit when they do not know something. They will ask for guidance or expert advice when they need it or will take the necessary courses and/or training to gain the skills and knowledge to succeed.
- *Natural at Networking:* Let's admit it (at the risk of sounding sexist), most women love to talk! Most self-employed women are willing to share valuable business tips with one another, serve as mentors to other women and young entrepreneurs, and give referrals to potential customers.
- *Not Afraid to Say "No":* They learn quickly that the "woman who can do it all" is a fictional character, and that they must

Get Real! Shadowing

If you really want to know what a self-employed woman's life is like, consider attending a women's entrepreneur conference, listening to business chats, and/or talking to as many self-employed women in your area as you can. If possible, shadow one or more of these women as they go about their daily schedules, and you will begin to see what is involved when a woman works for herself. You may experience the additional benefit of gaining a mentor.

"pace" their business activities even if that means turning clients away.

- *Good Managers:* Self-employed women are good time, financial, and people managers. They make the most of their time, monitor regularly their personal and business finances, price their products and/or services wisely, plan for their business and their retirement, and know how to treat customers and business associates with quality service and respect.
- *Multitaskers:* They are good at simultaneously juggling business tasks and, sometimes, personal ones as they go about their days' activities in order to accomplish what needs to be done.
- *Not Afraid to Have Fun:* They love being self-employed, either working on their own or running a business with employees, but they do not take themselves too seriously. They laugh at their mistakes, take time to build a snowman with their children, make friends with their customers, and exhibit joy and a positive attitude toward their work.

Your Family and Self-Employment: The "Balancing Act"

If you have children or are the primary caregiver of older parents or another person, you will face the challenges of performing your work interspersed with running errands, helping your teenager with a major homework project (due tomorrow, of course!), and maintaining the household. Women all over the world are facing the same challenges as they try to bring in an income and meet the needs of those they love.

Whether she works as an employee or for herself, each working woman has to perform her own "balancing act."

Preparation and Support

You will be more likely to succeed at your self-employment venture if you have your family's and life partner's support. Even when they do back you, it is also important that you discuss all the good (and bad) consequences of your decision. Here are some discussion topics and tips for preparing your family:

- *Time:* Let them know that you will be devoting a good amount of time to your new venture, but that you will be available "after hours" (which you will set) and, of course, for emergencies.
- *Sacrifice:* The household budget may be tighter, especially if you stop a full-time position to start your venture.
- *Help:* You are going to need assistance with errands, household chores, or business matters if you become busy.
- *Pluses:* You will have a more flexible schedule that may enable you to do some activities more easily than when you worked for an employer, such as attending sporting or community events in which your children participate.
- *Honesty:* Do not make big promises. Instead, tell your family that you are not exactly sure how your self-employed endeavor is going to affect the family and that there are risks. Emphasize that you will be "open" to frank comments at any time—and mean what you say.

Here are several suggestions to foster support from your family:

- *Delegate:* Ask family members to take over some of the household chores, according to their ages and interests. Do not expect "perfection" in how they do a task that you used to do. Let them do their household tasks while you work.

PROFILE: Bert Schwarz, Bucks Trading Post

Bert Schwarz, owner of Bucks Trading Post (www.buckstrading
post.com) exemplifies the self-employed woman's spirit in her persistence to learn what "she needs to know for her business." She
opened a retail shop twenty years ago in a barn located next to her
house, selling antique collectibles and furniture. She taught herself
computer skills and software use to manage her store's daily operations, bookkeeping, and customer mailing list, and she learned how
to use trade shows to market her products. Then she developed a
profitable sideline mail-order business selling lace curtains and home
décor items to customers all over the world. Next, Bert took her
business online with her Web site and is currently developing an informative e-zine for her customers. She never stops learning!

- *Respect:* Expect your family to respect your time and efforts for
  your venture; in turn, respect their opinions.
- *Communicate:* Schedule family meetings regularly and whenever
  a clash occurs. Have a family calendar in a central location and
  insist that everyone write down scheduled meetings, large homework projects, and other upcoming events to prevent conflicts.
- *Reward:* Pam, a self-employed bookkeeper, always took her
  family on a week's vacation at a nearby resort after her busy
  tax season. If you get a big contract or complete a demanding
  project, reward your family with a special outing or treat.

For many of today's women, working is essential in order to
bring in an income to help support their families, thus your family
is likely to find your becoming self-employed more acceptable than
did families of a few decades ago. Expect some adjustment at first,
which a good sense of humor can make easier—as can reminding
yourself that you are a role model to inspire your family to find
their ideal work someday.

Tips from Successful Women

- *Find other self-employed women and form a playgroup with your children.* As each mother takes a turn hosting the children, the others can get work accomplished in that block of time.

   Work "off hours" while your children or others in your home are sleeping, away at school, or at appointments; or work while a spouse or other family member relieves you.

   Two women, both software designers, "share" a nanny by having her come alternate days to care for their young children in their homes while they work. Other women hire a "mother's helper" for those after-school hours.
- *Simplify your life and prioritize.* Make a list of the most important people and activities in your life and make time for them, and cut back on some of your other commitments. Instead of being the head of a community group, volunteer to direct just one event or be a worker. Keep an hourly time chart of your activities for a week (be honest!) and then check it for wasted time. You must free up some time for your new venture.

HIRING FRIENDS AND FAMILY

In our country's past, families worked together in businesses, on farms, and in small shops. Children grew up learning the family business, which was often passed on from generation to generation. In the not-so-distant past, the owner of a large local car dealership had his three daughters work in his business as teenagers and then as college students. All three received graduate degrees as well as an astute sense of business management from that firsthand experience.

   Hiring family members has definite pluses: certain tax advantages, familiarity, and a legacy for future generations. On the other hand, hiring family members can lead to stress because treating each of them as "just another employee" can lead to arguments

Get Real! Home Sweet Home?

If you visualize working in your nice little home office while everyone around you stays happy, realize that you will have many extremely stressful days (probably more often than not) in trying to juggle your life and self-employment. Just when an important client returns your phone call, the doorbell will ring, the dog will bark, and your children will fight over who will answer the door. How can you deal with the daily stress? Here are several suggestions:

- *Give yourself periodic stress breaks.* Promise yourself you will take a hot bath, take a quiet walk, read a chapter from that exciting mystery novel, watch a movie or a favorite TV program, or engage in some other activity not associated with your work at all.
- *Work in blocks of time,* especially when you're unlikely to be uninterrupted.
- *Do not make your "to-do" list too long.* Try to pace your workload so you can realistically accomplish what you plan to do.
- *Keep a good sense of humor.* Laughter can help you get through most situations.
- *Learn to work midst the "chaos."* On days when you have child care, concentrate on the tasks that need complete concentration and save the jobs that can be done with the children around. Then, include them in business tasks they can handle. Make full use of technology— voice mail, cell phones (mute buttons to block out noise), fax machines, and e-mail to help you keep in touch with customers while you are dishing out a meal, refereeing a sibling squabble, or taking some family member to the doctor. Set limits for your children, but enjoy that time with them, too, as hectic as it may be. So, work in blocks of time, in-between the children's goings on.

and/or conflicts of interest. You may want to meet with a business consultant who specializes in handling family business issues.

If your business expands or has busy seasonal times, you may consider hiring a friend or two. As for pluses, you know the person's background and are likely to have fun working together. Minuses include the possibility of permanent damage to your friendship should hard feelings develop when your friend makes a mistake or misunderstands a payment issue.

If you, family, or friends know what is expected of one another and are able to keep a professional attitude, working together can be a fulfilling learning experience. It really is your "call," and one that you should consider carefully so that you do not alienate one another.

Choosing the Best Self-Employment Option

If you have been thinking of working for yourself, no doubt you have also given thought as to what you will do. But you are more likely to find the best self-employed option for you if you first do an objective personal assessment.

PERSONAL ASSESSMENT—KNOW THYSELF!

One good way to assess yourself is to write your resume, or update it if you already have one. A typical resume will list your qualifications, strengths, work history, education and training, volunteer and community participation, hobbies, interests, activities, and references.

Qualifications: The measurable knowledge and training you have gained through education, lessons, courses, on-the-job experiences, and apprenticeships.

Strengths: The intangible personality characteristics you possess. This is not always placed on a resume and may be difficult to assess. You can ask others who know you to give you their opinion of what inner qualities they believe you possess, what they believe you do well.

Get Real! Your Partner's Support

Okay, this is the start of the new millennium, when women do not need "permission" from their husbands or "significant others" to begin a venture. Still, if you share life goals together, discussing your work option with your life partner shows respect and consideration. Azriela Jaffe, author of ten books including *Honey, I Want to Start My Own Business: A Planning Guide for Couples,* advises, "Speak to him about what the benefits are for him, instead of trying to convince him to support the benefits for you!"

Work History: A listing of your present and former jobs, including each job's duties and responsibilities.

Education and Training: Part of your qualifications, but you can specifically list the institutions, schools, and/or any additional place(s) where you may have learned specific skills.

Volunteer and Community Participation: Organizing and directing a memorial sports tournament may not have paid you anything, but the leadership and organizational skills you gained are very important in directing your own venture. Such activities also enabled you to become acquainted with many people in your community who can be valuable sources of leads for potential customers.

Hobbies, Interests, Activities: What you do in your free time—usually what you cannot wait to do, often a passion for you.

There is one more personal question that usually does not appear on a resume: What is your dream(s)? A dream may be related to your listed skills and qualifications or something you have thought about many times, but never really experienced. If you would like to combine your dream and self-employment, then I say,

Smile!

When Pam, an independent sales representative, discovered that her three teenage daughters were putting clean clothes in the dirty clothes pile rather than putting them away in their closets or drawers, she marched them down to the laundry room and taught them how to do the wash. "From then on, their dirty wash was their responsibility," she said.

"Why not?!" As Dr. Norman Vincent Peale once said, "A dream and a plan equal a goal."

OVERCOMING FEAR

> *Do the thing you fear, and the death of fear is certain.*
> —RALPH WALDO EMERSON

Let's face it. Talking about starting a business and actually doing it are two different things! You may fear others' reactions and responses to your venture into self-employment and, worst of all, may fear failing. Yes, starting a venture is a risk and you may indeed fail at your first attempt of working for yourself, and you can expect to hear some negative comments from others. However, consider these tips:

1. *Don't be afraid of failure.* Business experts state that entrepreneurs average three attempts in starting a venture before they succeed.
2. *Learn from your mistakes.* In school you may have received an F on a test and never had a chance to retake that test. Fortunately, life is not like those school tests; you can become more knowledgeable *because* of your mistakes and failures. As you learn how to be successfully self-employed, the lessons you learn through experience will be much more lasting than those received as a red mark on a paper! As Winston Churchill said, "Never give in—never, never, never, never, in nothing great or small, large or petty, never give in except to convictions of honor and good sense."

3. *Inform yourself!* This bears repeating many times: Gather all
    the information you need before you start out; leave none of
    your startup questions unanswered. The more knowledge you
    have about your industry and what you can expect from self-
    employment, the less fear you will have. Thorough research
    may take you a year, but statistics show that an entrepreneur's
    success in a venture correlates directly to the amount of time
    spent researching the venture.
4. *Create your own support group.* Make connections with people
    who are informative, supportive, and also self-employed. Your
    business experts, mentors, and other entrepreneurs will be those
    you can turn to if you have a question or problem. So, though
    you may work alone, you will never really "be" alone.

FREE TRAINING

Many self-employed women today are using skills and training they
learned on the job. They apply those work experiences to their venture. One woman started her own bakery and breakfast café near
a railroad station after she had worked in a commercial bakery.

If you have a venture in mind, but desire to learn more about
that specific business or the industry in general, look for a job in
that industry. It will give you a firsthand picture of what a typical
day, week, month, or even year is like in such a job. Note, though,
that ethically (and maybe legally), you should not work at a company in which you will be a direct competitor and try to steal their
clients. It may be better from the start to be honest with your employer about the reason you wish to work for her. She may be one
of your first clients or she may refer clients to you that do not meet
the "target market criteria" for her business's products or sales.

PRELIMINARY RESEARCH

How does research help in finding your ideal self-employed venture? Thorough preliminary research can determine the following:

1. *Whether a potential market—customers—exists for your prod-
    uct or service!* No matter how unique or needed you think your
    product or service is, if your research reveals that no one wants

or needs what you have to offer (or will pay your prices), then you will not make money. It is as simple as that!

2. *What potential customers really want in a product or service.* If your product or service will save your customers time and/or money in some unique way, your venture should have the potential to be profitable.

3. *Whether there are potential customers whose needs are not being met.* If your research shows that your competition is not meeting the needs of certain customers, this may prove to be a "niche" market for you. For example, Maria, a licensed professional counselor and personal coach, developed a sideline coaching/counseling niche when parents of college students asked her to keep in touch with their children via e-mail.

"Matching" You and a Self-Employed Venture

Here is a list to help "match" you with your "perfect" self-employed venture. Answer "Yes" or "No" to the following questions:

1. Do you have any experience, training, or education in the industry of your venture?
2. Is this venture the kind that can be started on a part-time basis to test its profitability and potential growth?
3. Will you be able to afford the minimum startup costs and commitment of time this venture will require?
4. Have you researched the future prospects of this business—trend or fad?
5. Have you identified your best potential customers for this business and their location(s)?
6. Will this business integrate well with other activities and the important people in your life?
7. Will your product or service fulfill an untapped need?
8. Do you have a network of people, experts, and/or professional association members to whom you can turn if you need assistance with this particular venture?
9. Do you know your industry's pricing guidelines for this venture, and will your prices be competitive?
10. Is there an existing demand for your products or services?

SEW's Suggestions

Maria Bailey, CEO, BSM Media and founder of BlueSuitMom.com, states:

> Many women fear going out on their own. I make it a habit that when fear begins to surface, I always write down the "worst-case scenario." Most of us fear the unknown, but once you write down your worst fears, they are no longer unknown. They are in fact very clear to you. They are never as bad as you think they will be. As I tell my children, "You will never know unless you try." What's the worst thing that can happen? You quit your present job and don't have a paycheck for a few weeks, or maybe months? But what is the best thing that can happen? You follow your dreams and feel great because you succeeded. It's no wonder that my favorite saying is "If you do what you've always done, you'll get what you've always gotten."

11. Will you still like doing this work if some of your days require long hours of your time?

Rating

8–11 "Yes" answers	=	a good match
5–7 "Yes" answers	=	a possible match
4 or fewer "Yes" answers	=	probably not a good match at this time

(If you are still interested in this idea, do additional research.)

Goals and Plans

My mother once told me, "I do not have any formula to tell you how to be successful, but I do know that trying to please everyone will lead you to fail." How does this apply to you and self-employment? It is important in that your work will become an integral part of your life. Some will criticize you for your decision to work for yourself, while others will praise you, while still others really will not care because they're too busy with their own lives. Thus, the planning of your venture into self-employment is actually only part of your entire "life plan," and to try to live your life according to another's opinion of what you should or should not be doing is to be untrue to yourself and your dreams. Take your time to find the "real" you and be true to yourself.

BEING TRUE TO YOU

When you go about the planning and goal-setting process that will be discussed next, you may want to sit down and also figure how your venture will integrate with the aims and desires you have for the rest of your life. Sure, no plan will go exactly as was designed, because life is too uncertain; but to not try something because someone is against it robs you of the opportunity to know whether you would or would not have succeeded.

Now, conversely, you cannot completely disregard the opinions of those you care about the most (besides, they might have some good suggestions!). What is the solution? To be honest with yourself about what you really want from your life and ask others to respect that, as you will listen openly to their concerns and reasoning. But those who really care about you will not try to hold you back; instead, they'll be there as your supporters, as you would be for them. Being true to yourself by working for yourself may not make your life easy, but at least you can say, "I made my choices and without any regrets!"

BUSINESS PLAN BASICS

After some thought and deliberation, you have finally decided on an idea for a business. What's next? A business plan! Whether you put it on paper or just have one in your head, a good business plan is essential for moving your new venture forward.

A business plan is important because it is the "blueprint" for "constructing" your new home business. It really does not matter how lengthy a plan is, but a good plan should do the following:

PROFILE: Linda Pinson, president,
Out of Your Mind . . . and Into the Marketplace

Linda Pinson, president of Out of Your Mind . . . and Into the Market-place, www.business-plan.com, became a business plan expert after she attended an entrepreneurship conference and decided that she "was not very pleased" with the business seminars. She says: "After the conference, I approached colleges in my area and was immediately hired to teach entrepreneurial classes at five of them." Out of teaching those small business classes, her books were born. To accompany her books, she developed Automate Your Business Plan, software that is used nationally by the U.S. Small Business Administration's (SBA) Business Information Centers and other SBA offices.

- Provide an exact description of the products and/or services you are selling.
- Explain why you are qualified to run this business.
- Define your market—your best potential customers.
- Outline your sales and marketing plans, emphasizing the strengths and value of your business's offerings and how yours differs from your competitors'.
- Describe your business's operations—from where and how you will get your products and services to your customers.
- Include a financial plan that lists your present finances, the money your venture will need for startup, possible resources to obtain funds, and an estimate of business operation expenses.
- State your present and future goals that will be important in determining your ongoing business strategies.

Review your plan on at least a weekly basis, and do not be afraid to amend it as your new venture develops. Time spent in planning your business will increase the odds of it succeeding!

PLANS TO GOALS

Once you have a major business plan, you can then use it as the "master plan" to guide you in the specific steps you will need to take to make your self-employment a reality. Here are some tips in forming your goals for your self-employment:

- Identify your goals. Be specific.
- Write these goals down. Those who do this are more likely to accomplish their goals.
- Break down the goals into manageable steps and differentiate between the long-term and short-term ones.
- Prioritize your goals and decide which ones you can attain first.

ACHIEVING GOALS

Putting your goals on paper is one thing, but taking the action to actually achieve them is another. Here are some guidelines:

- *Be realistic in your expectations.* You may want to make a million dollars by the end of the year, but strive first to meet your venture's expenses; next, to earn a profit; and from there, see where your business grows!
- *Be prepared.* Look ahead for possible obstacles and consult with experts, if necessary, to help you get by them.
- *Keep going forward.* Even if you do not reach a specific goal as soon as you would like, just keep going ahead in your efforts. Your persistence will win out.
- *Evaluate your goals as you go along.* Your self-employment may take an unexpected turn, for the better, and you may have to revise them.
- *Enjoy the process of self-employment!* Many of your goals will require hard work and problem-solving skills, but you will derive a personal satisfaction as you accomplish each set goal.

Organizing

One of the drawbacks of starting a home business is that usually you will be responsible for *all* the operations of your venture, especially, at first when funds may be limited and you cannot afford

---

SEW's Suggestions

Deanne Bryce, owner of Leader Strength (www.LeaderStrength
.com), a corporate training company that specializes in implement-
ing leadership development processes inside organizations, offers
these suggestions for achieving one's goals:

> The most important element to achieving one's goals is desire.
> True desire is a feeling about something you want to do. It is
> a feeling that just won't go away even when you logically tell
> yourself that what you desire is hard, or doesn't make sense
> given your circumstances.
>
> Desire persists and helps you overcome obstacles like
> money, time, skills, personality styles, and knowledge. In my
> case, my personality isn't a typical entrepreneur personality. I am
> shy and prefer to be at home. I don't like being directive. In or-
> der to make it as a training consultant, you have to get out of
> the house and talk to people. I've learned to be directive in terms
> of telling people what I need . . . like telling the printer I didn't
> like the business cards he designed or telling a coach that she
> was not allowing me to make my own choices about my busi-
> ness idea. That nagging desire to design new learning processes,
> to communicate new ideas for businesses to get results from
> their employees, and to work with people to fine-tune their pur-
> pose is buried deep inside of me; and it keeps me going.

---

an office assistant. Thus, in addition to the services or products you
produce, you will also be handling your business's marketing, bookkeeping, customer orders and service, banking, and a multitude of
other tasks that normally would be handled by a paid staff in a
larger company. To efficiently manage your business's operations,
you will need to be well organized. Without good organization, you
will waste time and eventually lose money.

Debbie Williams, organizing expert and author of *Home Management 101: A Guide for Busy Parents*, recommends you consider

three organizing essentials when planning your work area: "(1) Start with a good plan; (2) Define your space; and (3) Utilize whatever storage solutions are necessary to help you keep your papers and products together."

Your home office does not have to look neat unless you want it that way (mine is not!!) or you plan to have your customers come to your office; but it *does* have to be organized in a way that works best for you. If you are having difficulty maintaining control over your work space, you may want to consult with a professional organizer (See the National Association of Professional Organizers information listed at the end of this section) who will be able to provide you with practical organizing solutions and even some helpful time-management tips. Your time is valuable and you do not want to waste it looking for a lost order or invoice!

YOUR WORK SPACE AND EQUIPMENT

A well-organized work space and the right equipment and technology for your type of work can be a major factor in the success of your self-employed venture. It is important to find a separate room or space that can be designated for your business and can remain undisturbed when you are not working.

Your work area should be free from noise and distractions; have good lighting and ventilation; have an efficient layout to allow maximum use of space and use; have adequate outlets and wiring for your equipment, phone lines, and computer hook-up; and include sufficient storage space. You will probably move your office/work space area a number of times as your venture grows or to find the best location.

You can save money by purchasing used office furniture or leasing equipment or joining an association whose membership benefits include discounts on business purchases. Your equipment should be in good working order and ready for you to use at any time. If you can afford it at your startup, purchase quality technology with enough power and capability to handle potential growth and expansion, so you will not have to continually update. If you cannot afford a large cash outlay, consider leasing or renting. Good technology is essential for controlling your output and staying in touch with your customers.

SEW's Suggestions

Here are some ideas for locating your work space:

- *Integration*—Using privacy screens, look for a quiet corner of a guest room, bedroom, study, or another room that is empty much of the day.
- *Unusual Spaces*—Transform spaces under stairways, in large closets, or even a screened-in porch, sun room, or a mud room.
- *High and Low*—Attics, basements, garages, and outbuildings are also possibilities if they can be easily remodeled to provide the right temperatures and protection from the weather.
- *Building from a Kit*—If you can afford it, you can build (or have built) a home office addition. Some companies manufacture prefab buildings specifically designed for home offices or offer modern "yurts" that can be used.

SCHEDULING

Time is a precious commodity for many of us these days. To be successful at your venture, you should schedule your activities and work to make the most of the time you have!

To organize their offices and work, most self-employed people use the following:

- *Main calendar:* Use a day planner to write in your personal schedule (do not forget to add in family time!) and your family's activities so you can coordinate them. One self-employed mother with four teenagers uses felt-tip markers, one color for each child, to highlight each family member's schedule. Other ideas include using a wipe board and carrying a pocket planner or using a well-known planner like Day-Timer (available in paper/manual and also as software). For customer service and a catalog, visit the Web site or contact Day-Timer Organizer, www.DayTimer.com, (800) 805-2615.

- *Computer:* You can use your computer to:
  1. Use online calendar services and operate contact manager software such as Contact Manager (Symantec's ACT, www.symantec.com).
  2. Keep track of business correspondence, to store letter templates, and to set up filters to direct and separate those e-mail messages directly related to your business.
- *Communications:* Use voice-mail boxes on both your ground line and cellular phones to separate personal and business calls.
- *Electronic Planners:* These are good for balancing your time between your venture and your home life, and for people who do not like to write lists. PDAs (personal digital assistants) are available through Sharp, www.sharp-usa.com.

To find a professional organizer, contact the National Association of Professional Organizers, www.napo.net/ P.O. Box 140647, Austin TX 78714; Referral Line: (512) 454-8626; Fax: (512) 454-3036.

Bookkeeping Basics

It is very important that you know the basic elements of bookkeeping and record keeping for your venture. Keeping accurate financial records is crucial for your business's growth and survival. You should know every day how much money is coming in from receivables and going out in payables and whether or not you are making a profit. A good bookkeeping system can do the following:

- Help you correctly price your product and/or service.
- Help you figure out your profits or losses on each job and whether you are running a profitable venture.
- Help you assess your cash flow—short and long term. Your cash flow is the money you have after all your expenses are paid. A long-term cash flow will indicate if you will be able to meet future bills and if you will be making a profit.

SEW's SUGGESTIONS

A good accounting software program is worth every dollar you spend on it—*when* it is suitable for your business and *when* you know how to utilize all its features. Software versions can help you keep track of local, state, and federal tax accounts; create a budget for your business; produce invoices; maintain payroll accounts; offer financial calculators for loans; and perform any number of other tasks that will help keep you solvent. Look to area colleges or business schools, Small Business Development Centers, Women's Business Centers, or even private tutors to help you learn the accounting program you need. Do not forget to check with your industry association or organization for software designed specifically for your type of business.

- Help you work with lenders. In loan applications or approaching investors, having your financial records and projections will demonstrate to potential lenders your capacity to pay back a loan.
- Keep you up to date with your tax obligations and payments.

CHOOSING FINANCIAL EXPERTS

Business experts recommend that you include a consultation with an accountant in your startup costs. Many accountants belong to local business organizations, or you can ask other self-employed women for referrals. An accountant may also be able to recommend a bookkeeper to help you set up and manage your accounts. One woman bookkeeper included training on popular accounting software in her small business services for her clients to make *her* job easier!

A FINANCIAL PLAN

Besides your business plan and managing your business's cash flow, you should form a financial plan that incorporates your business's income and your personal financial goals. Here are several questions you can ask yourself in formulating your financial plan:

- What are your immediate financial goals? For your business? For yourself?
- What are your future financial goals? For your business? For yourself? In one year? In five and ten years?
- Once you reach your financial goals, do you plan to continue to work for yourself?
- If you had enough money, would you expand your venture, try a different one, or maybe start a nonprofit foundation?

If you can afford it, consult a professional financial advisor or planner who will have many more questions for you. She can help you boost your cash flow, increase your profits, and assist you in planning for your retirement. You can find certified financial planners who specialize in helping small businesses or entrepreneurs. It is best to talk to more than one, and to check out the credentials and references for each of those you consult.

Tax Considerations

Keeping a regular schedule for doing your record keeping will make filing your taxes easier. Here are some tips:

- With your accountant's help, maintain a tax calendar listing your tax filing deadlines and payments.
- Document all business funds using your checkbook and/or a general ledger. This cash flow record is what may be needed should the IRS request to verify your information.
- Set up a separate bank account for your self-employment to document all your venture's financial transactions.
- Keep a record of all your cash expenditures and income.
- If you have access to the Internet, visit the SBA's Online Women's Business Center at www.onlinewbc.gov/docs/finance/. This site has a "Finance Center" that includes much information about bookkeeping and accounting. Also visit the IRS site (www.irs.gov/smallbiz), which has a special section for small business owners and the self-employed.
- When in doubt, consult with a tax specialist or your accountant.

PRICING GUIDELINES

Deciding the prices for your product or services is one of the most difficult tasks a self-employed woman must face. Many people, especially women, tend to undercharge. You will need to consider the costs involved, profit level desired, competitors' prices, the value you add to the product or service, and what your customers (your market) are willing to pay. Ask yourself: Will my product or service be exclusive, one-of-a-kind or mass-produced? Is my product/ service in high or low demand?

Your goal with pricing is to maximize overall profit, not the profit per product or service. It is an ongoing evaluation of the costs and time involved in running your business and meeting your customers' expectations. Here are some pricing tips:

- Use your business plan to determine your operating expenses (overhead, labor, and materials costs); taxes and insurance costs (including health insurance, if not covered); your time spent for management, marketing, and production; and the percentage you want to save for retirement savings. Keep accurate records to better analyze your time and expenses.

- Also use your business plan to determine a break-even analysis—when projected income equals costs. This figure will help you set your prices knowing that you must at least charge a certain amount to reach this point—and more than this to make a profit. For assistance in making these calculations, use accounting software specific to your industry or for businesses in general.

- Set an annual income goal but do not forget to factor in and add your taxes, overhead costs, and your profit margin. Find out whether your industry has pricing guidelines. Some trade associations publish and sell rate guides.

  (*Note:* As a one-person enterprise, it is impossible to work 2,000 hours per year—based on fifty 40-hour work weeks, with two weeks for vacation—as you will be involved in marketing and the other business operations. You will only be able to "bill" approximately 1,000 hours a year.)

- Research and compare your prices to your competitors' and set them accordingly. This does not mean you should offer lower

SEW's Suggestions

If you are so busy that you cannot schedule any more work hours, it is time to raise your prices. Two women who partnered a clowning business were overwhelmed with requests for their entertainment services, so they raised their rates. "We had fewer parties, but we actually made more, plus we had more time for planning and to be with our families," they said.

prices, as customers may be willing to pay more for personal attention, better quality, or for your special niche. Pricing is actually concerned more with marketing, not what your service/product costs.

- Analyze your competitors' services to see what they do not offer (such as free delivery and pick-up, estimates, discounts for referrals to other customers), and offer that as part of your business.
- Be flexible in pricing. Be ready to adjust your prices as your business grows or your market varies.
- Offer different prices and packages from which your customers can choose. Sometimes, too, how you present your prices influences sales. To state your rate at $100 an hour, clients may be hesitant to do business with you if they do not know how many hours will be involved. Instead present a total dollar amount for the entire project (based on your hourly rate).
- For products, be aware of the psychology of pricing (for example, $3.99 sells better than $4.00!).
- With a service business, factor some room in your estimates that allows you to provide extras your customers might request. Have a signed contract listing additional charges for options in the event that a project is more complex than anticipated.

Pricing is based on an ongoing evaluation of the cost and time involved in running your business and meeting your customers' expectations. Look for ways to increase your profits by lowering your operating costs, but not at the expense of the quality your customers expect. Your prices signify the value of your product/service to your customer. Meeting with your accountant each quarter—especially in your startup years—is one of the wisest investments you can make. She can help you set realistic financial goals while helping insure your business will continue to be a profit-making venture.

Legal Considerations

While working for yourself or starting a home business, you must not overlook the legalities involved. If you are challenged, pleading ignorance will not be accepted as a defense.

CHOOSING A LAWYER

Your list of professional experts should include a lawyer in the event you need one for your self-employed venture. Whether through assisting you in registering your name, setting up your legal structure, writing contracts, or representing you in litigation, your lawyer can help keep you out of legal trouble. To find a lawyer, seek referrals from those whose opinions you value, or contact a lawyer referral group in your area. Interview several lawyers before you choose one and make sure that she is familiar with self-employment and small business legal matters. (See chapter 4, Home Business Startup Basics, for more legal information.)

Insurance Concerns

Make sure you get adequate insurance coverage as a self-employed individual. Do not assume that personal insurance or home policies cover business liability and equipment. (*Note:* Some companies will require you to have a certificate of insurance stating that you have a certain monetary amount of liability coverage.) Talk to a licensed insurance agent who can make professional recommendations as to the types of coverage you need (different types of work require different insurances). Some agents specialize in just one type of insurance, while others handle more than one and will search for the best policy to fit your personal and self-employment needs.

Briefly, some of the types of insurances you may need for your home business include property, vehicle (especially if one is essential to deliver your goods or services), liability, business interruption, disability, and health insurance.

Talk with other self-employed women about their insurances and their coverage and talk to agents licensed in the specific insurance that you need.

Professionalism and Ethics

True, one of the advantages of working from home is that you can work in jeans and a sweatshirt (unless, of course, you meet clients in your home office), work when you want, and generally run your business your way. However, no matter how small or casual your business is, you must operate it with professionalism if you want to be taken seriously and respected by your customers as well as by others in your industry.

You are a professional when you . . .

- Treat all clients and customers as individuals and with respect.
- Deliver what you promise (and a little more) to clients and business associates.
- Project a polished business image through your promotional materials.
- Utilize effective communications that enable your clients to reach you.
- Return clients' phone calls promptly.
- Set regular business hours.
- Remember to say "thank you" to your faithful customers.
- Strive to be honest and ethical in your dealings with customers and other business owners.
- Stay informed about the latest information and technology in your industry.
- Keep thinking about new services or products your business can offer your clients.

- Conduct yourself in a manner that establishes you as an expert in your field.
- Project confidence in yourself and your work when you talk and network with others.
- Follow a fair set of standards and ethics on how you conduct your business.

Perhaps you can add your own definition(s) of "professional." One of these might very well be "A professional is ethical." Ethics are the principles that you believe in and exhibit with your actions. In business, this means to . . .

- Be truthful in your advertising.
- Accept responsibility for your mistakes when it is your fault and make appropriate amends.
- Stress the benefits of your products or services instead of denigrating those of your competitors.
- Return money or give credit to clients who might have overpaid you.
- Try do what is right by following your instincts and staying true to your values when making difficult decisions.

Critics may say these definitions of professionalism and ethics are standards set too high, but remember that word-of-mouth referral is one of the best ways to get more business—or to ruin a business! Get a reputation of being dishonest or unethical, and you will soon find customers going to your competitors.

Marketing

Marketing is the general term describing the overall methods entrepreneurs use to get customers to purchase their products and/or services. Marketing activities include market research, pricing, public relations, advertising, marketing communications, sales and distribution, and any other means designed to create a demand for those products and/or services. In other words, your quest as a marketer is to find the best ways to let your target customers know that your product or service will benefit them.

DEVISING A MARKETING PLAN

Just as a business plan is a "blueprint" for the foundation of your business, a marketing plan is composed of tactics you will use to reach potential customers most likely to want and pay for your expertise or product. Here are some basic components you will want to include in your marketing plan:

- *Assessment of Your Business's Position:* You will want to sum up in several sentences your business's concept, strong and weak points, and how you believe your customers view your business.
- *Objectives:* After evaluating where your business is now, you will want to decide in which direction(s) you want your business to head.
- *Target Customer Profiles:* Do thorough market research to put together a "typical" customer (or customers) profile.
- *Design and Deliver:* This is a crucial part of your marketing plan. You will list your marketing objectives and begin to design a promotional strategy for each one. List as many low-cost promotional ideas as you can—talks, classes, flyers, demonstrations, press releases, and other economical ideas that you can use to achieve each marketing goal. Being creative and thinking of usual and unusual ways to get your customers' attention can be the "fun" part.

Market research may take time, but it can save you a lot of money if it helps you create a quality product and/or service that will be in demand; in addition, good planning will help you avoid wasting your dollars on ineffective ads or promotions.

TRADITIONAL VERSUS CREATIVE

Experts estimate that new entrepreneurs spend as much as 75 percent of their time in marketing their new venture. Although this huge time commitment should eventually lessen, as a self-employed woman or business owner, you will always be marketing yourself and your services or products, through good times and slow economic times. Many traditional marketing methods that are very effective can also be expensive, especially for the newly self-employed. Traditional methods include advertising in printed publications, radio, and television; advertising on billboards or signs; advertising at trade shows; having your vehicle painted; or using other common methods of getting the attention of potential customers. These traditional methods continue to be effective for many entrepreneurs and business owners. If your advertising budget is small, however, you can find many low-cost and creative ways to market your self-employment venture. Besides, creative marketing, which originates with your ideas and resourcefulness, can be fun. Examples include having a contest, giving a demonstration at a community gathering, teaching a class on your topic at a school or senior center, setting up a display of your products at a local bank or town hall, giving away free samples, or otherwise highlighting your products and/or services and "grabbing" the attention of people in a unique way. The more creative your idea, the more noticed and remembered it will be. Once people know about you, some of them will ask about your business. That is your opportunity to provide them with more information.

MARKETING RESEARCH ESSENTIALS

Once you have gained recognition, you need to communicate to potential customers why they should purchase your product or service. You can do that most effectively once you can answer the following questions:

- What are the interests of your target customers?
- What are their concerns?
- What are their problems?
- How can your product or service solve their problems?
- Does your product or service have other advantages that will benefit potential customers?
- Who are your competitors, and what are their strengths and weaknesses?

If your marketing research answers these questions, you should have the base for devising an effective marketing plan and resulting strategies.

EVALUATION TECHNIQUES

You may use creative marketing to promote you and/or your business, but how do you know whether these methods are working? Here are several ways to analyze the effectiveness of your marketing strategies:

- Track your advertising and promotion results. Ask customers how they heard about you or assign a code to the ads you place requesting that people write or e-mail you for more information.
- Analyze your last month's cash flow to see if you are under or over your projected gross income.
- Review your marketing plan and strategies to see if they are getting the customer responses that you want.
- Count the number of contacts that are making business referrals to you to see if you need to do more networking.
- Evaluate how you are using the Internet for your marketing purposes and which one or ones are the most effective in garnering new customers. The Internet offers many marketing possibilities including, of course, a Web site and how it is ranked in major search engine listings; a regular online newsletter to customers; your contributed articles to sites related to your business with a tagline containing your business's contact information; a reciprocal link with other related sites and other ways to get you and your business's name noticed by potential customers. (For more information see chapter 10, Going Online.)

After your assessment, you will be able to concentrate your time and money on the most productive marketing avenues, but do not forget to do it periodically, because people's needs and desires constantly change according to the trends and the times in which we all live.

INTERNET PROMOTING: TO WEB OR NOT

Just a few years ago, we were exposed to numerous articles discussing whether or not entrepreneurs needed a Web site to promote their

Smile!

When Patricia Gallagher published her first book, she had her van painted with the book's cover and her 800 ordering number for people to view as she drove across the country to do book signings. She made it halfway across the country with her three children then had to turn around when she discovered she was pregnant with her fourth child! Her painted van, however, did garner good publicity and many newspaper interviews as well as a number of radio and television appearances.

---

products, services, or business. Now, despite the dot-com "dives" of many big companies in 2001, the Internet is here to stay and can offer many options to promote your self-employment venture.

"NET" PR

Of course, you can set up a simple (or complex) Web site. Even if your target customers live in your same neighborhood, you can use a Web site to provide them with information about what you are offering. Or you can reach new customers the world over. Additional Internet opportunities to promote your venture include joining newsgroups, selling items on auction sites, networking with other self-employed women using chats or Web rings, using e-mail for advertising, and sending press releases to online media.

The Internet may or may not prove to be the most effective strategy in your marketing plan, but it should not be ignored. The Web will continue to provide many opportunities for you and your potential customers to "connect."

Additional Considerations

If your self-employment venture is successful, you will reach a stage at which you make some decisions concerning the increased demands for your products and/or your services. How you handle

---

SEW's Suggestions

Solo Strategies

If you are working for yourself, try these marketing methods suggested by a number of self-employed women:

- *Get referrals.* Asking satisfied clients and other entrepreneurs to "spread the word" about their services and products is effective because people usually trust referrals from friends.
- *Talk it up!* If you do not have stage fright (or even if you do), offer to present talks in your community about subjects related to your venture—or, if your target customers exist all over the country, consider conducting online chats and writing articles for national publications.
- *Specialize.* Focusing on offering a "niche" service or product to potential customers who have a need for it can bring results that are profitable for you.

---

your growth is critical to your continued self-employment; if your business's growth is not managed correctly, you can be forced to stop.

Expansion Dilemmas

One woman who had a thriving dessert business began getting so many orders that she did not have any time during the holidays, typically her busiest times, to spend with her twins and husband. She decided she would still supply two of her commercial accounts—a cooking school and a caterer—but would not take orders from individuals during holidays.

"My individual customers were upset," she said. "In fact, one woman shouted at me, 'What do you mean you are not taking any orders on holidays?!' I told her I wanted to enjoy the holidays, too, and that I would be glad to take her orders at other times of the year. Fortunately, she did order later on."

If you do decide to "grow with the flow," here are some suggestions:

- Decide whether growing is right for your business financially and for you personally at this time.
- Find out whether investing in technology can assist you in handling the growth demands. For example, investing in a phone system with voice mail and several mail boxes will help you to better manage calls from potential clients and enhance your professional business image.
- Have a meeting place available for conferences outside of your home office. You can meet clients for coffee or a meal; rent office space by the day or hour; or ask other business owners with office space whether you can meet with your clients when the rooms are not in use.
- Decide what aspect of your venture that you and only you should handle, and then consider having the other parts—filing, billing, assembling, bookkeeping, mailings, and even some of the selling performed by others whom you hire.

HIRE OR SUBCONTRACT

If you are ready to ask others to assist you with your venture, here are some employment options:

Hiring

In deciding to hire extra help, you will have to consider your work area, familiarize yourself with the proper hiring procedures and guidelines, and other employer-employee concerns. Consult with your accountant and a human resources consultant if you need this information. Check with a local office of SCORE, www.score.org, for a free business consultation.

- *Family Members:* One mother who had a wallpapering and painting business hired her older daughter to help her do the painting and her younger daughter to apply the paste to the wallpaper.
- *Part-Timers:* High school or college students will often work for reasonable pay in exchange for the work internship and needed course credits. Senior citizens may want to supplement their incomes and may have the added benefit of valuable experiences.

- *Those Needing Flexible Work Schedules:* Flexibility can attract new mothers or fathers who prefer to work part-time hours around their families' schedules.
- *Temporary Workers:* Contact a temporary employment service for qualified workers that you can use for a short period of time at affordable rates.

Subcontracting

- *Independent Contractors:* Are also self-employed individuals who work independently of any company. If you hire one, a contract should be written. Consult with your attorney if you have any questions as to the legal wording.
- *Virtual Assistants (VAs):* VAs have become popular over the last decade. They can handle just about every task of your venture that you do not need to be doing, and the added benefit is that they do not have to live near you. Work is relayed to them via the Internet. You can find VAs at places like Assist University (AssistU, www.assistu.com) that not only trains VAs, but also has a referral list.

PARTNERING

Many self-employed women join forces with other self-employed individuals. One writer partners regularly with a photographer on her freelance assignments. A copywriter partners with a graphic designer to put together promotional packages for large companies. The partners' strengths and specific skills must complement each other's, and the partners must be able to work together in the completion of a project. A written agreement should state the responsibilities of each partner and terms of payment.

BECOMING UN-SELF-EMPLOYED

Working for yourself can be thrilling, challenging, and rewarding in many more ways than the money you can make. But after a period of time, your venture may actually grow away from your personal goals, and you may decide to either take some time away from it or head in a new direction altogether. Some self-employed individuals retire or even return to work as an employee (although those who have worked for themselves often find "taking orders" from a boss difficult). Many, however, go on to start an entirely new venture, perhaps one that will give them more "balance" and a little less hectic life. Should you become a self-employed woman, you may eventually decide to do something different. That is the exciting part of working for yourself—you can do anything your entrepreneurial mind desires!

Eleven Frequently Asked Questions About Self-Employment

1. *Q: Who would be classified as a self-employed woman?*
   A: Basically, a self-employed woman (or man) is someone who works for herself and is not an employee of another company. She can be an independent contractor (and subcontractor), a freelance professional or consultant, a sole proprietor, a partner in a partnership, president of her own corporation, owner of a home-based or small business, owner of a retail store or shop, or any other endeavor where she works independently for herself.

2. *Q: What is the difference between telecommuting and work-from-home?*
   A: Essentially, a telecommuting position is a work-from-home position, except that telecommuting is usually associated with working for someone else, whereas work-from-home can also imply that you are working for yourself.

3. *Q: Where is a good place to start to find out business information and do market research as well as to find suppliers, manufacturers, or distributors?*
   A: Your local public library or college library. There you will find the *Thomas Register of Manufacturers* (www.thomasregister.com) that lists manufacturers by classifications and geographic area. Many libraries' reference sections also include directories of associations that have listings of trade show and industry information; directories of manufacturers listed by state; demographic reports of your area; and a listing of local and regional business organizations and much more. Introduce yourself to the reference librarian who can inform you of the full extent of the resources on hand as well as additional

sources you may be able to borrow from other libraries through their inter-library loan system.

4. *Q: How much money will I need to start a self-employment venture?*

   A. Financial experts recommend that you overestimate the amount of money you will need to start a venture or to begin working for yourself. If you work from home, you will not have the expenses related to an outside office, but you will have to take care of setting up your office, fulfilling your basic equipment needs, and paying legal and accounting fees to register and set up your record-keeping system. Add to that the expenses you will need to cover operating expenses for at least a year and the money you will need to support yourself and any loan payments.

5. *Q: Is there a less risky way to start a self-employment venture?*

   A. Working another job on the side, or starting your venture part time while working your full-time job will enable you to get your venture started, build a customer list, and earn money to invest back into your full-time startup. Working this way, though, will require excellent time management and organization. Starting part time will also help you work out your pricing base and do some test-marketing. Realize it may take a year or more until you will be able to quit your day job and go full time.

6. *Q: How will I know when I'm ready to go out on my own and start advertising for clients?*

   A. You will know you are ready when you have taken the time necessary to . . .

   - write a complete business plan;
   - set up your work space and obtain your basic equipment;
   - figure your financial needs and set up a bookkeeping system;
   - determine who the best potential customers are;
   - fulfill the legal aspects of establishing yourself; and
   - devise your marketing strategy.

If you would like to have someone review your plans objectively, you can contact the nearest SBA Women's Business

Center, a Small Business Development Center, or SCORE office for a free or low-cost consultation. Ask a mentor if you are lucky enough to have one, or you can even contact the business department at a local college to have a professor or class give you some feedback. Then if you feel it is the right time for you and your family, go ahead and send out those first press releases to announce that you now are in business!

7. *Q: How can I find a market niche?*
   A: One way is to listen and if you hear people saying they wish . . .

   - There was a product or service that would make a task easier.
   - They knew of a time-saving device.
   - They could avoid doing some chore or duty.
   - A specific product or service was less expensive, or of better quality.
   - They could learn something new but do not know where to start.
   - There was a better way of doing or operating something.

8. *Q: What is one of the hardest things to face when you work for yourself?*
   A: The feeling of isolation is very common among the self-employed, especially if a former job involved much interaction in an office or work setting. To overcome these feelings, many self-employed women join their local chambers of commerce, women's professional associations, trade associations, or their own informal entrepreneurial group. These groups provide opportunities to discuss common problems and make contacts and possible leads. Often these groups will meet monthly for lunches at local eating establishments, have round-table discussions or speakers, and are usually very well attended. As one woman who attends such a group on a regular basis says, "Men 'do' golf; women 'do' lunch!"

9. *Q: What do business experts mean when they advise that I "define" my self-employment venture?*
   A: To define your venture is to ask yourself what you *really* do for your customers. If you are a computer consultant, for

example, do you spend your time helping clients get their computers and software to operate properly, or do you train your customers how to use specific computer software? If you grow herbs, do you grow them for direct sales to consumers, or do you grow them for wholesale markets? Sometimes, you may not realize what business you are *really* in until you work for a while and see what service or product is in the most demand. Common advice is to "Follow the money!"

10. *Q: Will it help me to succeed if I have a college degree or an MBA?*

A: That depends on what work you will be doing and what a higher level of education can do for your self-employment venture. If you are going into some type of consultant work or need a certain degree for a license or a certification, then you will have to have that degree or schooling to qualify you as the "expert." However, if you have work experience and are the type of person who knows how to find the answers to your business questions, college may not be necessary.

I would recommend that you do take some business management courses at local schools or business centers. Women's Business Development Centers (www.onlinewbc.gov) and Small Business Development Centers (www.sba.gov/SBDC) offer many low-cost seminars and courses designed for women and men to succeed in their own businesses.

11. *Q: Are there any special obstacles that women face in starting a self-employed venture?*

A: To say that obstacles no longer exist for women who wish to become self-employed would not be true. However, the effect of the growing women's entrepreneurial movement over the last decade has helped to provide many more resources to assist women in starting a venture than were once available. Today's women are overcoming the obstacles of financing, self-confidence, and lack of information.

Financing: In the last century, many women once had to have men cosign with them for a business loan. Now, many banks advertise how much money they lend to women entrepreneurs and some, such as First Union Bank (www.firstunion.com), even have financial information pages on their Web sites for women business owners. Of course, the U.S. Small Business Administration (SBA) has a number of loan programs for small business loans and a number of banks around the country are SBA-approved lenders. For information about SBA lending, visit the site www.sba.gov/financing/ or call the SBA Answer Desk at (800) U-ASK-SBA (800-827-5722).

Many more financing options have also opened up for self-employed women and these range from the establishment of women's venture capital firms like the Women's Growth Capital Fund (www.womensgrowthcapital.com/home.cfm) to small loans from nonprofit organizations such as Count-Me-In for Women's Economic Independence (www.count-me-in.org/).

Self-Confidence: Bolstered by education and entrepreneurial training, more women are exhibiting confidence in themselves and their entrepreneurial abilities that is enabling them to get additional funding, contracts, and customers. Education and training provided by the establishment of Women's Business Centers in all fifty states (www.onlinewbc.gov) and networking opportunities by such organizations as The National Association of Women Business Owners (www.nawbo.org) and Women Incorporated (www.womeninc.org/) are giving women the business skills and support necessary to start and operate ventures in every industry, even those considered "nontraditional," such as construction and manufacturing.

Accessible Information: With the growth of the Internet, many, many Web sites now provide answers to business questions that women have. With access to the Internet, a woman can find a business idea, do the market research for it, explore resources for her startup financing options, learn how to set up her office, organize her time, register her business, market her venture, and network with other self-employed women from around the world. For those who do not have access to the Internet, most public libraries offer sign-up times for members to use computers with Internet access.

If you persist, you can find the answers (they are out there!) as well as the right people to help, and you will succeed in your self-employment venture—whatever obstacles you may face!

Related Resources

WEB SITES

Creative Marketing Solutions, www.yudkin.com/marketing.htm — Many articles on marketing ideas and methods by marketing expert Marcia Yudkin, author of *Six Steps to Free Publicity* and other books.

Entrepreneurial Couples Success Letter (ECS). This is a free biweekly e-mail newsletter published by Azriela Jaffe and dedicated to helping entrepreneurial couples and families build a thriving business, marriage, and family at the same time. To subscribe to *ECS,* e-mail: azriela@mindspring.com

Goals and Jewels, www.goalsandjewels.com — "The women's wealth-building Web site." Includes information and tips for women in setting their financial goals.

IRS, Small Business and Self-Employed Community, www.irs.gov/smallbiz/ — Search here for wage and tax information about hiring family as employees. When in doubt, always consult with a tax specialist and/or your accountant.

Overcoming the Impostor Syndrome, www.impostorsyndrome.com — Web site of Dr. Valerie Young, national speaker and contributing author of *Not As Far As You Think: The Realities of Working Women.* She says: "If you secretly fear that sooner or later your customers, clients, vendors, financial backers, and others will find out that you are not nearly as bright and capable as they seem to 'think' you are, you may be suffering from the 'impostor syndrome.'"

Real Goals, www.real-goals.com — Business site that provides articles about achieving both business and personal goals.

Women's Online Business Center, www.onlinewbc.gov/docs/starting/preparing.html — "Preparing Your Business Plan" and Women's Online Business Center, www.onlinewbc.gov/docs/starting/goals.html — "Personal Goal-Setting."

Health Insurance Sites

www.Chubb.com, Chub Group of Insurance Managers — Insurances for specific businesses and professionals.

www.digitalinsurance.com — Health insurance resource Web site.

www.iii.org, Insurance Information Institute, 110 William St., New York, NY 10038. To improve public understanding of insurance.

www.insuremarket.com — Comparison rate Web site for all types of insurances.

www.quotesmith.com — Insurance quotes for all types of insurances from over 300 companies.

www.soho.org — Group insurance for members of the SOHO, Inc.

Self-Employment Sites

www.1099.com — Publication "1099" for independent professionals (archived articles only).

www.ChiefHomeOfficer.com/ — Site of Jeffrey D. Zbar's Goin' SOHO! consultancy.

iVillage.com, www.ivillage.com/topics/work/ — iVillage's Women's site with self-employment articles.

www.lmcint.com/ — Site of LMC International providing career transition services across Canada; good self-employment and related links for both Canada and the U.S.

www.WorkingSolo.com — Site of Terri Lonier, author and business expert.

Market Research Sites

Marketing Research Association, www.mra-net.org — MarketResearch.com is the leading provider of global market intelligence products and services; offers over 40,000 research publications (for a fee).

Organizational Experts' Web Sites
(related products, articles and other information)

www.HomeOfficeLife.com — Lisa Kanarek's site.

www.OrganizedTimes.com — Debbie Williams's site.

ADDITIONAL RESOURCES

Family and Business Matters

Family Business Magazine, www.familybusinessmagazine.com, Family Business Publishing Company; P.O. Box 41966, Philadelphia, PA 19101-1966. For subscription information, visit their site or write to the above address.

Books

101 Ways to Promote Yourself: Tricks of the Trade for Taking Charge of Your Own Success by Raleigh Pinskey (New York: Avon Books, 1997).

101 Internet Marketing Tips for Your Business: Increase Your Profits and Stay Within Your Budget by Jeffrey P. Davidson (Irvine, CA: Entrepreneur Media, 2002).

Business Etiquette and Professionalism by M. Kay duPont (Menlo Park, CA: Crisp Publications, 1998).

Business Etiquette: 101 Ways to Conduct Business with Charm and Savvy by Ann Marie Sabath (Franklin Lakes, NJ: Career Press, 1997).

Business Plans Made Easy by Mark Henricks (Irvine, CA: Entrepreneur Media Inc., 1999).

Essential Business Etiquette, Bottom Line Behavior for Everyday Effectiveness by Lou Kennedy (St. Petersburg, FL: Palmetto Publishing, 1997).

Feel the Fear and Do It Anyway, abridged ed. by Susan Jeffers (Niles, IL: Nightingale Conant Corp., 2001) Susan Jeffers, Ph.D., well-known personal development expert, presents practical, step-by-step techniques that readers can use to overcome common fears and improve their lives.

Handbook of Online Marketing Research: Knowing Your Customer Using the Net by Joshua Grossnickle, Oliver Raskin (New York: McGraw-Hill Professional, 2000).

Home Office Life: Making a Space to Work at Home by Lisa Kanarek (Gloucester, MA: Rockport Publishers, 2001).

Home Management 101: A Guide for Busy Parents by Debbie Williams (Vancouver, WA: Champion Press, 2001).

Marketing for the Home-Based Business, 2nd ed., by Jeffrey P. Davidson (Holbrook, MA: Adams Media, 1999).

Minding Her Own Business: The Self-Employed Woman's Guide to Taxes and Record Keeping by Jan Zobel (Holbrook, MA: Adams Media, 2000).

Money-Smart Secrets for the Self-Employed by Linda Stern (New York: Random House, 1997).

Uncommon Marketing Techniques by Jeffrey Dobkin, "Small Business Master Marketer," www.dobkin.com/(Merion Station, PA: The Danielle Adams Publishing Co., 1998).

Secrets of Self-Employment by Sarah and Paul Edwards (Los Angeles: J. P. Tarcher, 1996).

—Edwards' Web site with information: www.homeworks.com/.

The Sole Proprietor: 101 Lessons from a Lifestyle Entrepreneur by Jane Pollak (Berkeley, CA: Publishers Group West, 2001).

Working Solo: The Real Guide to Freedom and Financial Success with Your Own Business, 2nd ed., by Terri Lonier (NY: John Wiley & Sons, 1998) — Lonier's Web site with information: www.workingsolo.com.

Libraries

In addition to having access to the Internet, public and college libraries (especially those offering business degrees) have many resources that you can access for research such as the:

American Demographics Magazine, www.demographics.com — Latest news on trends and consumers.

Encyclopedia of Associations (Gale Research Publications), www.Gale.com — Includes a listing of trade associations that can provide industry data.

Thomas Register of American Manufacturers, www.thomasregister.com — Multivolume listing of companies. Good for identifying businesses and possible competitors in your field.

Software

Jian, www.jian.com

Out of Your Mind . . . And Into the Marketplace; www.business-plan.com, publisher of business books and business plan software (founded by Linda Pinson, business plan expert).

Accounting Software (two examples of the many available programs); for product information, call or visit the Web sites.

Peachtree Accounting Software, www.peachtree.com; accounting software for small businesses; (800) 247-3224.

Quickbooks (easier), www.Intuit.com/quickbooks, www.quickbooks.com — accounting software, business services; (888) 246-8848.

Tax Preparation Software

Intuit, Inc., www.quicken.com; 2535 Garcia Ave., Mountain View, CA 94043; Tax preparation products; also tax tips and information.

Tutorials

"The Overnight Bookkeeper," www.eaglevip.com/html/onb.html; Eagle Business Center, P.O. Box 1460, Wildomar, CA 92595-1460; (800) 943-2392; Fax: (909) 678-6566. Bookkeeping tutorials, home study courses, and Web site.

Associations

The Financial Planning Association, www.fpanet.org/ — 1615 L Street NW, Suite 650, Washington, D.C. 20036.

National Association of Professional Organizers, www.napo.net — P.O. Box 140647, Austin, TX 78714; (512) 454-8626; Fax: (512) 454-3036.

CHAPTER TWO

Women's Business— Past, Present, Future

Welcome to "Women's Entrepreneurial World!" In the past several decades, the growth of women's business has been phenomenal—not just in the U.S., but in countries such as Argentina, the United Kingdom, Canada, and others the world over. Here are some U.S. statistics from two 2001 reports put out by the Center for Women's Business Research:

- Women's businesses continue to grow at twice the rate of all other U.S. firms.
- These women-owned businesses are exhibiting greater increases in employment and revenues than all other businesses.
- Between 1997 and 2002, the number of majority-owned, privately held women-owned firms will have grown to 6.2 million, an increase of 14 percent compared to 7 percent for all firms nationwide, with sales estimates to surpass $1 trillion.
- Women-owned firms will employ nearly 9.2 million workers in 2002, up 30 percent since 1997.

(The reports, "Women-Owned Businesses in 2002: Trends in the U.S. and the 50 States" and "Women-Owned Businesses in 2002: Trends in the Top 50 Metropolitan Areas," are published by the Center for Women's Business Research [founded as the National Foundation for Women Business Owners], and underwritten by Wells Fargo and Company, and with the help of the U.S. Bureau of the Census.)

Home-based business startups also continue to rise dramatically. Exact numbers of those who work from home vary with the organization doing the reporting: For example, the National Home-Based Business Association reports approximately 45 million home-based workers, with about 35 million working formally and informally as small businesses; The American Association of Home-Based Businesses, www.aahbb.org, estimates an existing 24+ million home-based businesses.

Finding an exact number is difficult because some people work out of their homes, such as independent sales reps and those in networking businesses or service businesses; others start home businesses on the side while still working as employees and work out of their homes in the evenings and on weekends.

Estimates of the numbers of women-owned home-based businesses are also hard to determine. The Center for Women's Business Research findings show that approximately 66 percent of home-based businesses are owned by women. Thus, we can safely say that all the studies indicate that home-based businesses and women-owned businesses the world over continue to grow faster than any other business types.

Here are some additional interesting facts concerning women's business ownership:

- IDC/LINK, a market research firm, states that an estimated three out of four home-based women business owners are college-educated. These women home-business owners are more likely to be married, have children, and be in their thirties and forties.
- Compared to women starting businesses ten to twenty years ago, women starting businesses today have . . .

    more management experience and education;

    the same overall revenue and employment profiles as women who have been in business twenty years or longer;

    more access to capital in the U.S.;

    less credit card debt used to finance their businesses; and

more bank credit—over half of women business owners (52 percent) had bank credit as of 1998.

- The number of women minorities owning businesses has increased. As of 2002, an estimated 1.2 million businesses employing more than 822,000 people and generating $100.6 billion in sales will be owned by women of color in the U.S. (The Center for Women's Business Research).

Younger women are also taking advantage of the entrepreneurial opportunities opening up to them. Gayle Sato Stodder, a freelance business writer based in Redondo Beach, California, and coauthor of *Entrepreneur Magazine's Young Millionaires* (www .entrepreneurmag.com), says:

> Young women entrepreneurs today are an entirely different breed from the entrepreneurial women I was writing about twelve years ago. They have the skills, ambition, and confidence to go after whatever they want—whether that's multi-billion-dollar success or creative fulfillment. What does that mean for the future of women in business? Everything. I predict we're going to see more success and in a plethora of sizes, shapes, and forms. It's an exciting time for all of us.

Thus, the rapid growth of women's entrepreneurship, in the U.S. and throughout the world, is sure to progress as the twenty-first century progresses. As more women choose to be independent while stabilizing their lives, their families, and the communities in which they live, the number of female entrepreneurs—whether home-based, free agents, or located in an outside facility—will continue to increase.

Home Business "Truths": Myths and Realistic Expectations

In *More 101 Best Home-Based Businesses for Women* (1998), I wrote about common misconceptions and myths about having a home-based business and the realities of owning a home business. They included these:

Myth #1: A home-based business has no overhead.

Reality: As much as 50 percent of a home-based business's billing rate can go towards covering overhead costs, but you can deduct a percentage of these expenses from your income tax when you work out of your house (check with your accountant and/or the latest IRS guidelines about these home office/business tax deductions).

Myth #2: I will not need child care if I work from home.

Reality: It's true that a home business allows you the flexibility of working your own hours, around your family. However, depending on your children's ages, you may still need someone to help you either watch or "run" your older children to their activities to give you blocks of uninterrupted working time. As more and more women work from home, it is not uncommon for whole neighborhoods of home business moms to take turns hosting play groups to free up time for one another.

Myth #3: If I have a home business, I will have time to clean house, continue to volunteer at church and school, cook delectable meals, taxi the kids to all their activities, and have a meaningful, personal relationship with a "significant other."

Reality: Few "super" moms exist anymore (thank goodness!). So many women are working these days that they are learning to say "no" more often to extraneous activities so they can have more time for their families and their businesses. Typically, home-based entrepreneurs still work long hours, but they like the flexibility of arranging their own work hours. And they have not forgotten their communities; in fact, women lead the way in using their businesses for altruistic ways to help their communities.

Myth #4: I have a great idea that I know will make me lots of money, and I plan to start it next week.

Reality: My mission as a business author is to provide women with as much information and as many resources as I can to assist them in self-employed ventures. I cannot promise, however, that anyone will earn thousands a week, or even succeed in business. That is up to you. You will need at least six to twelve months to plan, research, and get some customer response to your business. As I emphasized in *More 101 Best Home-Based Businesses for Women,* you may wish to start your venture tomorrow, but first researching your business idea and planning your strategy will be more likely to lead to your making money.

Myth #5: If I work from home, I can be much more casual in both how I dress and how I treat my customers.
Reality: Casual dress is commonplace—even for employees at most of today's businesses. A home business, of course, can be conducted in jeans and T-shirts. Still, professionalism and business etiquette is very important for your business's image. There should never be anything casual about how you treat your customers and present yourself and your business.

A few more myths could be added, such as these: You'll never have to answer to a boss (the reality is that you *will* have to answer to your customers, distributors, the IRS, and to the toughest boss of all—yourself!). Working at home will be more quiet than where you worked before (the reality is that you may live next door to a neighbor whose dog barks incessantly at a hole he dug in a ground!).

Still many women home-business owners say that nothing can entice them back to working for a company again; evidently, the realities of working from home are not so harsh. Being aware of the realities of home-based entrepreneurship will help you prepare for your work ahead, and hopefully, enable you to say what one woman home-based business owner said: "I'm wondering why I waited so long!"

Ten Home Business Axioms

Axioms are self-evident truths. As a home business entrepreneur, you may hear these ten major home business "truths" over and over again:

1. Have Knowledge and Experience.

You *are* your business, so make sure you have the qualifications and preferably first hand experience necessary to operate it. You can take courses to become qualified and volunteer or work in a job to gain the necessary experience, but never stop your learning for your business and for personal enlightenment.

2. Be a Marketing "Maven."

Never miss an opportunity to market your business, and never stop looking for new ways to attract customers.

3. Love Your Business.

Business owners may not like what they do, which must make their lives not much fun. Try to choose a home business you love because you will be working many hours at it each week!

4. Never Stop Networking.

Networking is not just conversing with others to get more business for yourself; it is also thinking of leads for others. Offer to share leads and tips with those interested in entrepreneurship or even become a mentor to a new entrepreneur. Generosity always comes full circle.

5. Follow Your Vision.

Do not give up on your dreams and goals. Realize that you *will* make mistakes, and that mistakes are only bad when you do not learn from them. Keep going forward!

6. Make Your Customer First—and Have Lots of Them!

Customers pay for the value you offer in terms of service and quality. Treat them with respect.

My eighty-five-year-old father-in-law woke up recently on the coldest day of the winter to find he had no heat because his oil tank was empty. When he called the company, they said he had not paid a bill so they simply did not deliver more oil. My father-in-law was upset because the company he had patronized for some forty years (without missing a single payment before!) did not call to ask him what the problem was. Now the home oil company may lose a good customer to a competitor, as well as others through negative word-of-mouth.

7. Do Not Limit Yourself to Just One Customer or Client.

No matter how well one customer or client pays you, that's not enough. One glaring example of this is the many small enterprises that received up to 75 percent of their business from the bankrupt Enron power company in 2001. Several had to lay off employees when Enron ran out of money!

8. Surround Yourself with Good People and Build Your List of Experts.

Much as you'd like to run and manage your business without any problems, this can happen only in a "perfect" world! As you build your business, build your network of experts—accountant, business coach, insurance agents, lawyer, technology wizard, tax specialist, and others who will help you keep your business solvent. In addition, nurture relationships with people who will support you— friends, family, business associates, mentors, and others who will encourage you through the down sides of your entrepreneurial ventures. These people can also offer "constructive" criticism (preferably not "destructive" criticism) to help you learn from your mistakes and go forward. Choose these people carefully!

9. Be a Good Manager of Business—and Life.

Dreams are wonderful, but achieving them in reality requires *planning*. Your business's plan (which sets goals and objectives for your venture) and your life plan (which sets goals and objectives for your life) have to be compatible. A business plan outlines its mission, its purposes, and the methods you will use to achieve those objectives, while a life plan analyzes your present personal and financial situations and also sets goals. Both plans should be reviewed weekly, if not daily, to make sure you are taking the steps, right now, to achieve the goals you set down.

10. Care About Something in This World That Has No Connection to Money!

You often hear this statement, "Well, we can't save the whole world!" Although this may be true, a good response might be this: "No, but I can do my part in making it a little better."

At the risk of sounding sexist, I say that women tend to be more active in volunteer and altruistic activities; this applies to women business owners as well. Many, many men business owners also volunteer time and provide sponsorships to help their communities.

Smile!

When one mother began working from home, her thirteen-year-old son told her she should get a "real" job so she could afford to buy him expensive sneakers like his friends had. (She did not!)

However, according to statistics from the Center for Women's Business Research, seven in ten women business owners volunteer at least once per month and they are more likely to be in volunteer organization leadership positions. For example, Rochelle Balch, owner of a successful computer-consulting firm in Arizona, volunteers to help incarcerated youth. Another example is Barbara, an independent marketing specialist for major corporations, who does major work for a local organization that asks for good, pre-owned business suits and attire from professional women to give to low-income women who are starting new careers.

Women who are employed by companies also devote much time to helping others, but owners of home-based businesses generally have more flexibility that enables them to arrange their schedules to participate in volunteer activities. Business owners who volunteer also garner some good publicity for their businesses, but many say the intangible rewards go far beyond the monetary ones. It's a win-win-win situation: for those you are helping, for your community, and for you personally.

Common Home Business Problems and Suggested Solutions

Problem: *How do I say "No" to clients and customers who ask me to do work I really do not like to do?*

Suggested Solution: Take a personal inventory of the types of work you do best and really enjoy; stress those when you market your business. If a client asks you to do something you do not really want to do, you can refer the client to another business owner who specializes in that work area, subcontract that specific part of the work to another entrepreneur, or tell him or her that you will do it for him or her this time, but in the future would prefer to perform work with which you feel most comfortable. Honesty may lose you some business customers, but you will enjoy rather than dread your work.

Problem: *How do I handle the long hours a home business (or any business) requires?*

Suggested Solution: Successful home business owners learn to implement time management techniques that enable them to work more efficiently with the time they have.

Problem: *How do I start a business with little or no money?*

Suggested Solution: Finding financing for startup costs and continued growth can be a significant challenge. More financing resources are opening up via the Internet, and more types of small business loans are being offered by governmental agencies, and business groups and organizations. First, make an appointment with a local banker and ask her what her bank looks for in a loan application. She may even guide you through the loan process. Also contact a local Women's Business Center or U.S. SBA Small Business Development Center to see what government loans are available.

Ask other women entrepreneurs how they financed their businesses. They may be able to give you some practical tips, plus leads to financial sources of which you were not aware. Lastly, think of "creative" financing—selling items on an online auction, having a garage sale, doing odd jobs, and thinking of other ways to bring in money for your startup. If you can, avoid using personal credit cards; the less debt you have, the better chances you will have in getting a loan to fund your business's growth and expansion needs.

Problem: *How do I balance family demands, community activities, and a business along with everything else that is going on in my life? It can be very stressful—often overwhelming.*

Suggested Solution: Successful home business owners consider the impact their businesses have on their families and often involve family members in their business decision making. They also learn how to say "No," and to prioritize their commitments.

Problem: *In being a "one-person band," a.k.a. a home-based entrepreneur, how do I manage the responsibility of producing the products and/or services, and performing ALL the other jobs required to make a business successful—marketing, bookkeeping, doing business correspondence—that in a large company would be delegated to specific employees?*

Suggested Solution: Home business owners learn to focus their time on the profit-making tasks and delegate the rest of their business operations to their designated experts—accountants, business lawyers, Web designers, desktop publishers, virtual assistants, and other professionals.

Problem: *Statistics show that it takes on average three attempts to start a business until one succeeds. How can I minimize my risk in starting a home business and maximize the possibility of finding the ideal venture for myself?*

Suggested Solution: If possible, start your business on a part-time basis. Three-quarters of home businesses are started this way, enabling home business entrepreneurs to "test" the market for their products and/or services, in addition to providing a "learning curve" period to make and learn from any business mistakes.

Problem: *Why do family members, friends, clients, and/or financial institutions often value a business based in a home less than one with an office in a commercial district?* (Note: Local zoning laws vary widely pertaining to the permission of certain types of businesses that operate out of one's home, so check first with your local, state, and federal authorities to see whether the business you want to operate from home is legal.)

Suggested Solution: Acceptance is all about how you conduct your home business. Home business entrepreneurs should learn to set "hours" and limits to manage interruptions. Also, ten years ago, many people "hid" the fact that their businesses were home-based. As the number of home-based businesses has increased, especially those run by owners who are as professional and ethical as any located in a business district, so has acceptance for them. If you take your business seriously and are professional in how you operate it, others will take your business seriously as well.

Problem: *I enjoy my home business, but with all the demands of a new business, how do I say, "Time to stop working"?*

Suggested Solution: One excellent response from Sharon S., a wise woman who attended one of my online chats was this:

> Did you ever work outside of the home? Were you a workaholic there? Did you put in extra hours . . . ? Create a "workday" for yourself—start and finish times! Make your to-do lists: one got-a-do and one can-do-later! At the end of your (designated) workday, make your list for the next day and just transfer what didn't happen.
>
> I'm sure you're aware of the little quip that goes, "When you die, your 'in' box will still be full." I do not know how much you are earning, but I do know that nothing can replace the precious things in life—taking a walk, enjoying a garden. Slow down, girl!! It will all get done and if it doesn't . . . life will still go on. Trust me.

I would just add one additional tip: Let go of perfection as far as housekeeping, meals, and other household chores are concerned, so you will have more time to spend on your business, which will translate into having more "fun" time with your loved ones.

Problem: *How do I overcome my fear of starting a home business?*

Suggested Solution: Attend a woman's entrepreneur conference and/or classes, such as those held by many Small Business Development Centers (www.sba.gov/SBDC) and Women's Business Centers (www.onlinewbc.gov). They offer business-related workshops and networking opportunities with other women entrepreneurs to help give you the confidence, support, and knowledge to start.

Problem: *Everyone says to go with your passion. What if I'm not sure what that is?*

SEW's Suggestions

Janet Attard, author of *The Home Office and Small Business Answer Book* (Holbrook, MA: Adams Media Corporation, 2000) and an Internet expert (www.businessknowhow.com) states:

> The startup questions I see the most are related to finding customers—particularly when there is little or no money for advertising. One typical scenario is when the entrepreneur has spent all her money starting her business and has nothing left for advertising. Another is when the entrepreneur starts a business because it seems like something everyone will want, but she has done no real research to determine just what she will have to do to attract customers on a steady basis.

Suggested Solution: Here's a response from Mary S., another self-employed woman, on an online message board:

> Hi! I was in the same predicament not long ago. I had a college degree I was not using. I had been a waitress for 5+ years and going nowhere. I also tried selling cars and doing health club management. I hated all my jobs so much that I would cry on my way to work every day and only stayed at each one about six months. I felt destined to slugging away at some job I hated for the next forty years! I thought I would never find a job I liked. I was miserable and depressed and making my boyfriend miserable, too. To make matters worse, the love of my life was following his dream and passion as a singer/songwriter and doing very well.
>
> Everyone told me the same thing: "Find something you love to do." I felt there was nothing. I loved horses, but had already tried training and giving riding lessons, neither of which I wanted to do full time. But, I recently started a horse gift business. I am using my marketing

degree and am involved with horses as well!! I found a
job as a receptionist close to home and do my new business on the side. I hope it will become a full-time endeavor in the near future!!
Look for things related to what you love and then you
will find a job you love! Good luck!!

Being a home-based entrepreneur demands self-discipline, a
quest for learning, and at times an incredible amount of both physical and mental stamina. But the women (and men) home business
entrepreneurs I have interviewed say that, for them, the benefits far
outweigh the negatives. Besides doing work for which they have
"passion," the independence, achieving growth and personal balance, attaining pride and self-esteem, and gaining more "control of
their own fate" are just a few of the many reasons a home business
is started every eleven seconds in the U.S. (as stated in *Home Business Connection*). Most home business owners I've talked with have
said this about their venture: "It is fun, exciting, and *never* boring!!"
If you cannot say the same about your job, then consider starting a
home business. I can guarantee your life will never be the same!

Related Resources

WEB SITES

Wells Fargo & Company's "Resource Center for Small Business Owners,"
http://www.wellsfargo.com/biz/.

ADDITIONAL RESOURCES

Books:

*Careerpreneurs: Lessons from Leading Women Entrepreneurs on Building a
Career Without Boundaries* by Dorothy Perrin Moore (Palo Alto, CA:
Davies-Black Publishing, 2000).

Entrepreneur Magazine's Young Millionaires by Rieva Lesonsky and Gayle
Sato Stodder (Irvine, CA: Entrepreneur Media, 1998).

Tips & Traps for Entrepreneurs: Real-Life Ideas and Solutions for the Toughest Problems Facing Entrepreneurs by Courtney Price and Kathleen Allen (NY: McGraw-Hill, 1998).

Women's Home-Based Business Book of Answers: 78 Questions Answered by Top Women Business Leaders by Maria Bailey (Roseville, CA: Prima Communications, Inc., 2001).

Preparation

Energy, excitement, and enthusiasm is what I see and hear in the actions and voices of women who tell me, "I have this idea for a
business . . ." and then go onto describe one (or more) businesses they
would like to do out of their homes. One woman in an online chat I
was hosting told me, "I make flower arrangements, sell on online auctions, and refinish furniture. Which one should I choose to make into
a business?" I responded, as I often do: "Which one do you like to do
most and which venture has been showing some promising profits?"
The woman told me, "I love the furniture refinishing, and I have been
making good money with my online auctions." I then suggested that
she might narrow down those two choices by specializing in what she
sells online and doing something unique with her furniture refinishing.

For example, she could sell a certain type of collectible on the
online auction and become an expert; and, if she is artistic, she could
decoratively paint furniture for children's rooms or refinish only certain styles of furniture and even sell those through online auctions
or her own Web site. In other words, when choosing a business:

1. Pick something that you love to do and can do with your talents or training.
2. Specialize and find a market niche.
3. Make sure you have a sufficient number of customers who
   want or need your product and service and are willing to pay
   your prices.

To find this ideal business, you are going to need excitement, energy, and enthusiasm to sustain you through the startup phases and

SEW's Suggestions

Debra Cohen, president of Home Remedies of NY, Inc. (www.home
ownersreferral.com), a home-based homeowners referral service, offers these tips—individually or as part of an HRN business package:

> Regardless of your reasons for wanting to run a business from
> home, it's just as important to analyze yourself as it is to ana-
> lyze the market you plan to serve.

beyond. The more preliminary research and preparation you do, the
more likely you will find and have a successful home business.

1. *What are my strengths?*
   The answer to this question will provide the foundation on
   which you can build a successful business. Whether you're a
   people person, a computer geek, a number cruncher, or a
   craftsperson, your business should maximize your strengths.

2. *What are my weaknesses?*
   If you're going to conduct an "honest" self-evaluation, then it's
   important that you admit to your weaknesses. Perhaps you're not
   as disciplined as you'd like to be, or maybe you're not the best
   bookkeeper. Running a business will require you to handle a wide
   array of responsibilities, from sales and marketing to accounting
   and secretarial. If you overlook one aspect of your business or
   don't handle it efficiently, the business will suffer, or worse yet, fail.

Preliminary Research and Considerations

Do you have what it takes to be a home business entrepreneur?

Maybe a better question is this: Do you *realize* what it takes to
run a business from your home? Dreaming about working from
home is one thing, but the reality is another. Answer these personal
questions as truthfully as you can:

Entrepreneurial Characteristics: Self-Assessment

1. Do you get upset when your workday does not go as planned?
2. Are you able to say "No" and mean it?
3. Do you like people?
4. Are you a self-starter?
5. Do you persist in finding answers to questions?
6. Are you good with managing finances?
7. Do you have the knowledge and expertise needed to operate the business you want to start and the technology and equipment to run it?
8. Are you good at problem-solving?
9. Are you able to focus on the task at hand even amidst the interruptions of business and family activities that occur daily?
10. Are you unafraid of the "unknown"? If you are afraid of trying new things, do you still challenge yourself and try them anyway?
11. Are you determined that you are going to have a home business?
12. Do you have the ability to laugh at your mistakes, learn from them, and put things in the proper perspective of your life?

If you have more "Yes" answers than "No" answers, you are probably ready for the next steps of researching and planning your business idea(s). If you have more "No" answers, this does not necessarily mean that you should give up the idea of having a home business; however, you will have to strengthen your weaker personal areas or choose other people who are good in those areas to help you. Keep in mind that the real "test" comes when you actually start and operate a home business venture, including how you apply what you know and learn as you go!

CONFIDENCE AND SELF-ESTEEM

Having confidence and self-esteem can propel you to take those first entrepreneurial steps. Entrepreneurs in general are risk-takers. If, however, you do not feel good about taking this chance, here are some suggestions:

- *Look for motivation.* When Chrissy C. did not have enough money after living expenses to buy her mother a Christmas gift, she was determined never to be in that financial situation again.

Hot Business: Professional Coaching

In pursuing a work-life change, consider consulting with a professional coach to assist you with doing a personal assessment, setting goals, and achieving those goals. Professional coaching is one of the hottest businesses to develop over the last several years.

A professional coach's services include helping individuals and business owners to focus and follow through on their goals. Coaches monitor their clients to ensure that they follow through on daily tasks that will enable them to move forward to what they want to achieve. Coach training programs emphasize that coaches work with their clients in collaborative relationship, a type of partnership.

Terri Levine, M.S., a high performance coach who founded the coaching company, Comprehensive Coaching, www.comprehensivecoaching.com, as well as a coach training program for professionals, www.comprehensive coachingu.com, says, "Successful coaches have already been professionally successful in another career or venue."

Coaches are not counselors to solve personal and professional issues, but rather objective professionals who can work with clients to help them go beyond their expectations for a better life. They may be one of your experts to help you achieve your life and business goals.

International Coach Federation, www.coachfederation .com; 1444 "I" St. NW, Ste. 700, Washington, D.C. 20005. A professional organization with chapters around the country and a coaching referral service.

So, she opened her first comedy club and today has three clubs and enough money for a down payment on a new house. She makes all the arrangements from her home during the week for the Friday and Saturday night shows. Use that motivating reason to bolster your confidence.

- *Believe in yourself.* Sometimes the only one who believes in you is you. Oftentimes when a would-be entrepreneur hears, "You'll never make it," she becomes motivated to prove the pessimist wrong!
- *Set achievable goals.* Set your final goal and then work backwards. List the steps you need to achieve to bring you to that final goal and accomplish them one at a time.
- *Review how far you have come.* Sometimes you do not realize how much you have achieved and experienced in your life until you write it all down. The same applies to your business goals: Write down each little step you take, then periodically review those to help you realize that you *are* going forward even though it often seems as though you are going backward.
- *Prepare for the worst and hope for the best.* The more you are prepared with research, the more confident you will feel to start your business.

Success breeds success, so celebrate your successes, no matter how small, and add your "bragging rights" to your business promotional materials. Do not dwell on your mistakes. Learn from them and then move forward *(always forward!)* and your confidence and self-esteem will grow because you know you will be able to handle just about any business challenge.

KEY BUSINESS SKILLS (ESSENTIAL KNOW-HOW)

Every individual needs basic work skills—even for entry-level jobs. This fact also pertains to those who work from home—whether as a teleworker or a home business owner. Work-from-home success requires at least fundamental knowledge in the following areas:

Technology

You should have a basic operating knowledge of . . .

Word Processing Programs, such as Microsoft Word (www.microsoft.com), Corel WordPerfect (www.corel.com), Lotus Word Pro, for business correspondence.

Database Programs, such as Database Act! (www.symantec.com), Lotus Organizer (www.lotus.com), Microsoft Excel (www.microsoft.com) for spreadsheets, data, and information management.

Accounting & Bookkeeping Programs, such as Quicken or Quick-Books (www.intuit.com), to help manage your cash flow, billing, and overall business financial management and monitoring.

Industry-Related Software, such as CorelDRAW (www.corel.com), QuarkXPress (www.quark.com) for desktop publishers, and other specific programs related to your field.

Internet

You will need a basic knowledge of the Internet and e-mail capabilities for . . .

Business-to-Business Resources, to get competitive bids on goods and services and auctioning off overstock, bartering opportunities, and other Internet exchange sources.

Market Research, for potential customers or reviewing competitors' offerings.

Marketing Opportunities, to reach customers, worldwide, through one's Web site, e-mail newsletters, permission marketing, and chats.

Business Web Design and Marketing Tips.

Office Equipment

Even if all your office equipment has online or telephone tech support, you will save time and money (and time really is money when you work alone from home!) by learning the basic functions of your computer, fax, copier, cellular phone, scanner, and other equipment by . . .

- Reading the operating manuals!
- Learning a new function each day (if possible) for each piece of equipment.

- Knowing how to "troubleshoot," by being aware of potential malfunctions and their probable causes.
- Learning basic keyboarding or typing skills for speed in executing your daily business tasks.

General Business Management

Working from home or having a home business requires that you know basic business operations, such as . . .

- Effective marketing and sales techniques
- How to write a business plan
- How to meet customer demands
- Time management and organization skills
- Correct pricing of your goods and services.

If you feel you are lacking in any of the previously mentioned skills you can: take online courses like those covering Internet technology offered by ZD Net's Smart Planet (www.smartplanet.com) and other sites listed below; or take home study courses (write for a brochure or visit the Web site of the Distance Education and Training Council, 1601 18th Street NW, Washington, D.C. 20009, www.detc.org); or enroll in local business courses or adult evening classes held at many public schools and colleges; or contact a local SCORE office, a Women's Business Center, or Small Business Development Center (see "Government" in the Resources section). Your local (or online) bookstore, office supply store, or computer center is likely to offer a wide selection of guides and self-tutorial programs, such as *The Complete Idiot's Guides* and the *Dummies* books to help you learn office skills and technology at home.

It is imperative to maintain and periodically upgrade your business skills to stay both knowledgeable and competitive in your industry.

Advantages and Disadvantages of Home Businesses

Here are some advantages and disadvantages of having a home business:

Advantages: No commute, no traffic. Your office is just a few steps away.

Disadvantages: You can feel isolated from the outside world.

Advantages: You can work even if you are disabled or help care for children or elderly parents.

Disadvantages: You will be interrupted at times you are working and your family may resent the time you spend on your business.

Advantages: You can start a home business at any age.

Disadvantages: You will need stamina to work the extra hours that your business will often need.

Advantages: A home-based business is less expensive to start, especially if it is service-based, and can provide you with a number of tax deductions for your home office use.

Disadvantages: You still have to purchase or lease all the quality equipment you need to operate your business and be responsible for getting it repaired. If you were an employee, it would be the company's responsibility to repair or replace a piece of equipment that malfunctions!

PROS AND CONS

The pros and cons of having a home business include:

Pro: You have the flexibility to arrange your work schedule around nonbusiness activities.

Con: You still have to make up those work hours missed if you plan to earn any money.

Pro: The potential of money you can earn is unlimited.

Con: You get no regular paycheck, and may need a year or more before your business makes significant profits.

Pro: No two days are alike.

Con: Managing all the tasks required to operate a profitable home business can often be overwhelming.

Get Real! Interruptions

I have worked at my home business for fifteen years, and my family and relatives know this. Still, when they call on the phone, unexpectedly drop in at my house, or into my home office, I get comments such as these:

"I know you are working, but this will just take a minute . . ." (Never takes a minute!)

"Mom, could you wash these pants for me? Oh, by the way, I need them tonight." (He has five other clean pairs but he wants those.)

"Mom, this paper is due tomorrow. Would you mind looking it over?" (He needs me to help him find three more sources for his bibliography.)

"Well, you do eat lunch, don't you?" (My mom, stopping by unannounced.)

"Mom, Mr. Smith, the principal, wants you to call him . . . as soon as possible." (Did not take his hat off when he entered school!)

"Hon, was there a reason you had the oven on?" (Oops! Supper out tonight!)

Pro: Working from home you can save on food, commuting, and clothing expenses—except those related directly toward your business.

Con: If not covered by another family member's health-care plan and other insurances, you will have to pay for your own insurance plans and that can be very expensive.

Pro: You can shop or take vacations whenever it fits your schedule.

Con: You might have to work while you are sick or on vacation!

Pro: You have more control over your destiny and the direction of your life.

Con: I can think of no downside to that statement!

Be aware of both the benefits of working from home and the detriments; knowing the major advantages and disadvantage, pros and cons, will help you to know what to expect as a home business owner. However, exactly how a home business will affect your life and goals can only be understood through actual experience. Then, and only then, can you enumerate the advantages or disadvantages of your working from home.

Product or Service Business, or Both?

Is your business going to sell a product—such as food, clothing, or craft items? Or will you offer a service—such as consulting, tutoring, child care? Or will you be combining both—such as through selling handmade lampshades and refurbishing old lamps?

In general, a product-oriented business will be more expensive than a service-based one because you will either have to purchase the supplies to make your items or buy the products from your suppliers at wholesale prices to resell. If yours is a unique, one-of-a-kind item, you will have to introduce it to the public to create an interest and demand for it. Judy, a talented artist, designs and makes ceramic buttons, firing them in a kiln in her home. She has created a market for her hand-painted buttons by posting them on a Web site, exhibiting at craft shows, and having them sold in several special shops. She has also had a couple of feature profile articles by *Bead and Button* magazine that helped broaden her customer base.

Generally, products are sold in the following ways:

Retail: Directly to your customers from your home, home party sales, or at other locations such as shows and trade shows.

Consignment: A shop or gallery carries your item and takes a percentage of that selling price, a commission that was agreed upon according to a contract that you both should have signed. Every state now has a version of the Uniform Commercial Code (UCC), which protects your product should it be damaged as the result of the store's negligence. Special laws protecting craft-persons and artisans from bankruptcy and shop/gallery abuses have also been passed by over thirty states.

Do your research on the laws and the reputation of any stores you are considering consigning your products before you place any of your items with them.

Wholesaling: Selling your items wholesale is an indirect method of selling to consumers because you sell larger quantities at a "wholesale price" to the retailer, or owners of mail-order businesses, online malls, and other sales distribution programs. Success selling your products this way depends on the cost of your production and your pricing structure.

Experienced entrepreneurs who sell their handmade products wholesale recommend that you assess the total cost of making your product and be sure you include a profit when figuring your wholesale price. If you are thinking of selling your products this way, here are some additional tips and considerations:

- Be sure you can produce your item(s) in a time- and cost-efficient manner so you can fill and deliver orders within designated time periods.
- Use inventory and billing software for accounting, order sheets, and inventory and tax records.
- Use only good-quality promotional materials—featuring product photos and brochures, pricing and ordering sheets, and business cards when selling to your buyers.
- Learn the wholesale terms and the entire process *before* you begin selling in order to save time and aggravation.

SALES TAX NUMBER

If you sell products or goods in a state that collects sales tax, you must get a tax number from your state, even if you sell wholesale items. (*Note:* If you plan to purchase items at wholesale shows for resale, you will need a sales tax number to be admitted to these shows.) You send collected sales tax money to the state from the sales to the final user in your state. How often you file these reports

---

PROFILE: Sharon Apichella, Decorative Wood Products

Apichella, who makes handmade wood products from her home, likes selling at wholesale craft buyer shows because she only has to attend a few wholesale shows a year to get the sales orders she needs to make her target yearly earnings. After she exhausted her "supply" of babysitters by using them every weekend that she attended craft (retail) shows, she decided to see how her products would sell at a wholesale show near her home. Apichella came home with over $5,000 worth of orders. She still exhibits occasionally at retail craft shows to sell discontinued items; to see what the public is buying; and to test-market new product ideas.

---

depends on your state's requirements. For information, contact your state department of revenue (see State-by-State Information: Web Sites in the Resources section of the appendix). Your state will also inform you what sales taxes you do and do not pay as a seller of wholesale items. The information here is presented as an overview only; consult with an accountant and related agencies as to your specific tax requirements.

BASIC TERMINOLOGY

If you are intending to sell wholesale, familiarize yourself with the wholesaling terminology, such as:

Discount: The percentage a retailer takes off your retail price to arrive at the wholesale price she will pay for your product.

F.O.B.: These letters, which stand for "freight, or free on board," designate who is paying for the shipping of your item.

Markup: The percentage a retailer adds to your wholesale price to get the retail price at which she will be selling to her customers.

Pro Forma: This term on the invoice means that you will send the items to a buyer after you have received payment from her.

Terms of Sale: Specifies what discount you will give the buyer if she pays within a certain number of days and when full payment is expected.

Part or Full Time?

Three-quarters of all home businesses are started part time. Here are some reasons:

- A part-time business gives you a chance to test the profitability potential for your product or service.
- You need less money to start because you can buy the essentials for your business and add or upgrade your equipment and supplies as your business begins to make money.
- If you are working as a full- or part-time employee, you will still be covered by health insurance and other plans.
- Operating part time gives you a chance to make mistakes and learn how to operate and perfect your business operations.
- A part-time business will give you an opportunity to test the compatibility of a partnership and how the partners work together in a business arrangement.
- You can build a customer base until you reach the point when you will be able to go full time.

Here are some of the drawbacks to starting part time:

- It may take longer until your business begins to make a profit.
- You will have to give up some free time to run your business.
- You may not be considered a "serious" business by some suppliers, banks, or even prospective customers.

PART-TIME PREPARATION

Starting part time, especially when you have a family or are involved in many activities outside of work, requires some careful balancing. Here are some tips to help you get ready:

- List all your own and your family members' activities and see whether you can either eliminate a few or combine errands to free up some time for your business.

- Discuss all the ramifications with your family and stress the benefits.
- Do not work every free hour on this part-time venture. Schedule time for yourself and your family, and make sure you make that time!

PART-TIME OPTIONS

Here are some part-time options and related tips with each:

- *Weekend Business:* Often businesses involve weekend celebrations (weddings, anniversaries, birthday parties), gardening, shows and markets, and so on. Try not to work both days every weekend.
- *On the Side:* If your present job does not have a huge workload, you might start your part-time business during breaks or during your lunch hour. With the technology of cellular phones, e-mail, and the Internet, you can communicate with customers and other business associates. Ethically and legally, your business should not directly compete with the company for whom you work.
- *Seasonal:* You may be available part time to make holiday candy or gifts; run a lawn-mowing or landscaping business in the summer (if you are a teacher, for example); or offer a service in December to assemble gifts such as bicycles or furniture. Start researching any seasonal business ideas at least a year in advance, so you will be prepared to advertise for your first customers when that season comes around again.

Deciding whether to start out on a part- or full-time basis will depend on your time, personal relationships, finances, potential demand for your products or services, and the skills that qualify you to be a business owner. Only you can determine the best time to go full time.

Follow Your "Passion" in Choosing a Business

In my first book, *101 Best Home-Based Businesses for Women* (the third edition will be published in 2002), I included the following section and chart to help assist you in choosing a business.

How do you decide which business is the one for you? Think hard about what goals you want to achieve and what is important in your life. Then write them down. Visualize what you see yourself doing six months from now, a year from now, and five years from now. If you don't have a definite idea of what type of business to start, assess your skills and interests to narrow your business choices. Filling out the chart on page 78 may help you determine what business is right for you. If you need to, copy the chart onto a wide piece of paper and fill in your responses.

1. Jobs

List all the jobs you've ever held. Include part-time jobs and jobs held while you were in school. Under each job, include the following:

Education/Training. If you needed a degree, certification, or special training for any of your jobs, list that here. Having credentials can help establish you as an expert or professional to your customers. Print your credentials on your business cards and promotional materials if they apply.

Deborah Schadler's bachelor of science and master's degrees in education and her ten years of teaching experience were the basis for the successful tutoring center she began from her home.

Achievements. This is the time to brag about what you accomplished in each of your jobs! If you increased sales, started a new product line, organized a new program, or were responsible for any other important achievement, write it down. This process will help you analyze your strengths and give you more self-confidence as you list the results of all your work.

Skills Acquired. On-the-job training can be as valuable as completing courses in the same subject—in fact, even more so if you are able to transfer those skills to your business. Why? You have had firsthand experience and have seen what works and what does not.

What You Liked Best About the Job and Why. You may have hated a job, but not everything about it. If you write down and add up all the things you liked about your jobs, you may get a better picture of what you like to do. It usually follows that if you like what you do, you will work harder at it—and better your chance of succeeding in your business.

2. Volunteer Positions

Just because you were not paid does not mean you did not accomplish something. Volunteering your time shows dedication and direction of purpose. Write down any volunteer positions you've held and fill in the columns as you did with your paid jobs.

Women have traditionally been the volunteers in communities (which is one reason they have been willing to work for less than men) and often have been responsible for starting organizations. School parent-teacher groups, family support groups, and church committees are commonly directed by women. Fund-raising, organizing support, and leading the groups are just a few of the many activities an active volunteer contributes to an organization. Skills acquired and achievements made in your volunteer work are just as significant as those acquired in a paying job.

3. Military Service Positions

Relate any military experience, training, and education you've had to civilian occupations.

4. Hobbies

What starts out as a hobby for some people often turns into a full-time business. One woman made custom lampshades as a hobby, and then turned it into a part-time job. When her husband was injured in a car accident, she was able to increase her business to full time to cover their expenses until he recovered.

5. Interests

Write down your interests and examine them to see if you have the knowledge to adapt them to a service business. In selecting a business, feel free to think up new and different businesses or a new twist on a standard idea. One woman developed a sewing service for the physically disabled after a disabled friend requested clothing that would be easy to put on and take off.

SEW's Suggestions

Terri Levine, professional coach and coaching instructor, Comprehensive Coaching U, www.coachinginstruction.com, says:

Should a woman follow her "passion" in choosing a home business?

When thinking about a home-based business, first think about how much time, energy, love, and dedication you are going to put into that business. It will take you time to build, time to create. If it feels like something that is simply "work," or a "should" or "ought to," or if you select it because of the income it "might" bring, then you may feel burnout or anger toward the business, or lose your vision, passion, and focus.

In my experience coaching women in home-based businesses all around the world—especially those who are beginning coaching and consulting home-based businesses—I encourage each woman to get in touch with her burning desire, her intense passion. You only want to give yourself and your creativity, intelligence, energy, time, and other resources to those things that you feel a surge toward. That surge, or passion, will allow you to be pulled forward by your desire and your momentum. You'll create clarity and focus and will attract with more ease and less effort what you can envision, feel, touch, and have strong desire about.

In my opinion, you must have a burning passion, a fire-in-the-belly feeling about your product, service, and/or business concept to manifest what it is you are wanting.

Ask yourself:

What do I want?
What don't I want?
Why do I want what I want?
Why do I feel passion about this?

When you really feel the desire strongly, then you know you have found the business where you will be at home and FEEL at home!

Assessing Your Skills and Strengths

	Education/ Training	Achievements	Skills Acquired	What I Liked Best About the Job and Why
JOBS				
VOLUNTEER POSITIONS				
MILITARY SERVICE POSITIONS				
HOBBIES				
INTERESTS				

Sometimes our interests can lead us into related hobbies or work. For example, Linda always liked to take pictures. As her interest grew, she read everything she could on photography and, of course, kept taking lots of pictures. She later went to work at a photo store and also took a night photography course. Now a mother of young children, she has a home studio specializing in children's portraits and takes freelance photos for businesses and writers. Linda says, "I love being able to earn money doing something I enjoy!"

Remember: Don't be afraid to brainstorm for business ideas and to search for your particular niche. You just might find yourself in a business that is both special and successful!

PROFILE: Maria Bailey, CEO, BSM Media and founder of BlueSuitMom.com, a "Passionate Niche"

I am asked often by would-be entrepreneurs how to decide what opportunities to pursue. There are two schools of thought on the subject, and I follow a little of both. First, I think you must find a niche that is not being filled, whether a service or a product. Make sure the niche is large enough to need filling. You don't want to focus on a niche so small that it offers no room for growth or profitability. Also evaluate the spending power of your potential market. You don't want to fill a need with a product they cannot afford.

Second, follow your passion. I list this element second because it is possible to develop a passion for filling a particular niche or need. Sometimes you see the problem and then develop the passion to fix it, although some entrepreneurial experiences are created by a hobby becoming a profession. For me, I saw a niche with needs not being met in the executive working mother demographic. I then became passionate in helping other working mothers find work and family balance. From that passion emerged BlueSuitMom.com, the first Web site designed for executive working mothers, and "Mom Talk Radio," the first radio show in South Florida for busy moms.

Once you launch your own business, you will work very long hours—even when your eyes feel droopy and you want to go to bed—and all that will keep you going will be your passion to do it.

HOBBY VERSUS BUSINESS

If you use much of your free time to pursue a hobby or interest, you might at one time or another think, "Can't I do this as a business?" The answer is, "Yes, many businesses have started as an outgrowth of a hobby." However, there is more to a business than just being "good at what you do." To be a successful business owner, you also must know how to manage a business and how to market your product or service, and be willing to work long hours. Turning a hobby into a profitable venture, however much you may love it, can take the joy out of it. Too much pressure to make a living, too much uncertainty, and too much doubt about whether you can turn a hobby into a successful business are reasons some people give for not making their hobby their business.

Two strong indicators for turning your hobby into a profitable business are:

- *You know your hobby.* If you have been recognized with awards, featured in articles, and are considered a "master" at what you do, then you have the credentials and background to attract prospective customers willing to pay your prices.
- *There is a demand for your product or services.* Maybe you make one-of-a-kind artwork that people ask you to make for them or as gifts, or perhaps people ask you to tutor their children. This does not mean that these people will *pay* for these products or services, but it does demonstrate that your work is noticed.

If you really are enthused about turning your hobby into a business, the next step is to write a business plan (detailed later in this book); analyze your finances and set about financing your startup; create a marketing plan; and then set goals for yourself and your business. Many people want to keep their hobbies just that— for enjoyment and pleasure. But if you decide to combine your passion and your work, your challenge is to use your *head* to also create a profitable business while working from your *heart.*

Find a Market, Find a Niche, Find Potential Customers

What is a business "niche?" A niche defined in the dictionary is "a suitable place or position." Then you want to choose a business idea that is in a good marketing position in terms of meeting the needs of customers that your competitors overlooked or did not think were worth their time.

For example, one summer I helped my husband with a lawn-mowing business. All the area's larger lawn care businesses vied fiercely to do the surrounding bigger businesses' and organizations' lawns, but no one wanted to do the little townhouse or mini-lawns. My husband and I found that we had more business than we could handle with these niche customers, and that the bigger lawn-care companies referred others who had small lawns to us.

How do you find that perfect business niche?

1. Take the results of your personal assessment and several of the business ideas you have selected based on your skills and your preferences and see which ones match best.
2. Now, ask yourself: Which of these "matched" business ideas will satisfy me personally and provide me with the lifestyle I prefer?
3. Now, the important part: Look to see what similar businesses exist and who their customers are and what they offer their customers. If you can determine through your research that there are customers whose needs are unfulfilled, then that may be the niche your business can fill.

Of course, it will not be that easy to find an untapped market, but if you keep your eyes and ears open, you are more likely to find one. You should think "niche" if you hear people saying they wish . . .

- There was a product or service that would make a task easier.
- They knew of a time-saving device.
- They could avoid doing some chore or duty.
- A specific product or service was less expensive, or of better quality.
- They could learn something new but do not know where to start.
- There was another way of doing or operating something.

Taking the time to combine your best skills, your passions, and your life's goals with a business idea that is in a good position to meet the needs of potential customers, will result in much better odds of your business succeeding with ample profits—and without having to worry about the big competitors!

Make a "Mission Statement"

A mission statement is part of your overall business plan. It provides you with the reasons for your business's existence and its customer benefits. In other words, in an article for the "Work from Home" section of the women's Web site, iVillage, I wrote that a mission statement declares your business's purpose and the reason for its presence. For example, a representative of a large software company says, "Our mission statement, our guiding principle is to 'Focus our technology leadership to offer customers value, compatibility, and performance.'"

Susan Breslow Sardone, professional copywriter and the principal of Writing That Sells, www.writingthatsells.com, a company specializing in business-to-business communications, says this:

> Why should you have a mission statement? To keep your goals in focus . . . to increase understanding of them among both employees and clients . . . and to set an accurate and consistent tone for all company communications.

Other reasons why a mission statement is important include these:

- It will help activate your marketing plan in setting goals and objectives for you to accomplish in the future.
- A well-written statement can be an effective marketing tool and can be used as an introduction to prospective customers and capture their attention. You should be able to explain your business's fundamental nature, merit, and its undertaking in one or two well-articulated sentences—which you can readily pronounce to anyone who asks you, "What is your business?"
- It can help you define the type of customers your business will most likely be serving.
- It can help you focus on the benefits you promise your customers.
- It can help you better understand the purpose of your business and give you the inspiration and nerve to withstand the rigors that a business owner often experiences.

When written, a mission statement can be as long as a page, or as short as a few sentences or a paragraph. To help you in writing your business's mission statement, here are some content suggestions:

- Provide a description of your business as you "envision" it—how you wish your prospective customers to think of your business.
- Describe how your business meets the needs of your customers.
- Explain how customers will benefit from using your product or services.
- Include descriptive and active words and terminology easy for anyone to understand.
- Write with a "picture" of your target customer in mind.

After you have written your statement, put it away for a few hours or until the next day so you will have a "fresh" outlook on it when you re-read it. To include all this in a paragraph or single page is not easy! Write and re-write your statement or write several and get some feedback from other business owners, business experts, or friends and family.

When you have finally decided on your mission statement, use it as a valuable guideline in the decision-making process of your business's operations by reading it to yourself daily.

Before You Quit Your Day Job

You may have dreamed of starting a home business for various reasons, but before you tell your boss off and quit your day job, ask yourself these questions:

1. While at your present job, have you . . .

   - Checked your company's benefit plans to see if they will increase in value, and if and when you might receive money from them?
   - Scheduled routine physical, dental, or eye examinations for you and your family covered by your company's health insurance?

- Determined the cost of the health coverage if you have to pay for it (and looked for the best plans if you have to find your own coverage)?
- Updated your references, including any written commendations you might have received for doing an exceptional job?
- Enrolled in any courses, training sessions, or seminars that were paid by your employer that could be used in a future business?

2. Have you prepared yourself financially by . . .

- Paying down as much debt as possible and made sure you have established good credit?
- Saving at least six months to two years of living expenses so you have the money for the basic startup costs? (When you own your own business, you can't assume you'll always have that money coming in.)
- Looking into getting a severance or retirement package that could help finance a business or pay living expenses?

3. Have you . . .

- Asked yourself, and the honest opinion of others, if you have what it takes to be a business owner?
- Evaluated your skills and/or education to decide if you need additional training for your venture?

4. In preparing for your business's operations, have you . . .

- Written (or are in the process of) a business plan you could take to a banker?
- Conducted thorough market research for your business idea?
- Developed a business network of experts and contacts in your industry and in the community in which you will be doing business? (These will be invaluable in getting referrals and clients.)
- Set goals—long range and short term—to establish a plan of action?

5. With your family have you . . .

- Discussed the impact a business startup could have on their lives? (Their backing will be important to your business's success!)

By heeding practical tips like these, your business will be more likely to succeed when you walk out the door for the last time and into the door of your own full-time home business.

Tips in Preparing Those Who Live with You

You may be excited to start your business, but your immediate family and/or significant other may not be so happy, as they fear what may come. How can you prepare them? Here are some suggestions:

- Have that family meeting (if you can get everyone together at the same time!) and discuss the specifics of your business plans: the financial impact, your work area, what you expect from them while you are working, and what kind of assistance you will need.
- Stress the benefits of your being home while working, but do not paint too rosy a picture.
- Be honest and tell them you will have less time to do some of the household chores and errands, but you will promise to always schedule some of your free time with family.
- Set the rules or guidelines of interrupting you, using your office supplies, answering your business phone line; but in exchange, tell them you will set regular business hours and keep to that schedule so that you are available when you are finished for the day.
- If they are old enough, ask whether they would be willing to help you out if needed. When they do help you, treat them as employees and do not scold them if they make mistakes. If you can, reward them with payment or a treat.

Get Real! "DO IT NOW!"

Judith Burnett Schneider, author, lecturer and cofounder of The Frantic Woman's Movement, www.franticwoman .com, says,

One of the grandest mistakes frantic women (those who are overscheduled and under-rested) who long to start a home-based business make is to "wait." So often I hear women say, "I'm going to start my own business when the kids are in school full time." Or they say, "I don't have the time (or money) now, but in five years, I'll be able to do more." My answer is always, "Do it now." Take it from many experienced frantic women/business owners—it doesn't get any easier. It isn't likely that you'll ever have huge blocks of time to invest solely in your home-based business. That's why they're "home-based"—so you can continue with the life you've chosen—including the house, the spouse, the kids, and the dog— *and* have your business, too!

So what can you do? Abandon that search for free time and start now. If you are enthusiastic enough about your home business idea, you'll *want* to spend your time working on it as opposed to talking on the phone or watching a nighttime drama series. Step one: Pinpoint where your time is being wasted and use it constructively to research and expand your home-based business idea.

- Inform them that you are always willing to listen to complaints and feedback about your business activities and how they are affecting their lives.
- Realize that it will take time for everyone to adjust to your home business. If you stay positive, manage your time wisely, and do your best to keep to your announced business hours, you will have a happier family, as well as providing them with a role model for their future work.

Additional Work-from-Home Options

A number of additional work-from-home options exist that women have operated from a home base for years and still do very successfully today. If you choose one of these options, you have the advantage of having the support and backing of an already established company. One disadvantage is that you may not have the right personality to sell these companies' goods and services. Also, be wary of illegal pyramid schemes masquerading as legitimate businesses. As with any business idea, do your homework and investigate the company and how an opportunity operates before investing any of your dollars.

NETWORK MARKETING (PARTY PLANS), MLM, AND DISTRIBUTORSHIPS

Both direct selling and MLM (multilevel marketing) pertain to "network marketing," in which you, the "distributor," purchase the rights from a company to market its products to customers within a given territory (though not always exclusive).

As a distributor, you are self-employed and set your own hours. Generally, you purchase a starter kit with order forms, samples, and supplies for direct sales to consumers. Popular items sold this way may include toys, cosmetics, children's books, and other items. Distributors sell one-on-one to customers, through party plans, or a combination of both methods.

In MLM, distributors not only sell a company's products but enlist others to sell these products/services under their supervision—called "downline." You, the "recruiter" (or "sponsor") would then receive "compensation"—a percentage of your enlistees' sales.

If network marketing and direct sales are something you are considering, here are some guidelines to consider:

- *Research the company.* Do not let yourself be rushed or pressured.
- *Ask about the initial investment.* Legitimate network marketing companies usually offer affordable startup materials.
- *Like the products or services you are selling.* If you would not buy them for yourself, how can you convince someone else to buy them?

SEW's Suggestions

Marla Berchard, a network marketing professional/consultant, advises:

> To maximize financial success, it is critical to select a company that has four elements:
>
> 1. a compensation plan rewarding part-time distributors and full-time professionals, but not at each other's expense;
> 2. a stable company providing outstanding customer service;
> 3. products that are competitively priced, get results, and are consumable (very important!); and
> 4. duplicable training, support systems, and mentorship. This is where the phrase, "You're in business for yourself, but not by yourself" comes into play.
>
> Do your company research with calculator in hand and your common sense, as well as your intuition, highly activated. Learn how to sort through company and product "hype" and apply proven business principles to make a sound and informed decision. Tap into resources to help you learn what pitfalls and "red flags" to avoid. Above all else, find a good mentor. This is a great industry that presents tremendous opportunity for women entrepreneurs.

For Marla Berchard's free report, "The Simple Formula for Evaluating Network Marketing Compensation Plans," send an e-mail to mbhb@shaw.ca, or write to 2028 Carrick Street, Victoria B.C. Canada, V8R 2M6.

- *Approach network marketing as a business.* Keep records, plan, and follow the company's marketing strategies.
- *Invest in only one company at a time, and give yourself at least six months to a year, if possible, to see the results of your efforts.* Do not compare your results to others'. Remember any

WARNING!!: Watch Out for Pyramids!

What are pyramids? Pyramid business scams (which are illegal!) operate where a few people at the top make money from the many at the list's bottom who generally lose their initial (and often substantial) investment. Many pyramids disguise and tout themselves as legitimate MLMs and will imitate their multilevel structure. Pyramids will ask you for a substantial investment of money that you are to give to someone higher in the structure and then you are supposed to ask others to do the same. Of course, eventually the pyramid collapses and most of those who invested their money will lose it. Pyramid schemes seldom sell a product or service and only pretend they are selling a business opportunity. Their main goal is to recruit as many people as possible to add more money to the scheme.

---

new venture will entail a learning curve that takes a commitment of time and work.

- *Check on the company.* Contact the Direct Marketing and Multi-Level Marketing International Association to see if a company is a member and also check for any complaints with the Better Business Bureau's and attorney general's offices in the state of the company's headquarters.

If you want to check the legitimacy of a company, do one of the following:

- Check with a local chapter of the Better Business Bureau or visit their Web site at www.BBB.org.
- Contact the Multi-Level Marketing International Association at www.mlmia.com to see if the company is a reputable member.
- Contact The Federal Trade Commission (FTC) at www.ftc.gov or Federal Trade Commission, CRC-240, Washington, D.C. 20580 to see whether any complaints have been lodged against

the company. The FTC does not resolve disputes, but complaints against a company can help them spot illegal business practices. For more information or to file a complaint, visit their Web site or call (202) 326-2222.

HOME-BASED FRANCHISES AND BUSINESS OPPORTUNITIES

The publication *Small Business News* (Philadelphia/New Jersey), www.sbn-online.com, said in its April 1999 issue, that around 3,500 companies are franchising in the U.S. today and that franchises account for $800 billion in sales each year, with some 8 million employees. Home-based franchise fees can range in price from a couple of thousand dollars to many thousands of dollars. Types of franchises vary from children's products and services to pet care and miscellaneous services.

FRANCHISE BASICS: QUESTIONS AND EVALUATIONS

What is a franchise?

A franchise is a business opportunity in which the franchisee (you, the buyer) pays an initial franchise fee, startup costs, and often ongoing royalties (a percentage of monthly gross sales) to the franchisor (the owner of the franchise) for the right to sell and distribute the franchisor's products or services and use its trade name, trademark, or service mark. The franchisee operates the business following the standards and guidelines set by the franchisor.

Non-franchise business opportunities include dealers/distributorships, licensees, network marketing, vending machines, and co-operatives (a licensing-type agreement).

ADVANTAGES/DISADVANTAGES OF INVESTING IN A FRANCHISE

Pros

- There is less risk of failure in investing in an established operation than starting a business from scratch.
- Franchises have product-name recognition with which customers are already familiar.
- Franchisors can help provide professional startup advice and assist franchisees with any operating difficulties.

WARNING!!: Business Opportunity Scams

A business opportunity is a business venture sold by a company or entrepreneur who wishes to expand the company or sell the idea to others who want to start a similar business. A business opportunity is usually a "package" complete with a manual, business forms, and sometimes the equipment. Customer support may or may not be included—which is crucial to your success with the opportunity.

For example, one older couple answered an ad from a company selling a number of work-at-home business opportunities: medical billing, a home-based travel agency, and other so-called businesses anyone could "run from their kitchen table." Thinking they could do these businesses in their retirement years, they refinanced their home for $15,000 to purchase several of these at-home businesses. Unfortunately, the computer and software that came with the deal were not only out of date, but the couple received no instruction in how to operate them. Even worse, the couple received no training in how to market these "opportunities" or how to run a business. Had the couple invested that money in a business in which they had some experience *and* for which there was an existing market in their community, the results would likely have been much better.

The company (advertised as a family business with values!) was ordered to stop by its state attorney general's office and ordered to return the money to people who purchased their bogus opportunities. But most of that money was gone, so most of those customers lost all their money! Legitimate business opportunities do exist, but be very cautious of those that are anything but legitimate!

Cons

- Franchises can be expensive to acquire.
- Franchises can be restrictive in their operations for the franchisee.
- Franchises are not really your own business, but a contract to operate that franchise that may or may not be renewed at the end of the contract period.
- Some require a minimum of years of commitment. Be sure this is something you can do for years!

Questions to Ask Before Investing in a Franchise

- *Is this the right franchise for me?* From the over fifty different industries from which you can choose, select something that suits your interests, talents, and life's goals.
- *What is the future of this franchise?* Is there a market in your area for this type of franchise? Is the franchisor aware of the future trends in the franchise's industry, and is he or she making sure they will meet the demands of future customers?
- *Do I have professional advice?* Have I spoken with a banker, lawyer, and accountant who specialize in franchise business to get their opinions about this specific franchise?
- *How much do I know about a particular franchise's operations?* Have I spoken to other franchisees of the company that interests me to get their feedback? Have I spent some time observing or working in this franchise so I have an idea what a typical day is like?

One former career woman spent a year researching the franchise that interested her before deciding to invest in it. She talked to other franchisees with the company about their experiences and made a visit to the company's headquarters to interview the executives and employees. Franchise business experts advise you to prepare yourself and take your time to thoroughly investigate any franchise and business opportunity.

UFOCs

You should not even contemplate purchasing a franchise until you receive and analyze its Uniform Franchising Offering Circular (UFOC) and its franchise agreement, which state and federal laws require the company supply you within ten days after your first personal meeting or ten days before any agreement is signed or a down payment put down. A UFOC includes standard items that must be disclosed to you, the prospective franchisee: a business description, contract obligations of you and the franchisor, any lawsuits or bankruptcy history, and much more. Let your business experts also look over the UFOC and the agreement to get professional opinions.

Related Resources on page 99 offers a listing of some recommended organizations, books, articles, experts, and Web sites to help you learn everything you might want to know about acquiring a franchise contract. Take advantage of their available information to help you make the decision whether franchising is the best home-based business option for you.

STARTING YOUR OWN FRANCHISE, NETWORK MARKETING OR BUSINESS OPPORTUNITY

After working in direct selling and network marketing, or if you have a successful business, you may think of developing it into a franchise or a business opportunity. Business experts advise that your first consult should be with professionals—legal, financial, and management consulting firms that specialize in franchise and/or business opportunity development. They will be able to tell you if your home business is suitable for this type of expansion.

Debra Cohen of Home Remedies of NY, Inc. (see Profile) and Paula Kay of Ageless Placements, a service in Florida that uses seniors to help other seniors with household chores in their homes, both expanded into selling business packages—so other entrepreneurs could start similar businesses in their areas.

Some factors to consider:

- Your business should be suitable for franchising or starting up in many other areas.
- It should have a universal demand and have a good profit potential for those who purchase it.
- You will need to make a plan of development.
- You will need to follow all the governmental regulations and guidelines in selling to others.

If your business is very successful and many people are asking you how to start one, you might just consider going this route with your home business.

WORK-FROM-HOME

Many people ask about (legitimate) work-from-home options for various reasons: They do not have the funds, time, or inclination to start their own home business; their health is poor or they have a limiting disability; they are the primary caregiver of children or an elderly relative who need constant care; or they have some other reason that requires them to stay at home.

So, the question is this: "Can you find legitimate work-from-home jobs?" The answer is: "Yes, but these jobs are difficult to find!"

Here are some of the reasons:

1. *Certain types of home work are illegal.* Some regulations by federal and state governments forbid companies from hiring home workers for certain jobs involving sewing, jewelry-making, and other industries. These laws are the result of past home worker abuses by employers. For information, contact your local and state officials and visit the Department of Labor's site and search for "home work," www.dol.gov.

2. *IRS independent contractor (IC) guidelines are complicated.* Employers may wish to avoid hiring home workers because of the complicated IRS guidelines they must follow as to who is and who is not an IC or an employee. (For more information, see "Legal Considerations," Independent Contractor Issues, in chapter 5.)

3. *There are many, many home working scams.* Scam artists abound everywhere, including the Internet, to take money from those who wish to work from home. Follow the adage, "If it sounds too good to be true . . . ," and never send any money for information! Legitimate industries that use home workers do not ask for money. The Web sites of the Federal Trade Commission, www.ftc.gov, and the National Fraud Information Center, www.fraud.org, regularly feature some of the latest work-from-home and Internet scams.

PROFILE: Debra Cohen, president of Home Remedies of NY, Inc.,
www.homeownersreferral.com, a homeowner referral network

Several years ago when Debra Cohen and her husband purchased
their first home, she was five months pregnant and working fifty
hours a week. As she began to develop a list of dependable contractors, Cohen came up with an idea to create a "personal agency
for the home," and formed Homeowner Referral Network. As her
business grew, others became interested in starting a similar business, so she documented all her business's startup and management
steps that she put into a manual, *The Complete Guide to Owning
and Operating a Successful Homeowner Referral Network.* Cohen
is now selling her business idea as a home business opportunity in
the form of several business "packages" that include the manual
and different levels of support.

---

4. *Employers are hesitant to hire an unknown worker.* Few employers will trust a person they do not know with company
   materials or responsibilities. Those new workers they do hire
   often come from referrals by present (trusted) workers and only
   after an interview and a trial working period. Therefore, when
   seeking a work-at-home job, a person should first search in
   their own area for home work opportunities. Note, too, that it
   just makes more practical sense for employers to have employees in one location in terms of quality control, cost, health and
   safety, and of course, liability issues, rather than having workers "scattered about" in private dwellings.

Thus, if you are seeking a work-at-home job, you should first
assess your own skills, and second, ask around your own neighborhood for businesses that may need part-time help. If you become a valued employee, and the job can be performed (legally) in
a home setting, then your employer may permit you to take the job
home. Many companies these days will often "outsource" certain

kinds of work to independent contractors, depending on their skills and qualifications.

Another question would be this: "What types of work are people doing from home?" Just a few of the many ingenious ways people are earning money from their own and others' homes include sitting in people's homes to wait for repairpersons or deliveries; being greeters at real estate open houses; getting paid for their opinions online; and doing telemarketing or other types of communications work. (*Note:* If in doubt, consult with a tax specialist about reporting any income you make for tax reporting purposes.)

Buying a Business

Most newspapers, especially the larger ones, will have in their ads various businesses for sale. Sometimes these will also be home-based businesses. Depending on your finances, buying an existing business may be an option for you.

(*Note:* If you are in the process of starting a business, you should periodically scan for sale ads because you can often get great bargains on good, used office equipment and supplies.)

Here are some items that you and your experts—legal and financial—should check to see if the business for sale is a good buy. For larger businesses, you can also hire a business broker to represent you.

- *Financial Statements:* Preferably a certified public accountant (CPA) will look at the business balance sheet and its profit and loss statements.
- *Assets:* The business should have more assets than liabilities.
- *Marketing Analysis:* An analysis of the business's current marketing methods to see if they are adequate or should be updated and revised to bring in more customers.
- *Fair Price:* The price you pay should allow you to get a fair return on your investment and not be high-risk.
- *Smooth Transition:* If it is a one- or two-person business, loyal customers may not like the way you handle the goods or services, so you will want to consider whether the transition in ownership will be acceptable to the existing clients.

- *Observation:* You should observe the typical workday or workweek of this business to get an idea how the present owner operates it.

- *Temporary Assistance:* Sometimes after a business's sale, the owner will commit to a period of time to help you ease into the management of it. See if this is a possibility.

- *Disclosure of Negatives:* There may be some negative aspects of the business you are buying, so it is important that you consider all the information you gather from your experts and the seller to see if these minuses can be overcome.

Buying an existing home business can bring you a steady income immediately or it can bring you headaches. Only after a thorough evaluation of the business can you decide whether it is a good "fit" with you and your goals. You may just decide to start your own business from scratch instead.

MULTIPLE BUSINESSES?

Many business experts advise against having two separate home and/or small businesses, especially when starting out, for obvious reasons: You're likely to spread your resources of time and money too thin and be unable to focus enough on any one business to make it successful.

Of course, there are always exceptions. One single young woman, Regina, supported herself with a full-time cleaning business but also had a passion for creating her one-of-a-kind jewelry. She would do her cleaning during the day and make her jewelry at night. On weekends, she would sell her jewelry at art shows and sometimes work part time for a jeweler to perfect her skills. Regina's goal, though, is to be able to support herself with the sales of her jewelry. She is slowly building a steady, repeat-customer list toward that goal.

What Regina and Nancy Cleary (see Profile to follow) have in common, is that after establishing their first business both started a business on the side, their "passions." In Regina's case, her two businesses were totally different. In Nancy Cleary's example, her boxes are an extension of her graphic arts skills.

PROFILE: Nancy Cleary, Wyatt-MacKenzie Publishing,
www.Box-is.com

Nancy Cleary, publisher at Wyatt-MacKenzie Publishing and creator of Box-is.com, which is dedicated to helping women entrepreneurs package and sell their ideas, says this:

> I run my graphic design studio full time (40+ hrs/week) which, for now, financially supports my new company, my passion—my publishing company. I struggle every day to juggle the two companies and two small children; but I believe this is my purpose, and I am helping other women (work-at-home moms especially) in the process.
>
> I come in before 9:00 A.M. to work on publishing projects and back in after dinner for four to six hours a few times a week. My weekends and holidays, I dedicate to myself by working solely on publishing projects rather than client work.
>
> My mission is to intrinsically combine the work of the two companies. This is part of my marketing plan. I trade graphic design services for cooperative marketing and co-branding of my publishing products. I understand the difficulties women entrepreneurs face when packaging and marketing their ideas, both creatively and financially. So, while there is no immediate financial gain, I am building a powerful brand and an army of grateful women to promote it!
>
> The reason I started my publishing company was the same reason people leave their "regular work." I spent my days making everyone else's dreams come true but my own, and I would end work at night with a paycheck—but nothing else to show for my hard work.
>
> I wanted to leave a legacy! I wanted *my* name on the products I designed (actually the names of my two children!).

Some other tips if you decide to operate more than one home business are:

1. *Keep your business's operations separated wherever possible.* This includes your business checking accounts, bookkeeping and business records, voice mailboxes, e-mail addresses, post office boxes, and any other functions that are related to each of your ventures.
2. *Monitor the cash flow of each business to make sure one business's profits are not being drained by another.*
3. *Keep other aspects as your life as simple as possible.* Get help to handle the business's paperwork and your household work so you still have time for your loved ones and some personal time!

Whether you have one, or eighteen businesses like one man in my town, each one needs its own individual business plan with its goals and objectives. If you want to take on the challenge of balancing two or more businesses along with your personal life, then go ahead. But take time off to enjoy life, too!

Related Resources

WEB SITES

Bizy Moms, www.bizymoms.com. Web site of home business author, Liz Folger, offers chats with business experts and entrepreneurs, home business e-books and online classes, and other related information.

It's Your Life is a free e-newsletter, at www.Changingcourse.com that offers articles, a large "Resources for a Change" section, a bulletin board to put you in touch with others making the leap to self-employment, a bookstore, and the inspiration you need to help you to escape the traditional job world and create a more satisfying life working at what you love.

"Entrepreneurial Assessment" by Judith Dacey, CPA, at www.easyas123 .com/selftest.htm.

The Edward Lowe Foundation's "Entrepreneurial Edge," www.edge.lowe.org. "Search" in its documents for "Mission Statement."

Entrepreneurial Parent, www.en-parent.com/. Information and tips for balancing running a business and parenting.

FranInfo, www.franinfo.com. Gives basic information about how to choose a franchise; also provides information about franchising your own business.

Hewlett-Packard, www.education.hp.com/. Offers online courses, such as building Web pages, Photoshop basics, graphic design for nondesigners, and more.

Home-Based Working Moms, www.hbwm.com. An online community of work-at-home parents; articles, work-at-home kit, and related information.

HomeWorkingMom.com, Mother's Home Business Network's Web site. Telecommuting, freelance and home business information and ideas.

MyJobSearch.com, www.myjobsearch.com/advancement.html. This site's "Career Planning" section offers links to a number of free (and some for a fee) personal assessment sites for further self-evaluation.

Work-At-Home Moms, www.wahm.com. Work-at-home online magazine for mothers; articles, forums, home jobs and telecommuting listings, and more.

Online Courses

"Breakfast with Dell," www.dell.com/breakfast. Periodic online sessions for answers to technology questions.

ThirdAge's, "Learning Center," www.thirdage.com/, and others offer classes that range from free to fee-based.

BOOKS

101 Best Weekend Businesses by Dan Ramsey (Franklin Lakes, NY: Career Press, 1996).

101 Best Extra-Income Opportunities for Women: Special Money-Making Ideas for Women Who Run Out of Money Before They Run Out of Month by Jennifer Basye Sander (Roseville, CA: Prima Communications, Inc., 1997).

The 220 Best Franchises to Buy: The Source Book for Evaluating the Best Franchise Opportunities, 3rd ed., by Lynie Arden, Constance Jones, Philip Leif Group Staff (Broadway Books, 2000).

The Artist-Gallery Partnership: A Practical Guide to Consigning Art by Tad Crawford and Susan Mellon (New York, NY: Allworth Press, 1998).

Building a Successful Network Marketing Company: The Systems, the Products, and the Know-How You Need to Launch a Successful MLM Company by Angela L. Moore (Roseville, CA: Prima Communications, 1998).

Coaching for an Extraordinary Life by Terri Levine (Buckingham, PA: Lahaska Press, 2001).

Finding Your Perfect Work: The New Career Guide to Making a Living, Creating a Life by Paul and Sarah Edwards (New York: The Putnam Publishing Group, 1995).

Finding Your Niche: A Personal Guide for Entrepreneurs by Laurence J. Pino (New York: Berkley Publishing Group, 1994).

The Franchise Bible: How to Buy a Franchise or Franchise Your Own Business by Erwin J. Keup (Grants Pass, OR: PSI Research/The Oasis Press, 2000).

The Franchise Fraud: How to Protect Yourself Before & After You Invest by Robert L. Purvin, Jr. (New York: John Wiley & Sons, 1994).

Home Businesses You Can Buy: The Definitive Guide to Exploring Franchises, Multi-Level Marketing and Business Opportunities Plus How to Avoid Scams by Paul and Sarah Edwards and Walter Zooi (New York: Putnam, 1997).

Inside Network Marketing: An Expert's View into the Hidden Truths and Exploited Myths of America's Most Misunderstood Industry (revised and updated) by Leonard W. Clements (Roseville, CA: Prima Communications, 2000).

Homemade Money: How to Select, Start, Manage, Market and Multiply the Profits of a Business at Home, 5th ed., by Barbara Brabec (Cincinnati, OH: F & W Publications, 1997).

How to Raise a Family and a Career Under One Roof by Lisa Roberts (Moontownship, PA: Brookhaven Press, 1997).

The Mission Statement Book: 301 Corporate Mission Statements from America's Top Companies by Jeffrey Abrahams (Berkeley, CA: Ten Speed Press, 1999).

Mompreneurs: A Practical Step-by-Step Guide to Work-at-Home Success by Ellen H. Parlapiano and Patricia Coby (New York: Berkley, 1996).

The Pathfinder: How to Choose or Change Your Career for a Lifetime of Satisfaction and Success by Nicholas Lore (New York: Simon & Schuster Trade Paperbacks, 1997).

The Shoestring Entrepreneur's Guide to the Best Home-Based Franchises by Robert Spiegel (New York: St. Martin's Press, 2000).

The Stay-at-Home Mom's Guide to Making Money: How to Create the Business That's Right for You Using the Skills and Interests You Already Have, rev. 2nd ed., by Liz Folger (Rocklin, CA: Prima Publishing 1997), www.bizymoms.com.

Strategies for Successfully Buying or Selling a Business! by Russell L. Brown (Niantic, CT: RDS Associates, 1997).

To Build the Life You Want, Create the Work You Love: The Spiritual Dimension of Entrepreneuring by Marsha Sinetar (New York: St. Martin's Press, 1995).

Ultimate Guide to Network Marketing: Your Step-By-Step Guide to Wealth by Russell Paley (Franklin Lakes, NJ: Career Press, Inc., 2000).

What's Your Sabotage? The Last Word in Overcoming Self-Sabotage by Alyce Cornyn-Selby (Portland, OR: Beynch Press, 2000).

The Work-at-Home Sourcebook, 7th ed., by Lynie Arden (CO: Live Oak Publications, 1999).

Work Yourself Happy: A Step-by-Step Guide to Creating Joy in Your Life and Work by Terri Levine (Buckingham, PA: Lahaska Press, 2000).

Which Business? Help in Selecting Your New Venture by Nancy Drescher (Grants Pass, OR: Oasis Press, 1997).

ADDITIONAL RESOURCES

Publications

The Crafts Report, www.craftsreport.com. Includes business articles and features for professional artisans and craftspeople who make a living from their work; also lists craft retail, wholesale, and trade shows.

MLM Woman Newsletter, www.mlmwoman.com; Regent Press, 2081 N. Oxnard Blvd., #251, Oxnard, CA 93030. Linda Locke, editor/publisher.

Step into Success, www.stepintosuccess.com; P.O. Box 712, Lakeland, MI 48143. A print magazine for women in business providing ongoing education and motivation and concrete business-building methods. "A 'must-have' for direct sellers!"

Magazine Web Sites Listing Franchises

(They also have regular print issues featuring a listing of home-based franchises.)

Entrepreneur, www.entrepeneur.com. Also has a section, "Women in Franchising."

Home Business Magazine, www.homebusinessmag.com. Publishes a special annual issue featuring home-based franchises and business opportunities.

Market Research Sources

American Demographics (magazine), www.demographics.com; P.O. Box 68, Ithaca, NY 14851.

Marketing Research Association, www.mra-net.org; 1344 Silas Deane Hwy., #306, Rocky Hill, CT 06067.

Organizations

The Better Business Bureau, www.bbb.org. Go to their Web site to find a local chapter to check the credentials of a locally based company or to file a complaint.

The Direct Selling Association, www.dsa.org; 1275 Pennsylvania Ave. #800 NW, Washington D.C. 20004. This national trade association of the leading firms that manufacture and distribute goods and services sold directly to consumers has a "Code of Ethics" for members.

Multi-Level Marketing International Association, 119 Stanford Ct., Irvine, CA 92612. Web site: www.mlmia.com/.

The National Consumers League's National Fraud Information Center (NFIC), www.fraud.org; (800) 876-7060 (Canada, U.S., and Puerto Rico).

Associations

American Association of Franchisees and Dealers, www.aafd.org; P.O. Box 81887, San Diego, CA 92138-1887. "A nonprofit trade association representing the rights and interests of franchisees and independent dealers throughout the U.S." Has publications on buying, financing, and other franchise information.

American Business Opportunity Institute, c/o Andrew A. Caffey, 3 Bethesda Metro Ctr., #700, Bethesda, MD 20814. Regulation information about business opportunity and franchise investments. Send a business-size, self-addressed stamped (first class) envelope for more information on publications and programs.

International Franchise Association (IFA), www.franchise.org/; 1350 New York Ave. NW, Ste. 900, Washington, D.C. 20005-4709; (202) 628-8000; Twice a year, the IFA publishes the *Franchise Opportunities Guide* containing important franchise buyers' information and can be purchased online or at major bookstores. The IFA has a "Women's Franchise Committee" to help encourage women to take advantage of franchising opportunities.

Booklets

The Federal Trade Commission has a number of consumer guides about buying franchises and business opportunities. Visit the Web site www.FTC.gov to read or call (202) 326-2222 to request these free booklets.

International Franchise Expo

www.betheboss.com, and other franchise information.

CHAPTER FOUR

Home Business Startup Basics

W hy do so many women start home businesses? Barbara Mainhart, a marketing communications professional with over twenty years' experience in all phases of corporate, product, and technical marketing communications, says that a number of things made her decide to work from her home. "Being able to do what I truly enjoy for multiple clients in multiple industries and markets is creatively and intellectually energizing," says Mainhart. "Within a corporation, you focus on one market or industry in depth, which can make you an expert but is also limiting. And the inevitable focus on corporate politics can eat up a huge percentage of the job."

After college, Chris Carroll was hired as a manager in the retail business. "They made us work forty-eight hours, but we were only paid for forty. Those forty-eight hours almost always turned into sixty hours. I thought, *If I'm going to work, I'm going to work for myself and get paid for it.* On my days off I started cleaning windows. One job led to another and my cleaning business was born."

Here are just a few additional reasons so many people are starting home businesses:

- Affordable technology and increased capabilities of computers and the related software have made operating all sizes of businesses from home easier.

- The Internet enables a person to reach a global market, have "virtual" business partners and collaborators, communicate easily with customers and business associates, enroll in business and technological courses, and obtain business know-how on just about every entrepreneurial topic that exists—all from one's home computer. Faster Internet connections are becoming more accessible and affordable.

- Home entrepreneurship is appealing to more people as the lack of job security is increasing and people are searching for the ideal combination of work and life.

- Although most home business owners have some sort of child-care coverage, a parent can be home for their children if they are sick and when they come home after school (a time that many children—elementary and teens alike—end up being "latchkey" kids, with no adult supervision).

- Depending on the type, many home businesses can be conducted from just about any location, permitting the owners to choose their ideal place to live.

- Home offices are generally healthier than many office buildings. It's your home and, of course, you can set the temperature, adjust the air flow and air quality as you and your family are accustomed to having it and might need it if you suffer from seasonal allergies, for example.

- While many couples have to work almost two and a half jobs just to meet their living expenses, the profit potential for running a home business is higher than working for an employer. According to a number of sources, the average home business earns an average of $50,000 per year, with around 20 percent earning more than $75,000 per year. Compare this to the U.S. Bureau of Economic Analysis that as of 1998, the U.S. per capita income was only $28,518. Home businesses can provide a supplemental income to those in retirement.

There are many more reasons for wanting to start a home business; in fact, each new entrepreneur has her own reasons. Whatever your reasons, they will help sustain and drive you to find a successful and satisfying home business.

Steps to Startup

Here is a (general) suggested timetable of steps that you can check off as you start up your business.

ONE YEAR BEFORE YOUR STARTUP:

Selecting a Business

__ Read books and articles on specific businesses and make a list of those that interest you.

__ Assess your skills and preferences.

__ Assess the impact a home business will have on your personal and/or family life.

Investigate

__ Contact entrepreneurs with similar businesses or in the same industry to see whether they will answer your questions and even permit you to "shadow" them for a day or two to get an idea of what is involved in such a venture.

__ Read industry manuals, books, and publications specific to the business that interests you.

__ Begin to discuss your entrepreneurship plans with your family.

Qualify Yourself

__ Contact schools, colleges, Women's Business Centers, SCORE offices, and/or Small Business Development Centers to enroll in courses or seminars that you will need to improve your business and management skills, get certification (if necessary), or obtain government or other financing.

__ Enroll in courses specific to your product or service, especially if you are planning a business different from your background.

__ Another option is to get a full- or part-time job, or volunteer in a similar business in your industry to gain practical, hands-on knowledge.

Six Months Before Your Startup:

Define Your Business
__ Specify the product and services your business will offer.

__ List your primary competitors.

__ Begin writing your business plan.

Determine Your Potential Customers
__ Survey, interview potential customers.

__ Research the demographics of these potential customers.

__ Analyze your competitors' present customers.

Further Study Your Industry
__ Use the Internet to gather information about trade associations in your industry by accessing their Web sites and conversing with other entrepreneurs in online chats or news groups.

__ Contact the information sources that align best with your interests.

Gather Your Experts
__ Get referrals from your local business organizations for a business lawyer, an accountant, and an insurance specialist.

__ Interview and select candidates then follow their professional recommendations needed for your business, such as clarifying legal requirements, setting up a bookkeeping system, and getting your business and you and your family covered by the proper insurances.

Four Months Before Startup

Take Care of Legalities
__ Determine your business structure: sole proprietorship, partnership, or corporation.

__ Register your name of business, DBA (doing business as), or your fictitious name.

___ Obtain a Federal Taxpayer ID Number (EIN).

___ Check with your local municipality about zoning regulations and required licenses; likewise with your county and state.

___ Apply for a sales tax permit.

Establish Networking Contacts

___ Join a local business organization.

___ Join a trade association.

Choose Part Time or Full Time

___ Analyze your personal financial situation to see if you have enough money to sustain you and your family for six months to a year if you start full time.

___ If not, decide your strategy as to how you will work your part-time business into your present work and family schedule.

THREE MONTHS BEFORE STARTUP TO OPENING DAY

Finalize Your Plans

___ Finalize your business plan and begin to implement your advertising and marketing strategies: press releases, opening promotions, talks, seminars, and advertising plans.

___ Have your promotional materials printed: business cards and brochures, stationery, advertising specialties.

___ Develop a daily management plan.

Set Up Your Office

___ Lease or buy the basic equipment and technology needed to start your business off.

___ Get connected to the Internet and designate a phone line with voice mail to handle customers' inquiries.

___ Decide and set up your working space in your home.

Finances

___ Arrange financing (if needed) and set up a business checking account.

___ Figure your probable costs. Establish pricing by checking with the current market and trade sources.

STARTUP DAY

Announce that you are open for business! Send press releases to newspapers and to print and online publications.

STARTUP COSTS

If you have decided what kind of business you are going to run or are still considering one, you will naturally be considering the basic startup costs. The total of these costs will be important in deciding when your "open for business" date will be, whether you will be applying for a loan, and how you will determine your fixed expenses.

Generally, a home business will cost less to start than a business located in a building in a commercial district, and generally a service business will cost less than a product-oriented one. Other factors will also influence your startup expenses as some businesses will require extra licenses, special equipment, and high-tech equipment.

STARTUP EXPENSE LIST

If you are a new entrepreneur, it is important to thoroughly research how much your chosen business idea will realistically cost to start up. Resources that can provide you with at least an idea of the startup figures include trade associations (they usually have guidelines for their specific industry); counselors at Women's Business Centers, offices of SCORE, or Small Business Development Centers; books, publications, and/or startup guides for specific businesses; business consultants and small business coaches; and, of course, other women and home-based entrepreneurs.

Here is a basic startup expense list to assist you in determining what funds you will need:

Basic Startup Expense List

Work space (your home office space) remodeling,
decorations   _____

Furniture and fixtures   _____

Equipment and installation   _____

Office supplies and services   _____

Utilities and installations   _____

Professional fees (legal, accounting, other)   _____

Permits, licenses   _____

Insurances (business, disability, disaster, health, other)   _____

Signs (outside, if permitted by zoning; vehicle)   _____

Business and/or trade association memberships   _____

Promotional materials (business cards, signs
[outside, if permitted by zoning, vehicle]
brochures, banners, other)   _____

Startup stock (product inventory if you produce goods)   _____

Internet expenses (connection; Web site; marketing)   _____

Miscellaneous (or unexpected) expenses   _____

Cash reserve (to sustain your business in its
beginning months until it begins to make money)   _____

Estimated Total of Startup Expenses   _____

ESTIMATED MONTHLY OPERATING EXPENSES

Once you have an idea of your startup expenses, estimate how much
it will cost you per month to run your home business. Your estimated
monthly expenses will be a combination of fixed expenses—insurances, professional costs, utilities, membership dues, Internet connection fees—and other expenses not affected by your revenues. And
variable expenses will be part of your monthly expenses—marketing

expenses, supplies, postage and mailing, gas for vehicles, repairs, and additional expenses that are affected by your business's income. Here are some basic considerations in estimating your monthly operating costs:

Basic Monthly Operating Costs

Living expenses (see financial plan)   _____

Your salary   _____

Home equipment maintenance/repairs   _____

Outsourcing (if you need extra help)   _____

Advertising   _____

Supplies (office, product-/service-related)   _____

Insurance fees   _____

Utilities (specific to your business)   _____

Professional fees (consulting, legal, accounting)   _____

Taxes   _____

Postage/shipping   _____

Internet (connection, Web hosting, design changes)   _____

Interest   _____

Credit card fees   _____

Depreciation   _____

Travel (trade shows, visiting clients, seminars)   _____

Education/training   _____

Membership dues   _____

Estimated Total of Operating Costs   _____

Figuring these startup and estimated monthly expenses will provide you with an idea of how much money you will need for a startup and to operate each month. It will also help you determine the following financial figures (all discussed later in this book): the prices for your products and/or services, your overall financial plan (discussed later), your cash flow, and your income projection. A good guideline is to always overestimate rather than underestimate your future expenses!

Home Business Dilemmas

ISOLATION

If you come from a work experience background where you had lots of interaction from other employees and the business's clients, you may feel isolated in operating your business (or may feel relieved if your previous job was too hectic!). Isolation can seriously sabotage your ability to work effectively if you do not deal with these feelings early on in your home venture. Recognize what is making you feel isolated and compensate for it. Here are some methods to handle home business isolation and loneliness:

Handling Isolation

- If you are missing your former coworkers, join a business ownership organization and participate in their monthly activities.
- If you are missing your support staff and hate doing all the "business-side" activities, then barter or outsource the duties you hate or need assistance with to other home business workers or business support services.
- If you are missing support from others in your industry, join that trade group and attend conferences and workshops they may hold in your area. Some industry trade groups have Web sites with ongoing chats and message boards where you can ask questions. Also look to join e-mail discussion groups. To find a list, search online, One List at www.onelist.com or www.lsoft .com/lists/listref.html; or start your own free list at Yahoo!, One List, or eGroups (www.egroups.com).
- If you want an informal home business group, form a home-based mother's group to meet at a member's house to discuss ongoing business problems. As mentioned previously in this book, you can also help one another by taking turns hosting a children's play group to free up several hours a day of uninterrupted

time to work. A benefit of joining with other home-based moms is that you may be able to partner on some work projects.

- Set regular business hours (best related to your schedule) and also some time each day to take a walk, read a favorite book, go to a local gym or your public library, or even just run an errand.
- Volunteer for a one-time project or for a regular commitment. Outside activities can be inspiring.
- Become a mentor to another aspiring home-based entrepreneur.
- Teach a course at a local school or community college. You not only get to interact with students, but you may also pick up a new customer or two.

AT-HOME OR FROM-HOME?

When choosing a home business, consider the type of work you will be doing and where you will be doing that work: primarily at-home or from-home? At-home businesses are those such as graphic design, at-home child-care service, pet grooming, custom design, freelance writing, information preparation, virtual assistance, and others for which the work is performed in your home office or workshop. From-home businesses include catering, landscape design, event planning, cleaning, professional consulting, and other ventures for which you have a home office, but generally go to your clients to do the work.

Many home-businesses are a combination of at-home or from-home: You do the planning, marketing, and record keeping from your home office, but also go to the clients' workplaces to conduct some of your business. Such businesses include bookkeeping, interior decorating or designing, errand running, and others for which you do some work in your office and the rest at your client's home or work-place. While searching for the business that suits you best, remember to consider how much "interaction" with other people will be required and whether you do or do not like to be with people.

PROCRASTINATION

I am sure you have all heard the axiom: "Work expands to fill the time." This is certainly true when you work from home. In a regular job, you generally avoid distractions such as laundry, cleaning,

---

SEW's Suggestions: Set Your Daily Intention

Terri Levine, professional coach, author of *Work Yourself Happy* and *Coaching for an Extraordinary Life,* suggests:

> Every single day, set your intention. Before you do anything, think of how you want to experience your day. When I get up in the morning, I set my intention of how I want my day to be; what I see myself accomplishing, and especially what feelings I want to have. Then I go about my day keeping my intention with me. It is amazing that if I intend to feel more joy, have more ease, and feel more productive, and if I focus on that intention, then I create that. I share this tip because when I first started my business I had no intention. Each day I was overwhelmed, felt distracted, and ran from thing to thing and call to call and idea to idea. With this focused intention, I have created an amazing income with ease and joy! Building a business can be easy and fun if you set out for it to be so.

---

walking the dog, pulling weeds, receiving packages for neighbors, and a myriad of other sidetracking chores.

The reasons people procrastinate vary. If you find yourself putting off work with your home business on a regular basis, take time to analyze why you are avoiding tasks. People generally procrastinate when . . .

- The tasks are not meaningful or important;
- They are perfectionists and cannot possibly attain the standards they have set;
- They lack confidence in their abilities to do the tasks;
- They are overanxious about the responses they might receive about their work;
- They may not understand how to tackle the task; or
- Some other factor keeps them from completing those tasks.

Some tips to help you overcome procrastination:

- Make a "to-do" list for each task each day, but break it down into smaller steps so you can achieve success, little by little. Reward yourself with each step.
- Mix your workload with a relaxing or fun activity every so often.
- At the beginning of a project, make a timetable calendar, with the due date listed. Then list the steps you need to take, day-by-day or week-by-week, to finish your work on time. Give yourself a few days of leeway for "emergencies" when you may miss some work time.
- Be kind to yourself. Remember that you are not superhuman, so make reasonable expectations of yourself.

If you cannot seem to stop procrastinating, you may want to consult with a business coach, a time-management expert, or another professional who may be able to provide you with some good tips to help you.

BALANCING FAMILY ACTIVITIES

Though you may start your home business to have more time with your family, there will be no "perfect" balance between the two. Actually, the challenge of a home-based business is the "juggling" of three important elements: your family and/or life partner, your home business, and your personal time.

As previously discussed, most home-based business mothers will have some sort of child-care support or arrangement. Depending on the situation and the business, many women will take their children with them on a job, as Joanne did when she had her daughters assist her in papering and pasting wallpaper during the summer. However, for certain projects, interviews with prospective clients, and certain kinds of operations, it is not possible (or professional) to have your children with you or in your office.

Here are some suggestions to keep your personal life and home business "balanced."

- *Define your work space*—even if it is just a curtain or panel, and try not to let too many papers or work-related items "stray" to other places in your home or apartment.
- *Set regular hours.* Define startup times, mealtimes, work days, end-of-work times, and off-times; but keep your schedule flexible so you can participate in activities that are important to you—family, spouse, health issues, "fun" time.

  One full-time bookkeeper told her clients that Mondays would be her make-up day if she missed a regular appointment due to her children's school activity or an illness, or for another reason. "I inform new clients that my family is my priority, and that I will make up work I might miss due to a family commitment," she says. "I tell the new clients that I will be happy to refer them to another bookkeeper if they cannot deal with this arrangement. Thus far, my clients are fine with this arrangement."

- *Set limits.* Cut down on interruptions by setting the rules with family and friends as you work. You probably have heard mothers say, "I tell my (older) children that, unless the house is on fire or someone is bleeding or not breathing, they can wait until my break to talk to me." Now this may sound tough, but if your home business income is helping to support your family, it is not too much to ask of them to respect your time when you are working. With extended family—in-laws, parents, and grandparents—interruptions are unavoidable at times. However, if you have an answering system and/or voice mail, you can screen your calls or review your calls during work breaks. Just make sure you "close up shop" at regular times so you can spend time with those important people in your life.
- *Set a routine.* People are creatures of habit, so if you set up a routine just as if you were going to a regular job, you will develop good work habits. Your family will be more likely to take your work seriously, as they observe you "going to work" every day.
- *Have a backup plan.* Know whom you can call to help you with office support if you have a sudden demand for your product or services. Have emergency child care ready if the

school calls you to pick up your sick child while you are near-
ing a deadline.

- *Get respite care if necessary.* If you are the caregiver of an elderly parent or a disabled relative, take advantage of adult day
  services and respite care to give yourself a break and your relative some new activities.
- *Plan some personal time for yourself.* Take time to lunch with
  friends, enjoy a hobby, read the latest novel by your favorite
  mystery author, or volunteer in your community. It satisfies
  your soul.

You will have days when everything is off-kilter and nothing
seems to go right, but that happens even to those who are employed
at a 9-to-5 job. So, when your bad day is over, get back into your
schedule as soon as possible. "Juggling" your business, your family, and your needs will become easier when you persist!

HEALTH AND FITNESS

Being an entrepreneur requires extra mental and physical energy. If
you are the sole owner of your business, you are responsible for
producing your goods and/or providing your services, even if you
do have assistance. If you neglect your mental and physical health,
you and your work will suffer. Here are some practical tips to help
you stay fit and smart.

- *Eat healthy!* Follow the food pyramid recommendations and
  eat lots of fruits and vegetables. Keep healthy snacks handy and
  avoid foods with fat and sugars, which can make you drowsy,
  not to mention increase your waistline!
- *Get the rest you need to operate.* Doctors recommend six to
  eight hours of rest a night, but some people can work on less.
  One advantage to working at home is that you can take an af-
  ternoon nap if you choose. Do not let sleep deprivation rob you
  of your concentration and health.
- *Exercise.* Studies show that exercise is not only good for your
  heart and circulation, but that it also keeps your brain active
  and nourished. Take walks on your work breaks; or if the

weather is bad, get on your stationary bike or treadmill. Stretching also keeps your muscles from cramping.

- *Stay mentally fit.* Meditate, pray, read motivational books, and stay positive. If no one else does it, compliment yourself each day about something you have accomplished or done well that day.

Take care of yourself because, yes, your family and customers are depending on you!

STRESS

I once heard on a science program that prehistoric man (and woman) only had to work approximately twenty hours a week to supply their basic needs. Sure, they did not have indoor plumbing, but you cannot beat the hours! The hours and pressure you will experience with your home business combined with running a household will undoubtedly cause stress.

Here are some tips to manage the running of a home business:

- Use yoga techniques or one of your favorite "stress-busters" when you feel the tension building inside of you, like exercise, music, dancing, or getting out of the house. Treat yourself to a session with a massage therapist.
- Envision a project from start to finish—get a mental picture of it and how you will tackle it. It will help calm you and let you concentrate on the tasks before you.
- Set aside blocks of time to handle each business task and clear your mind of it until that time rolls around.
- Always overestimate the time you think you need to complete a project to allow for unexpected delays or interruptions. If you do finish early, you will have more time to check over your work.

Keep Your Work Fun

You'll feel less stress and enjoy life more if your work is fun. Here are some ways to make your home business more fun:

- *Remind yourself why you are in business.* Do not overschedule your day and pace yourself. Smile every chance you get, even when it gets crazy with your home business and household. Learn to laugh at your mistakes and the crazy things that can happen as a home business owner. Remember how fortunate you are that you can do work you (hopefully) enjoy and get paid for it. (Or turn on the morning news during rush hour and you're likely to see the traffic jams you're missing by working from home!)

- *Keep your sense of humor!* Medical studies have proven that humor and laughter can improve your health.
- *Be around children and teens.* This will lighten up your life—really! Young people look at life so differently. (Notice how children laugh so many more times a day than adults do!)
- *Read a humorous story or watch a comedy* on television or a video.
- *Smile!* It will brighten your face and help your attitude.

You will face a variety of other home business dilemmas, but if you remain calm and know where to turn for help, you will overcome the problems.

Training and Education

Many companies provide ongoing training and workshops or tuition reimbursement to keep their employees' skills and knowledge current about the latest trends and/or technology in their industries. As a home business owner, however, it is *your* responsibility to take the courses and get the training you need to stay competitive with your business's offerings. Your customers expect you to be the expert. Therefore, you will need periodic training and education in your field. The good news is that education and training is much more accessible and affordable. Of course, each business has its standards, with some professions requiring licensing, others only experience.

One woman was turned down repeatedly when she approached medical offices to start a medical transcription service business. "They looked at me like I was crazy when they found out I had no training, so I enrolled in local classes at a local business school. After I completed my course, every medical office I solicited contracted with me!"

SOURCES FOR TRAINING AND/OR EDUCATION NEEDED FOR YOUR BUSINESS

If you plan to start a business or have already started one, you have a good idea of what skills or knowledge are important in operating your business. Talk to people in similar businesses and to members of trade groups and associations to see what training or courses they recommend. Of course, some professions or businesses require standard training before you can apply for a license.

Assess your present qualifications and ask yourself what skills or training you need to run and operate your business. Then find educational and training corresponding with your needs that is most accessible and affordable.

Work experience is important as well, so the sooner you get the basic training you need to open your business, the sooner you can get your business going and learn as you go. Here are some business-related resources:

- If you are still working at a job, take advantage of any courses you can take with your company's sponsorship or reimbursement that will also help you in your future business.
- Contact the Women's Business Center (www.onlinewbc.gov) or Small Business Development Center (www.sba.gov/SBDC) closest to you to find out about ongoing seminars and courses geared to entrepreneurs.
- Contact local schools, technology schools, and community and four-year colleges for credit courses, adult continuing education courses, and online courses they may have on entrepreneurship.
- Attend business expos and industry trade shows and entrepreneurial conferences, all of which offer speakers and demonstrations and workshops.
- Ask industry associations about any manuals or training programs they may offer.
- Ask local business organizations about any mentoring programs they may offer for members.

- Take advantage of other learning opportunities, such as home study programs, book and CD packages, online courses, video- and audiocassette tapes, CD-ROMs, and instructional guides.
- Get a job or volunteer in the industry that you would like to have a business to receive "free training."
- Subscribe to at least one industry publication that will help you keep abreast of the latest advances in your field.

Maryanne Burgess, author/publisher of the Designer Source Listing, and lifelong learner, says, "Savvy entrepreneurs never stop learning. Whatever your plans, be assured that information is developed today for the one-person operation just as it is for big business. Knowledge of your subject always gives you the (competitive) edge, so go for it!"

Three Essential Plans:
Business, Financial, Marketing

Though you may wish to start your "hot" business idea tomorrow, you must take the time to plan for your home business. In fact, it often takes a year from the time an entrepreneur decides on a business idea until she actually "opens" her business's doors. Three essential plans that you will need to create are: the business plan, which defines your business and sets your goals; your financial plan, which concerns financing and making your business profitable; and your marketing plan, which provides how your business will find and keep its customers. These plans will help to define your business and make it a success.

BUSINESS PLAN

After gathering information about your business idea (or your present one), you can start writing your plan. Business plans consist of a few to many pages; are simple or complex; are modified according to the type of business; and can be revised as goals or markets change.

Here are the major components of most plans, each of which can be written briefly or expansively:

Cover Page: Business's name, address, telephone and fax numbers, e-mail and Web site addresses.

Executive Summary: This is a summation of your business plan—and the most important part because it clearly explains the entire concept and purpose of your venture. Although listed at the plan's beginning, write it after your plan is finished for a more comprehensive summary.

Table of Contents: Just like a book, this section lists what is included in your business plan.

Statement of Purpose: Clarifies why you wrote this plan: For a loan application? For potential investors? For a personal business guide? Other?

Mission Statement: As listed previously in this book, a mission statement explains the purpose of your business and how it will benefit your customers.

Business Description: This section provides the specific details of your business's operations, its products and/or services; its legal structure; the goals and objectives you have set; and what factors you believe will be its keys to success.

Competitor Analysis: The information in this section should have been obtained in the pre-startup checklists, because it should list any potential competitors, their basic operations, and the assets and drawbacks of their products and services. These details will assist you in describing how your business will stand out from this competition.

Marketing Plan: A marketing plan includes profiles of your potential customers, describing their specific likes, dislikes, and expectations. This section also includes your sales strategies: pricing and sales terms, selling methods of products or services, and advertising plans.

Your Qualifications: This section will answer this question: "What qualifications—education, training, and/or work experience—do you have to run this business successfully?"

The Product or Service: This section will provide a detailed description of what product and/or service you will be selling, the exclusive features that will attract potential customers, and what methods you will use to meet the timely demand of products or services.

Operating Requirements: This section will list the equipment and supplies needed to provide your product and services, any special set up you may need (such as a workshop or licensed kitchen), and what hours you will be "open" for your customers.

Financial Information: This is one of the most important parts of your business plan, so consult a professional—accountant, banker, SCORE consultant, financial specialist, business plan specialist—if you need assistance in compiling your financial information. If you want to see sample business plans, ask other entrepreneurs if they would share theirs with you, or visit your local library.

Include startup costs, a cash flow statement, a balance sheet, a profit and loss statement, and a break-even analysis (the number of units you need to sell to cover all your fixed and variable costs without generating any profit or loss). This analysis can put an unrealistic idea into perspective, or get you to raise prices or expand or contract your products or services. Add a cash flow prediction.

Summation: A short listing of your goals and objectives, plus a statement of your commitment to your business's success.

Appendices: The supporting documents, quotes, estimates, articles, and market research data relevant to your plan.

Use your plan's guidelines to guide your startup (or to later expand your business) to evaluate the marketing plans, monitor expenses and profits, focus your business's direction, and anticipate potential problems with preparation of fall-back plans.

Review your plan on a regular basis, but do not hesitate to change and adapt it as your business develops in one or more directions. This planning process will direct your business to focus on its future growth and stability. Remember, a business plan is the

WARNING!!: Do Not Fail to Plan

Dr. Robert Sullivan, business expert and author and founder of the entrepreneurial resource Web site "Small Business Advisor" (www.isquare.com), says:

I think the most common mistake is lack of planning. I don't mean to imply that a sophisticated business plan is required, but a basic "strategic" plan is mandatory. Writing this plan will force you to think through what you are doing, why you are doing it, and how you are going to do it. Sounds basic, but without a plan there is no basis for making good decisions. The plan should include the scope and mission/purpose of the business, assumptions, goals and objectives, risks, and strategies for dealing with risks you have identified. Fail to plan and you plan to fail.

most important step you can take towards making your dream of owning a successful business a reality!

FINANCIAL PLAN

A crucial part of your business plan is the financial planning for your business startup.

Here are some important components you will want to include and consider in forming your business's financial plan:

- *Your startup costs.* Include everything you think should be part of the startup costs.
- *A business budget.* Create a budget for everything you think you will need to get your home business up and running.
- *Financing details.* Specify what kind of financing you will need and some actual or potential sources of this financing.
- *Planned use of funds.* State how you plan to use the funds for your business and the amount that you need.
- *A personal financial statement.*

EXTRA!!: Sample Business Plans

If you are writing a business plan for the first time, viewing sample business plans may give you a clearer understanding of its structure and composition. Here are several sources:

- Other entrepreneurs. If you belong to a chamber of commerce or women's business organization, ask one of the members who composed a business plan if she would mind sharing her plan so you can review it. She may also be able to provide you with some tips and what she learned from writing it.
- *Gale's Business Plans Handbook,* 9th ed. (Farmington Hills, MI: Gale Group, 2002). Look for this reference book in your public or college library. It contains twenty-four sample business plans of real-life entrepreneurs who used these plans to find financing for their manufacturing, retail, or service industry business.
- PaloAlto (software) Web site: www.bplans.com/; provides 60+ free sample business plans you can view online.

- *Projected cash flow.* This will be discussed in detail later in this book.
- *Time-line for use of money.* Specify when you will need the money and what aspect of your business will it be used for first.
- *Description of other funding strategies.*
- *Review of your financial plan.* Make sure your plan includes everything that bankers or other lenders will want.
- *Details of the methods you will use to generate the money to repay any loans.*

Have your accountant or small business financial expert review your financial plan to see whether anything is missing. Then, using

---

SEW's Suggestions

Dottie Gruhler, HerPlanet.com Network (www.HerPlanet.com) states:

> Before you start a home business, no matter how small it may be, always plan out two years financially. One of the main reasons women fail in business is because they start without planning for even six months down the line. All the money is spent before any comes in. If you know your monthly costs are going to be $300 a month, make sure you can cover that for at least one year out. Revenue does not always come right away, and if you are not prepared for your "growth time," your funds will run dry before you have time to replenish them.

---

leads from other entrepreneurs, begin to approach the lenders and investors that they recommend to apply for their assistance.

Thorough planning for your business's startup and continuance can make the difference between a business that not only survives but thrives!

Marketing Plan

Marketing is an ongoing process to keep "connected" to loyal customers and to find new ones. Marketing "feeds" your business as it brings your customers to buy your services and products. To keep that marketing "flow" ongoing, you need a marketing plan.

An effective marketing plan does the following:

- Profiles potential customers' likes, dislikes, and expectations.
- Explains sales strategies: pricing and sales terms, selling methods of products or services, and advertising plans.
- In other words, a marketing plan details all the methods a business owner uses to reach the best customers for her business.

Jeffrey Dobkin, marketing expert and author says, "To me, the definition of marketing can be reduced to five words: Marketing is 'selling to a defined audience.' Sales are to anyone, but when you pare down that number of folks to whom you are selling—to a more targeted group—that's marketing."

Marketing Plan Components

Just as a business plan is a blueprint for the foundation of your business, a marketing plan is composed of all the tactics you will use to connect with potential customers who will most want to pay for your expertise or product. Here are some components you will want to include in your marketing plan:

1. *Assessment of Your Business's Position.* Sum up in several sentences your business's concept, strong and weak points, and how you believe your customers view your business.
2. *Objectives.* After evaluating where your business is, decide in which direction(s) you want your business to head. Be specific here, listing new approaches for reaching more customers, such as educating customers as to the ways they can use your product or services and expanding your customer base or otherwise enlarging your marketing target.
3. *Target Customer Profiles.* Do thorough market research to put together a typical customer (or customers) profile—age, income level, preferences, and so on. If companies are your customers, profile their size, needs, spending budgets, and so on. Pay attention, too, to future predictions of trends in your industry so you can be ready to offer the latest advancements to benefit your customers.
4. *Design and Deliver.* This crucial part of your marketing plan will list your objectives and begin to design a promotional strategy for each one. List as many low-cost promotional ideas as you can and do not be afraid to use your creativity in thinking of usual and unusual ways to get your customers' attention. It can be the fun part.

Marketing Plan Assistance

You can get assistance in devising a marketing plan from the same sources that provide business plan help. You can also seek guidance in laying out your marketing plan from marketing specialists and consultants, or from marketing interns or marketing classes at nearby colleges.

A marketing plan is not a once-and-done project. Because marketing is a daily business process, it is ongoing. Whether simple or complex, your plan must be effective in helping your business grow or it will be nothing more than words on paper. Here are some tips to help you:

Create a marketing calendar. Marcia Yudkin, marketing expert and author of *Six Steps to Free Publicity* and several other books, offers this tip for an entrepreneur when she begins to write a marketing plan:

> To make marketing manageable, it's important to incorporate the element of timing by creating a marketing calendar and not merely a list of things to do. A marketing calendar involves scheduling the to-do's for times that are realistic and can actually get accomplished. Also, when things must be delivered at a specific point in time, you need to work backward through the process of preparing that marketing piece to schedule the steps and get started in enough time to complete the job well.

Stress the benefits. Customers—whether consumers or businesses— want to know how your product or service is going to benefit them in terms of time or money (or both). The challenge, then, is to communicate in your promotions how you can do this better than your competitors.

Understand the financials. Jeffrey Dobkin, marketing expert, says this:

> You've got to have sales and profits in the plan. No sales, nobody eats; no profits, nobody eats for long. These two items must be addressed from day one of the new business. If you can dial in sales and profits from the "get-go," you're going to be successful and everything else will fall into place.

Find Your Business's Best Position

Positioning in the marketplace means how you will make your product stand out from other similar products or services. You can do this with a catch phrase or slogan, name, or a special identity of your product or service—such as a computer expert's "The Home Business Computer Consultant," or a handmade soapmaker's "Natural Soaps, for Simple Skin Care."

Make Your Customers Your Partners

Futurists say that customers of the future will be more educated and expect more from those from whom they purchase items and/or services. To succeed in business, you must earn the trust of your customers, who want to know you will be there should they have a problem. You and your customer may form an ongoing relationship or partnership in which you work together to fulfill their needs.

Join Forces with Competitors

There are benefits of joining forces with other business owners (to be discussed later in this book); and believe it or not, this also includes competitors in your same industry. For example, an owner of a home-based antiques store joined other antique business owners in her county to print up a free road map with the locations of each participating store to give customers. She says, "We know from experience that people who are looking to buy antiques enjoy going to more than one shop when they go on 'antiquing' excursions. Having this map makes doing so easier for them."

Use Technology to Help Corner Your Market

We all know by now that Internet use is here to stay, with newcomers coming online every minute. The Internet enables a small business to reach a very specific niche market of potential customers around the world at an affordable cost. You can provide customers with information, free sample downloads, feedback opportunities, and the ability to place orders, and so on. Remember to think in terms of a worldwide market if you do sell via the Internet.

Make a Marketing Plan for Now and for the Next Century

After your business is operating for several months, look at your marketing methods and ask yourself honestly whether it is working. If it is not, you have the advantage (over larger companies) of being more flexible and able to change direction. If your marketing avenues are leading toward increasing sales, give yourself a quick pat on the back, but beware of being complacent. Keep abreast of the latest developments in your industry and consumer buying trends—especially those predicted in the next few years. If you do not stay current, you risk losing new customers and even loyal ones should they feel your operations are outdated.

Marketing is an ongoing (daily) process of testing and evaluating your methods, based on your sales and customers' responses. The key to a successful marketing plan is to balance your current endeavors with goals you can adjust for future growth—and to develop your business's own unique identity, which will attract the steady flow of customers needed to produce a successful and thriving business.

Home Office Setup

If you have the funds, you can hire an architect and an interior designer to help you find the best location in your house and design the ideal home office setup for you; however, all you really need is some space, a chair and desk, some shelves, and a computer and other communications equipment.

DESIGN AND LOCATION

There are as many different home office setups as there are home offices. The objective is to find the arrangement that works best for you. Do not be surprised, however, to find yourself moving your home office more than a few times to accommodate changes in your life and in your business. As you plan and assemble your home office, consider incorporating these suggestions:

- *Make a list.* List your business's basic needs: the amount of work space (an at-home business or work-from-home office), basic equipment, and storage requirements. Organize the list in order of importance and preferences: what equipment and furniture must be purchased now and what can be bought later.
- *Select and assess your location.* This will depend on the space you have available, whether you will be receiving customers in your home office, whether you want to be close or isolated from others in your home or apartment, what is convenient for you, your preference (a room with a view?), your comfort and safety, whether anyone else will be working in the space with you, and whether the room has access to the power you'll need to operate necessary equipment and lighting.
- *Review and evaluate your choices.* Consider all the potential spaces you listed and evaluate which ones would work best for you, your business, and for those who live with you.
- *Look at examples.* To get some ideas, look at books, home office publications, and home remodeling television programs, or visit the offices of other home business owners.
- *Consider the possibility of adapting your available spaces.* Whether it's a basement, porch, attic, attached garage, large closet, or just a corner of a room, compare these spaces to what you have seen and decide whether they can be adapted to include the features you like.
- *Put it on paper.* Before you purchase or build any office furniture, take graph paper or use design software to lay out the plan of your home office.
- *Set up a "mock" office.* Using the approximate measurements of your furniture and equipment, create a floor plan of your office so you can better visualize how the setup will work. Consider the work area "flow" or arrangement: the "L" shape works well with corners; the "U" shape will give you essentially three work surfaces; and the parallel work area will feature your desk facing into a room with auxiliary space behind you.

Other setup options could include built-in spaces, work "islands," or all-in-one office units or stackable pieces. If you are an

Smile!

Phyllis H. moved her home office into her son's bedroom when he married. Unfortunately, he and his wife divorced two years later so he moved back home. The woman then moved her office into a corner in her bedroom, often using her bed to lay out paperwork. When her son found his own apartment and moved out, the woman again commandeered his bedroom as office space. "I told him I loved him, but that he lost his bedroom for good now," she said with a laugh, "and that if he moved back again, the couch would be his permanent bed!"

---

artist or artisan, then you will have a number of other considerations for your work area, such as safety, proper use of materials, ventilation requirements, storage for inventory, and areas for packing and shipping preparation.

These are but a few of the many ways to acquire an affordable, yet efficient and comfortable, home office setup. By using your ingenuity, time, common sense, and creativity, you can have an office that is both functional and attractive.

OFFICE CENTERS, SUITES

You may have times when you need to meet with clients or work away from your home office. Maybe your office space is not suitable for meetings with clients or you wish to hold a larger meeting with several clients, or you may be traveling and away from your home office, or you need a larger space to teach a class. Here are suggested alternatives for professional office rooms and buildings you might use:

- Rent shared office space on an as-needed basis in an executive business center and pay for the use of the office support systems that you use.

Money$aving Tip: An Economical Setup

Print publications such as *Home Business Journal* and *Home Business Magazine* often feature photos and examples of home office options, as well as reviews of the latest home office technology and furniture that will accommodate all kinds of business budgets. As a number of women quoted in this book have recommended, be thrifty when you start your business and do not overspend. You will need every dollar possible to market and operate your new business until it becomes profitable. Here are some money-saving tips:

- *Look at garage sales, auctions, and thrift shops for used pieces of furniture.* You can also get excellent deals on good used furniture when schools upgrade office furniture or companies go out of business or move out of the area.
- *Be creative.* Turn cabinets, kitchen tables, entertainment centers, and other items into pieces that will hold your supplies. If you or a friend or spouse are handy, you can take standing file cabinets and place cut-out plywood (covered by hardboard to keep it smooth) to create a low-cost work arrangement.
- *Consider leasing.* Leasing equipment can be expensive, but it may be a better option at first.
- *Recycle whatever supplies you can.*

The more money you save at the startup, the more you will have to sustain or grow your business later.

- Contact the Office Business Center Association (see their address on page 173), whose members are located across the country, and rent rooms by the hour, day, week, or year.
- Contact a local chamber of commerce or women's business organization to see if you can rent one of their rooms or a member's office for your meeting.

WARNING!!: Avoid Making Home Office Mistakes

- *Get a good office chair.* Don't just use a kitchen chair! Besides your computer or a piece of equipment essential to your business, your office chair is extremely important. It should be comfortable, provide proper support for you and your back, and be adjustable. Rebecca Boenigk, CEO of Neutral Posture Ergonomics, Inc., a company that makes ergonomically designed office chairs, says this: "If you put your body in a chair that puts you in the wrong posture day after day, you will hurt yourself."
- *Keep equipment convenient.* Avoid inappropriate heights or distances of your chair, work space, keyboard, monitor, and/or printer. Make sure your chair is high enough in relation to your desk area and that it has a five-base caster bottom for more stability; that your desk area is not too low or high for you to comfortably sit; that your keyboard is positioned at an appropriate angle to avoid wrist injury, commonly known as carpal tunnel syndrome; and that you need not reach too far for your most-used supplies or to use equipment such as your printer.
- *Use appropriate lighting.* Avoid harsh lighting or too little light, both of which can lead to eye strain and headaches. Also, sunlight or indoor lighting can cause a glare from your monitor. Position your computer or computer correctly to avoid this.
- *Do a safety check, especially if children will be present.* Neglecting to check your home office for frayed or loose electrical cords or small items like paper clips can lead to serious injury of a child or damage to equipment. In one young mother's home office, her three-year-old stuck an entire box of paper clips through her floppy disk drive! "That was a costly trip to the computer repair shop!" she said.

(continued)

WARNING!!: Avoid Making Home Office Mistakes *(continued)*

- *Soundproof your office as much as possible.* Not trying to (somewhat) soundproof your office will lead to distractions from barking dogs, lawn mowers, and noisy children. If you want to hear what your children are doing while you are working, install a wireless intercom in their rooms.
- *Keep pets out of your office.* Pet hair can get into and damage your equipment, and animals can become entangled or shocked by electrical cords.

- Ask whether your local community college has any conference rooms.
- Check to see if your local public library has a quiet room available.
- Meet at a restaurant or coffee shop, preferably during its off-hours.
- Barter a product or service with another woman business owner who has a free office you can use for your meeting.
- Contact a small business incubator near you to see if they have office space available.
- Check, too, with a local motel or hotel for available rooms. Many have large rooms you can rent to conduct seminars.
- Plan to meet with your client in her office.
- Be creative! For example, an elementary school music teacher who had been let go because of budget constrictions subcontracted with several school districts to give music lessons to their students. She parked a large, carpeted van at the schools, in which she gave music lessons to students.

LEASING VERSUS PURCHASING

Leasing your equipment is an option for equipping your home office, especially if you do not want to borrow money to buy equipment, do not want to spend all your money when you start your home venture, or do not qualify for a loan. The SBA says that 80 percent of all U.S. businesses have leased equipment—from office furniture, computers, and copiers, to machinery and cars and trucks—at one time or another. Another reason entrepreneurs lease equipment is that their business's operational needs demand the latest in technology, and leasing allows them to have equipment they could not have afforded otherwise.

Before you decide whether or not to lease, take the following benefits (and drawbacks) into consideration:

Pros of Leasing

- Frees up business capital.
- Provides flexibility to allow companies with uncertain profits to have the equipment they need to stay competitive.
- Enables you to regularly upgrade equipment rather than be stuck with out-of-date technology.
- Can be deducted as business expenses.

Cons of Leasing

- Leasing can be expensive in the long run because you are paying for the use of the equipment, its depreciation, plus the interest.
- A lease contract stipulates you must make all the lease payments.
- You may discover additional costs are involved, such as document preparation fees, one-time lease fees determined by the state in which you will be conducting business, state taxes that are factored into the lease payments; plus you may need to purchase additional insurance to cover the leased equipment.

Many firms and institutions lease equipment—some offering reasonable rates, others not-so-reasonable rates. Be sure to read the terms of the leasing contract carefully and, if you have questions, have your lawyer review it with you. Take special note of the contract's renewal terms, penalties if you cancel, what happens to the equipment after the lease is ended, and the renewal options. Oftentimes you can negotiate for better terms.

Leasing can be an effective option to furnish your home office, but make sure you understand all your responsibilities.

TECHNOLOGY

Technology today is enabling small and home-based businesses to compete with much larger companies, and to find customers all over the world. Affordable technology is one reason the number of people working at home has increased. For what I once spent for a computer and printer, I can now buy a desktop computer, monitor, color printer, and a multifunction machine (fax, copier, answering machine, speaker phone).

Your pieces of equipment are the tools for your business. Of course, your specific home business will dictate exactly what you need to produce your product and/or services. A desktop publisher will use more sophisticated publishing and drawing software than someone operating an errand service. So when planning your business startup, you will want to plan for (1) your general home office equipment; and (2) the technology and/or machinery necessary for your particular business.

As you plan and purchase your equipment, follow these guidelines:

- *Choose equipment that will help you be more efficient and proficient.* Do your product research before you shop and know what "job" each piece of equipment is to do for you.
- *Compare prices.* See Related Resources for ideas, and look for good customer support and guarantees (very important!). Decide whether those maintenance agreements are worth the extra expense.
- *Follow your business's industry recommendations.*
- *Ask other entrepreneurs for recommendations for good companies and dealers.* Ask especially those whose staff members are knowledgeable about the equipment, rather than just salespersons.
- *Keep a file of information pertaining to your equipment.* Keep a folder with all your receipts and return policies, equipment manuals, and warranties in the event a piece of equipment malfunctions. Keep the customer support phone numbers handy.
- *Be sure you buy from reliable dealers.* Check with your local Better Business Bureau office or consumer's office to see if any complaints have been filed against a dealer.

Choosing Computers

There is no question that every business needs a computer, even businesses that provide services out of the home office. Before you purchase a computer, ask yourself these three questions:

1. *What kind of system do I need?* That, again, depends on what you will be doing with it for your business. Graphic artists will be running more sophisticated software and many prefer the Macintosh computer's capabilities, as opposed to a bookkeeper who needs a basic PC to operate her accounting software. You should also foresee your needs for your computer's capability about two years ahead.
2. *What size computer should I buy?* Desktop computers are larger and relatively permanent as opposed to laptop computers—which are becoming more affordable and popular, take up less space, and can be transported wherever you go.
3. *Where should I buy a computer?* You can buy one either through a reputable retail store or through the mail. Visit the computer manufacturers at their online sites for prices, customization options, comparison shopping, and for ordering once you have decided.

If money is an issue, new home business owners often use their family computer, buy a secondhand one, or even get one from someone who is giving one away. But buying a new one will give you more up-to-date features for customer service and support. You can buy the latest model a manufacturer advertises; however, if you go for a model that came out only six months ago, you will probably have plenty of power and capability for less money than the new one advertised. If in doubt, make an appointment with a computer consultant who can help advise you as to the best system for you and your home business needs.

Your system should have at least 64MB, preferably 128MB, of RAM, a fast processor (such as a Pentium III or AMD chip), a CD-ROM drive (speed 24X), at least a 3GB hard drive, and one or more removable disk drives with as many gigabytes of storage space to handle the operations and graphics you will need to conduct business. Most major computer manufacturers are online: Compaq (www.compaq.com), Dell (www.dell.com), Gateway (www.gateway.com), Hewlett-Packard (www.hp.com), IBM (www.ibm.com), and Apple (www.apple.com). Or visit your local office supply and technology store or contact the companies directly for their current catalogs.

Here are some basic considerations for your computer-related equipment, software, and technology:

Keyboard: Look for ones that are ergonomically designed to help prevent repetitive injuries like carpal tunnel syndrome and those with added keys that direct your Web browser, e-mail, and CD software.

Monitor: Purchase ones that give you high resolution (no less than 640 x 480), and at least 15 to 17 inches of screen.

Printer: Get as much speed as your finances will allow, and check first to see how much the toner and color inks cost. Good color inkjet printers, such ones made by Epson (www.epson.com) or Hewlett-Packard (www.hp.com), are priced under $500. Compare their features for envelope printing and other options you can use to create your own promotional materials.

Scanner: These are very affordable and enable you to place images and photos into your computer and load them onto your Web site, where you can use them to illustrate your marketing materials, to send as e-mail attachments, or to help sell items on auction Web sites. You can also use them to transfer text to your computer that can be read by optical character recognition (OCR) software. Flatbed scanners are generally the easiest to use though upright scanners take up less space.

Software: Look to see what software already comes with your computer. If you do need to buy software, look for home office suites that have word processing, database management, accounting, spreadsheets, and Web browsing and design. You can also find software programs designed for almost any specific business. You will want to load and use software designed for your business type. Other core applications to assist you in operating your business are schedulers, contact managers, and other business-related software to help with tasks such as shipping, inventory control, and credit card processing. You may also want to consider voice recognition software for your computer.

In addition to being an aid for persons who cannot type on a keyboard due to a disability, this software, with a little practice, can also save anyone time and increase productivity as it can go as fast as a person can talk as well as cut down on spelling errors and offers other advantages over the traditional use of a keyboard.

Internet Connection: You will need to be connected to the Internet to do research, to keep in touch with customers via e-mail, or to maintain a Web site. To display Internet documents, you will need Microsoft Explorer or Netscape Communicator, which you can purchase or download free from the Internet.

Modem: A modem (internal or external unit) connects you to the Internet. Modems come in different speeds, which control how quickly your computer can receive information. You should have at least 36.6 Kbps (kilobits per second), but can go as high as 128 Kbps, depending on the type of Internet connection. Common options include:

- *Dial-up connection:* You use an existing phone line. This is the slowest way to connect, but is usually the least expensive per month.
- *Cable modem:* If your cable service has this available, you can get a fast, direct connection.
- *DSL (digital subscriber line):* Has to be offered by your local telephone company, and uses parts of your phone line not used by your voice. Your residence has to be located relatively close to the telephone switch that supports it.
- *Other options:* Options that do not use a modem include ISDN (integrated services digital network) through a special phone line, WebTV (a device using a regular telephone jack), wireless, and satellite.

Here are additional equipment items that you are likely to find useful in your business:

Photocopier: This can save you many trips to the print or office supply shop. The cartridges (consumables) are expensive for the lower-priced copiers. Use office supply centers and stores like Kinko's for multiples of copies should you need them and save your copier for your basic office use.

Digital camera: Instead of film, these cameras store photos digitally that are then transferred to your computer with a card, cable, or floppy disk. Inexpensive ones can be purchased for around a hundred dollars; cameras with a higher number of pixels that give a better quality photo are more expensive.

Fax (facsimile): You can purchase a single unit or have a fax modem or software installed so that you can transmit faxes from your computer. Plain paper machines are easier to operate. Also look for features such as delayed sending and broadcast faxing to save costs. Multifunction machines that can scan, print, and fax directly from your PC are worth considering when you first start up if your budget is tight.

Your technology will involve a considerable amount of your money and time, so use devices and software such as the following for protection of your investments. (*Note:* The brands listed do not constitute an endorsement. Compare similar products to choose the ones that best suit you and your home office technology.)

1. *Protecting against power outages:* Somewhere in the world at any moment, there is a power outage due to a storm, an overload of demand for power, or technology failure. Use UPS (uninterruptible power supply) devices to keep your PC running during a power failure so you will have time to save your work and shut safely down; and use surge suppressors to prevent loss of power (and data) during power brown-outs. Company: American Power Conversion (APC), West Kingston, RI 02892; www.apc.com.

2. *Protecting against computer viruses:* To protect against the latest virus, use virus protection software, and download regular up-

dates to fend off the latest Net "intruders." Company: Norton AntiVirus Symantec Corporation, Cupertino, CA 95014; www.symantec.com (also makes "Norton SystemWorks," which combines virus protection, disk repair, and other functions).

3. *Protecting data:* Install software that schedules automatic data backups like Backup Exec made by SeaGate Software and uses external zip (hard) drives like Imation SuperDisk. As one computer expert said, "It's not *if* your computer's hard drive will crash someday, it's *when* it will crash!" Be prepared! Companies: SeaGate Technology, Scotts Valley, CA 95066; www.sea gate.com/; Imation Corp., Oakdale, MN 55128-3414; www .imation.com.

4. *Videoconferencing:* Now that high-speed Internet access is available for home and small-office use, videoconferencing and video-based chat is increasing in popularity as a way to "meet" with clients and business associates around the world. Video-conferencing is an exchange of sound and video images among two or more distant individuals. All who are involved in the conferencing can hear and see in the real time mode over the Internet. Images that can be transmitted include date from graphics, applications or files, video streams, and immovable images of object.

In order to conduct a videoconference, you will need a sound card, speakers, a microphone, a Web camera, videoconferencing software, and access to the Internet via high-speed cable or DSL. Of course, both parties must have a similar equipment setup for the videoconference to be successful. Take note, too, that some conference centers and office centers such as Kinko's rent video-conferencing meeting rooms.

Advantages of videoconferencing include savings in time, travel, and phone bill costs, and the ability to hold virtual meetings that may lead to faster business decisions. The drawbacks: not everyone's office setup has videoconference capabilities; the quality of the equipment used may vary, resulting in poor sound or video; and the cost, though it is becoming more affordable, may be prohibitive for home office budgets.

As the technology continues to improve and prices decrease, you should consider installing videoconferencing equipment.

5. *Mobile technology:* When you leave your home office to travel around town, across the country, or even around the world, mobile technology can keep you connected to those involved with your business. If you already have a home business, you probably have at least one piece of equipment that travels with you.

Typical mobile technology that you might pack up and take with you to access people, files, or the Internet includes laptop computers, remote access software, personal organizers, pagers, cellular phones, a national Internet service provider address like Hotmail.com or AOL, contact managers, adapters to hook up your equipment to alternative power sources (or a backup battery), and fax software or fax service such as eFax (www.efax.com). Here's some advice on buying and using mobile technology:

- Even if you can afford it, do not buy all your mobile equipment at once. Learn how to operate the pieces that you use most, and purchase other technology as you need it.
- Learn all the capabilities of each piece of equipment and software program to maximize its capabilities.
- When you travel to other cities, know where an office center, cyber café, or even a local chamber of commerce office is located should you need to borrow or rent equipment if yours fails.
- You might try using automatic follow-me services like those from BigPlanet (www.bigplanet.com/) or 800Voice mail.net that, for a fee, will relay incoming messages to your pager, handheld, or cell phone.

The good news is that the right technology can enable people to find you wherever you are in the world; the bad news is that you are never really away from your office or work.

Desktop Publishing (DTP)

Even though the Internet has opened a whole new world of cybermarketing, we sometimes forget that hard-copy (print) promotional materials—brochures, fliers, newsletters, and even business cards and labels, are important in bringing in new customers. Your basic word-processing software has some excellent features in its design capabilities and clip art, and is a good place to start when you design your first materials. However, eventually, you will want to expand your options and capabilities.

You can expand those DTP options using software such as Microsoft Picture It! Publishing 2001 and HomePublisher for Mac (Adobe), both of which are very good. DTP professionals prefer the more complex (and expensive) Adobe PageMaker or QuarkXPress. Of course, you will also need publishing software printers (quality laser and small color printer); and will find it helpful to have a flatbed scanner, removable storage drives, and a digital camera.

The following technology considerations will enable you to do most of your own desktop publishing tasks:

- Have a fast modem.
- Have adequate memory available. Graphics programs take up large amounts of memory space, so your computer should have an adequate amount of random access memory (RAM) and hard drive memory.
- Have the capability to write to removable hard drives so you can back up your hard disk data and transmit files.
- Look for scanners with good input resolution and with software that enables you to obtain and edit art right away.
- Consider investing in a PostScript printer, which DTP professionals prefer.

Take DTP courses through continuing education classes at local public schools and community colleges to improve your skills and get the most out of your DTP software. Unless you are artistically inclined and able to produce a professional look, you might have an artist design a logo for your business. You can then scan and place it on a disk for use whenever you need it for marketing materials.

First impressions are important, and with today's DTP software, you should be able to do a great job designing and producing your own promotional materials. If you do not have the time or prefer not doing it, ask your entrepreneurial network for recommendations. If you receive many compliments on your DTP designs and copy, however, you might have new sideline home business—producing materials for other home business owners!

Home Networking: LANs

Ongoing improvements in technology, affordability, and increased demand—due to family members' various study, banking, online research, home business use, telecommuting, communications, and other computer uses—have contributed to the fact, that as of the year 2000, the Census Bureau (www.census.gov) reported more than half of the country's 105 million households owned computers.

Because of this multiple-PC trend in homes, consumers began to seek technology that would allow them to connect their home computers to one another—"home networking"—in the same way computers in traditional office settings have been linked for years. Here is a brief overview of this growing home-technological trend:

Benefits of Home-Networked PCs
- Files and backup storage systems, printers, and other peripherals can be shared.
- If you travel or telecommute, some networking products enable you to connect a laptop computer to both a corporate LAN and a home network, thus giving you flexibility in where you can work.
- You can save money by having your PCs share simultaneous Internet access with just one ISP account.
- Kids can participate in playing games between their computers.

Drawbacks of Home-Networked PCs
- Choosing which networking technologies will best suit you and your home office can be difficult.
- You may experience technical difficulties, such as getting networked computers to "recognize" one another in terms of files, printers, and other peripherals.
- Installing and setting up a networking system can be frustrating and confusing. Companies' products and tech support vary in setup ease and support.
- Not all commercial ISPs will allow more than one person to access the Internet at the same time.

EXTRA!! Home Networking Definitions

Home networking: Connecting two or more home computers together in order to share resources and information.

NIC: Network interface card (needed to install in some computer systems that enable networking).

LAN: Local area network (the connected PCs, etc., in an office or home setting). The two kinds of networks are *client-server,* in which a main PC with major processing and power storage capabilities is connected with other computers via NICs and cables; and a *peer-to-peer* network, in which two or more computers are connected, with neither being more powerful than the other.

ISP: Internet service provider (local or commercial access such as AOL)

ICS: Internet connection sharing is the technology that uses Windows 98, for example, enabling several computers on a home network to connect into the Internet using only one phone line.

Platform: General term used to describe the technology and wiring that enables home networking to occur.

Networking Connections Platforms

- *Ethernet network:* Conventional technology that is used by many corporate networks. For home networking, Ethernet requires installing NICs and cables, and PCs need to be in the same or nearby rooms.
- *USB Ethernet networking:* This newer technology also involves cables but is easier to install and more portable. However, it can only connect two PCs whose distance cannot be more than sixteen feet.

- *Phone line networking:* This platform uses a home's existing telephone wiring, adapters, and a company's related software. For example, Intel Corporation's The Intel AnyPoint (www .intel.com/anypoint) connects PCs via home telephone jacks without interrupting your ability to make and receive phone calls while sending data across the network. The unit is easy to install and reasonably priced.

- *AC power-based networking:* This technology plugs into your AC outlets, but experts say it is still a bit slow and can blow a fuse on your home's electrical systems when too many PCs (and household appliances) operate simultaneously.

- *Wireless:* This platform uses airwaves and adapters with antennas to connect PCs anywhere within your home. The available products vary in complexity of setups and prices.

Home networking is just part of the whole future trend of the new "wired" homes. Before you embark on installing a LAN, take time to research these new trends. (The resources listed on pages 172–175 are excellent ones to introduce you to this topic.) Even as you read this, home networking, Internet access connections, and overall remote technology is improving, expanding, and becoming more cost-efficient. This exciting technology has the potential to create opportunities for more of us to work from our homes while sharing time and experiences with those important people living with us.

Phones

Install at least two phone lines (most newer homes already are wired for two separate lines), or one with multiple rings, and consider dedicating a third line to your fax and/or a modem. Use a headset to prevent neck strain if you use the phone frequently.

- *Voice Mail Systems:* Phone companies also offer low-cost digital subscriber lines (DSL) as alternatives to dial-up and cable modem. If you receive frequent customers calls, have a system that will play music or messages while your customers are on hold or use the voice mail with your phone company or your cellular phone. A real person sounds the most professional, however (and people like talking to a "real" person), so you might want to hire someone to handle the phone calls during your busy times or seasons.

- *Cellular Phone:* A cellular phone is good for keeping in touch with customers (and your family) as you travel outside your office. Because costs can add up quickly, it's important to compare plans in terms of the areas covered and the rates. You can save money by purchasing prepaid cellular phone service and paying for additional minutes as you need them.

Phone Etiquette

Despite the increased use of Internet e-mail, your first contact with customers will often be over the phone. Having a voice mail system on your ground line and cell phone will help your professional image. Here are some phone etiquette suggestions:

- Do not talk business or let your cell phone ring (you can put it on vibrate) where it will disturb others.
- To protect yourself and others, do not drive with one hand and hold your cell phone with the other. Look for a safe pull-off space and make your call. (Even if you have hands-free attachments, your main concentration is not on your driving.) Set business hours and do not answer either your office number or cell phone number after those hours.
- Do not give out others' telephone cell phone numbers unless you have their permission.
- If noise outside your home office suddenly occurs, either use your mute button or ask your caller if you can hang up and call back later.
- Do not send a fax to a client unless they are expecting it.
- Do away with call-waiting (rude!) and instead have a phone system or answering service that can take calls while you are on the phone.

These are among the most annoying phone abuses, but there are others (you are sure to have some of your own!).

Teleconferencing

Teleconferencing is another way to talk to multiple computer users at once. You can use your PC and dial-up connections or a phone unit that can handle two or more calls coming in on separate phone lines to have a "meeting" from your home office. Check your computer's hardware and software manuals to see whether your system is capable of handling teleconferences.

Another "virtual" meeting option is paying to use a Web conferencing service like the services of MeetingPlace, www.meetingplace.net. All you need is a telephone and a Web browser to communicate with others in real-time.

ERGONOMICS

The Bureau of Labor Statistics reported in 1997 that repetitive stress traumas accounted for 64 percent of the approximately 430,000 total reported workplace illnesses in 1997. The U.S. Department of Labor asked The National Academy of Sciences (NAS) to look into the issue of ergonomics in the workplace, and in two reports since 1998, NAS estimated that $50 billion a year is lost by businesses from sick leave, decreased productivity and medical-care costs linked to repetitive stress injuries. Repetitive motions performed in work tasks lead to strains, stiffness in joints, tendonitis, and nerve damage like that in carpal tunnel syndrome. Ergonomics is concerned with fitting the job with the worker to create the ideal working environment.

So you do not suffer from a repetitive strain injury (RSI) in your home office or related work, take advantage of the ergonomic products now available and follow these tips:

- Take regular breaks from intensive tasks, at least every hour.
- Warm up your muscles and ligaments with stretches, as you would before an athletic workout.
- Have your home office furniture and equipment fit your needs (see Related Resources). If you sit at a desk, your chair and work space should be at the right height for you to prevent back strain.
- Sit, walk, stand, and, especially, lift with good alignment and posture.
- Try to get regular physical exercise such as lifting light weights or doing aerobic activity to keep your muscles strong and flexible.

EXTRA!!: What You Can Ergonomically Protect

- *Your neck:* If you use the phone, you can use a speaker phone or a headset that will keep your neck and head straight. *Company:* Hello Direct, www.hello-direct.com
- *Your spine and arms:* An ergonomically designed, adjustable chair will do much to prevent back pain and strain. *Companies:* Neutral Posture Ergonomics, Inc. (see Related Resources) or Haworth Furniture, www.haworth-furn.com
- *Your wrists:* To keep them at the proper angle use wrist rests. *Company:* 3M, www.mmm.com
- *Your upper arms and forearms:* Split and angled keyboards can make working at a computer much more comfortable. *Company:* Kinesis Corp, www.kinesis-ergo.com
- *Your mouse finger:* Specialty mouse designs and pads prevent hand and finger soreness. *Companies:* Kensington Technology, www.kensington.com; 3M, www.mmm.com
- *Your eyes:* To prevent "computer vision syndrome," eyestrain caused by glare from light that bounces off your computer screen, use a special computer light that sits on top of your monitor. *Company:* One Tech, www.computerlight.com

Check your local office supply store and office equipment catalogs for more selections.

Employees seldom have as much control over their work areas as do those who work at home, so take advantage of your opportunity to set up an efficient, pleasant, and ergonomically designed home office that will keep you happy and healthy as you operate your business.

Safety: OSHA, Hazards

The federal Occupational Safety & Health Administration (OSHA) and state laws require that you know all "recognized hazards" in the workplace, which can include the long-term effects of chemicals and pollutants. This does not mean that OSHA inspectors are going to come in and inspect your home work area or office. But if you have some employees in your home or involve them in work with you outside your home office, you should be aware of your responsibility for the safety of those workers.

For example, if you have a home workshop manufacturing a handmade product, you should know what toxins are in the materials with which you are working and what protective measures you should have in place: goggles for eyes; masks for fumes; a proper ventilation system to remove dust and fumes; and other safety provisions. If you have employees, you should have written safety guidelines. OSHA has made home inspections mainly to inspect the homes of workers who worked at home for their employers, but not for home offices.

Even if you are the sole worker, it makes sense for you to provide yourself with a safe working environment. For more information about OSHA regulations, visit the office's Web site, www.osha.gov.

TECHNOLOGY FOR ENTREPRENEURS WITH DISABILITIES

The U.S. Census has revealed that people with disabilities have higher rates of self-employment than people without disabilities. Technology and adapted equipment—hardware, software, adapted equipment, home office furniture, and other uniquely designed items—have assisted many persons who are "differently abled" to work independently or operate home businesses from their homes. Here are a few examples of the available adaptations and technology for various disabilities:

- *Hearing Impaired:* Products that use visual adaptations.
- *Communication Impaired:* Products assisting persons with dyslexia, sensory perception, and other impairments.
- *Vision Impaired:* Products assisting individuals with low vision to blindness, such as large-sized text, tactile and sound enhancement items.
- *Mobility Impaired:* Products for those with limited physical movements, such as voice recognition software and alternative keyboards.

Visit trade shows like those sponsored by Abilities EXPO, www.abilitiesexpo.com, and you will see many, many assisted living products and technology. Check also with the organizations listed here and later on in this book for additional resources; and check with your state government to see what technical, financial, and rehabilitation services they have available for persons with disabilities (Pennsylvania, for example, has allocated funds to help persons with physical impairments to modify their homes).

POSTAGE

If you are tired of standing in long lines at the post office, you may want to consider having in your office a mail meter or use an electronic postaging system. Besides helping to enhance your business's image, metered mail enables you to assign the exact postage and in different classes, get feedback on responses to direct mailing campaigns, and save you trips to the post office.

How it works: You need a postage meter that you rent, along with a base and a scale that you can buy if you want. Or you can use your computer and the company's software or hardware device to print certified postage directly onto envelopes and mailing labels. Costs range from a few hundred dollars to several thousand dollars. If you only send out a few pieces of mail a day, the investment may not be worth it for you. However, if you launch a direct mail campaign, it can save you time and money while reaching potential customers.

As with all your business's purchases, shop around and compare prices to find the best company that fits your mailing needs.

Protecting You and Your Home Business

(*Note:* The information in this section is presented as an introduction and overview of the types of insurances available to protect you, your family, and your home business. To ensure adequate and comprehensive coverage, speak with one or more insurance company representatives and/or independent agents who are licensed and qualified.)

We all hope for the best, but should also prepare for the worst. To protect your person, property, and livelihood, it's important to have insurance should a disaster occur despite your taking precautions.

INSURANCES

If you operate a home business, you will have to approach insurance coverage just as you would if you owned and operated a business out of a commercial building. As a home business owner, you will also have a responsibility you never had to think about as an employee of a company—finding health and other types of business insurance. Part of your preliminary startup business research should include deciding what types of insurances you will need. Do this now, rather than after something has happened. Here are some guidelines:

Separate your home (building) insurance from your home business insurance, or add to it as recommended by your agent. Most home insurances do not adequately cover home business needs or the potential liability you take on when you start a home business. Generally, homeowner's policies do not cover any business equipment or liability; therefore, if you are sued, a lien could be put against assets, including your home.

Business insurance policies may seem an unnecessary expense when you start your business, but without insurance, you take a risk that you may regret later. Home and small business owners often purchase these kinds of insurance policies:

Incidental Business Endorsement: Attached to your existing homeowner's policy to cover loss of equipment and structure as well as liability coverage for certain eligible types of businesses. These endorsements are usually much more affordable than commercial insurance policies. If, however, your business specifically requires a commercial policy, your independent agent should also be able to help you or refer you to other agents who handle that type of insurance.

Home Office Coverage: This type of insurance covers your office equipment and supplies, and any buildings that house your business. Your business inventory may or may not be included under property insurance so you may need a commercial policy for this. Check, too, to see if your home insurance covers the possessions and property of clients and others located in your home office.

If you use a car, truck, or other vehicle for business, again check with your agent to see if you can just add an endorsement or if you need a separate commercial policy.

Business Owners Package Policy: If an endorsement to your homeowner's policy is not possible, ask your agent about a business owner package, called a BOP.

In-Home Business Owners Policy: Some insurance companies offer policies that cover both your business and your home. Often these are more affordable.

Commercial Business Policy: Depending on the type of home business you operate, your business may only qualify for commercial coverage. Of course, rates vary according to the nature of your business, but many commercial policies combine both loss and liability. *Note:* Clients often request a certificate that you have insurance—usually pertaining to liability issues—before they will do business with you. Just ask your agent to send such a certificate to your client.

Disability Coverage

If you were unable to run your business tomorrow, due to an illness or injury, who would pay your bills and support your family's needs? Being self-employed, you do not have workmen's compensation to fall back on. Therefore, if you should be injured on the job and cannot work, you do not earn any money. If you are permanently disabled, qualifying for social security disability benefits could take years.

Disability coverage rates will vary with the type of insurance you choose, the risk of your particular work, the length of time (after the accident or illness) it takes to receive disability payments, and for how long your coverage will run.

Depending on the insurance carrier, you may have more or fewer options, but you'll choose from three general types:

Business Overhead Expense Coverage: If you cannot work, this will cover rent/mortgage payments, utilities, phone, employees' pay (if you have any), and other business expenses.

Income Replacement Coverage: Covers your lost income, usually a percentage of what you made before you became disabled.

Buyout Protection: This usually applies to a partnership in that the policy provides money for your partner(s) to purchase your interest in the business.

Some people do not believe it is beneficial to have disability insurance, even though safety specialists state that most accidents occur in the home! Check with your local chamber of commerce to see whether they offer members disability coverage. Discuss all your options with a qualified insurance agent. Together you can make the decision best for you.

Business Continuation and Interruptions

This type of disaster insurance covers your net profits and expenses should a fire, flood, tornado, hurricane, earthquake, or another misfortunate occur and you would be unable to operate your business from your home office. Compensation is usually calculated by figuring out an average of your business's income over the previous twelve months before the catastrophe. If your business income is the sole or main support of you and/or your family, it is especially important that you have this type of insurance.

Health

One drawback of being self-employed is having to pay for your own health insurance—even though you can deduct a percentage of your payments from your taxes (check with your accountant for the specifics). At this time the U.S. is in a health-care crisis, with the federal government estimating that almost 40 million people are without health care! (For more information and health-care options, visit the Web site, CoverageForTheUninsured.com.) As an entrepreneur, your quest is affordable health insurance that will best serve your needs. Here are options you might investigate:

1. *COBRA (Consolidated Omnibus Budget Reconciliation Act):* If your previous job provided health benefits, a 1985 federal rule says a former employer must offer the option of continuing your health coverage for eighteen months. Of course, you pay the

premiums. Be aware, too, that you and your employer may have to meet additional criteria to be eligible for this program.

2. *Associations and Organizations:* Business owner groups like local chambers of commerce, your national trade or industry group, or organizations for professionals, such as bar associations for lawyers, may offer group-rate insurance as part of their member benefits.

3. *Health Alliances:* These are set up just to purchase health insurance and offer members a number of plans from which to choose.

4. *Individual Plans:* Experts recommend you talk directly with an independent insurance agent. She can answer your questions and may be able to offer you a variety of plans to best fit your situation. Make sure the agent is licensed in your state and is knowledgeable in the area of health plans for the self-employed!

When you go to talk to an insurance agent or go online for health insurance quotes, you will be asked to consider major coverage types such as these:

Indemnity: The traditional coverage, a.k.a. "fee for services," that reimburses expenses and has no health-care provider limitations.

Preferred Provider Organization (PPO): Offers reduced costs if you use the suggested network of physicians.

Point of Service (POP) and Health Maintenance Organization (HMO): Predetermined health-care providers provide the regular health care.

Other Options: You may want to also talk to your agent about medical savings accounts (MSAs) that are tax-advantaged personal savings accounts to be used for health care not covered by insurance, including deductibles and co-payments. Another option is catastrophic insurance (which has a huge deductible of $2,500 per person or $5,000 per family), along with a money market account to which you make deposits each month to be used specifically to pay medical expenses.

A number of Internet sites (see page 171 in Related Resources) provide health insurance information, rate comparisons, quotes, and even online purchasing of plans (subject to state regulations). Again, thoroughly check to be sure that an online insurance company is licensed in your state and is following state guidelines for selling via the Internet. Make sure it is a legitimate company, not a scam!

Experts advise you to ask hard questions about any health insurance plan you consider before you sign up for it so you know exactly what health care costs it does and does not cover. The Web site of the Agency for Healthcare Research and Quality (www.ahcpr.gov/consumer) provides health insurance information, including such articles as "Checkup on Health Insurance Choices" and "Choosing and Using a Health Plan."

You'll find no perfect health insurance coverage, but exploring the different plans available will help you find the best available coverage for your circumstances for the best price.

Liability

This type of insurance covers against bodily injury or property damage inadvertently caused by you to others. Besides protecting you from paying an expensive judgment, liability insurance gives you access to legal representation—your insurance company—which will fight to resolve any lawsuit on your behalf. Again, depending on your business, basic liability may be included in a homeowner's endorsement.

Three kinds of liability protection are available:

1. *Product liability* protects you in the event your product injures someone or causes damage from its use.
2. *Professional liability* (also called malpractice or errors-and-omissions insurance) protects you from malpractice suits claiming your advice or services were not provided as agreed upon. This is one of the reasons you have contracts for projects.
3. *General liability* gives you protection if a client or delivery person is injured at your home.

Other Types of Insurance

Here are several additional types of insurance that may be important and applicable to your business as it expands and/or if your business product or service is very unique and not covered under standard policies.

SEW's Suggestions

In order to assist your insurance agent in selecting the best insurance policy for you, consider these questions:

- Will you be hiring any (outside) employees?
- What is your business product or service and what impact does it have on your customers?
- Are you a consultant or professional who provides knowledge-based services, giving advice that can affect clients personally or their business's decisions?
- Do customers or delivery persons come to your home?
- Do your customers require a certificate of commercial insurance from you?
- What is the value of your business-related equipment?
- Do you have clients' property at your home?
- What certifications and training have you had in your field?
- If you do work at a client's home or business site, what equipment of yours do you use and what of your client's do you use?
- What security, fire prevention, and other safety features do you have for your home office and/or equipment?

You want to strike a balance between how much insurance you need and how much you can afford. A good agent will help you find this balance and also review your policy with you periodically to assist in helping you adjust your policies as your business also grows and changes.

Employee: If your business grows to the point you need to hire employees, you are required to provide all your workers with workers' compensation insurance should an employee become injured or ill due to a work-related injury or condition. If your business is incorporated, you may be eligible for workmen's compensation if you should suffer an injury.

Key Man (Woman): Sole proprietors generally do have this type of insurance, but this type of policy covers "key" people—employees vital to your business—should they for one reason or another be unable to work. Oftentimes, lenders such as banks will require you to have this type of insurance so you will be able to repay their business loan.

Specific Business: Specific businesses sometimes require more coverage or that special policies be underwritten. For example, a retired schoolteacher/herpetologist gives demonstrations at state fairs with his reptile show. Though he does not have any venomous snakes, he still had to go to an insurance company that specializes in unusual ventures like his to get coverage.

Life: With most families dependent on two sources of income, you should consider having a life insurance policy that pays death benefits if you should die that will help your family or beneficiaries to pay living expenses and continue your business if they choose. The unfortunate events of September 11, 2001, made all of us wonder what would happen to our loved ones if we suddenly died or were killed.

DISASTER PREVENTION AND RECOVERY PLANS

It can happen to any business or home—fire, weather damage, or another unexpected catastrophe—as the book *The Worst-Case Scenarios* demonstrates. You should plan for just that—the worst-case scenario, such as the destruction of your home office, your home, or home-based buildings, or the loss of equipment or property destroyed in a client's building.

You will more likely recover and be able to afford to rebuild your business if you follow these disaster restoration plan tips:

- Have a list of all your equipment and business property, along with their purchase receipts (to assess their value) and guarantees in a safe place, such as a bank safety deposit box.
- In that same safe location, keep contact information for your insurance agent, your customers, suppliers, and other important people.

- Make sure your insurance policy covers the *replacement* value, not the current value of your used equipment.
- Keep accurate records of the equipment and other assets you have insured—in a safe place outside your home. Hire an inventory specialist to catalog your equipment, products, etc., if your insured property is large (many of these specialists sell inventory kits for you to do your own cataloging). Some provide a videotape of your protected property and contents.
- Have business interruption insurance (also called business income, or BI, coverage).
- Ask your insurance agent what are the procedures her company would like you to follow in an emergency.
- Update your coverage of your business as it changes.

If the worst-case scenario should happen, first take care of yourself and family, and then notify your insurance agent(s) as soon as possible. When everyone is safe, sit down with your family and agent and create a plan to start rebuilding your life and your business again. If your area has been declared a "disaster area" by government authorities, you may qualify for low-interest loans to help you rebuild your home and business. Unfortunately, this may take months, and even years, but if you have been able to cover your business with adequate insurance, and have a good insurance agent to assist you, your business may someday be back and better than ever!

Business Experts and Associates

When people do the research for a home or small business startup, they often forget that they need some help along the way. You will not be able to do it all! Judith E. Dacey, CPA (www.EasyAs123.com), a nationally recognized small business consultant, says this:

> As the head (and only) honcho, it is easy to fall into the trap of running the business by the seat of your pants. Women have a tendency to run their business on a shoestring. It's second nature to buy office furniture economically, shop for office supplies, and disparage soft expenses like a lawyer or

accountant. A good team of advisors is not an expense. It is an *investment in yourself*. You create the only limits placed on your business. To grow your business, you must grow. Use advisors to educate you: to challenge your thinking, to provide wisdom and encouragement. Business is a team sport. Loners rarely experience more than moderate success and often have a higher likelihood of failure.

So, who do you turn to to assist you in your business startup and its operations? Again, ask for referrals from other home and small business owners, or contact the professional associations for people located near you. You will want to have the following experts available:

ACCOUNTANTS

It is nearly impossible for the home-based and small business owner to stay current with tax laws and changes, so having an accountant (and a bookkeeper if you need help with your record keeping or to keep up to a growing business) can help set up your bookkeeping structure, review your business's current financial status, and help you plan for future growth.

Judith Dacey says this about the importance of having an accountant:

> Before starting a home-based business, it's smart to seek advice from an accountant who is experienced in working with SOHO (small office/home office) businesses. Why? Because even though you are the sole owner of your business, you have a silent partner . . . the IRS.
>
> Use a pro to show you how to keep your profits out of Uncle Sam's pockets. Cutting costs and raising prices can grow your bottom line, but that only increases your biggest expense: the government. Expect to pay typically 40 to 50 percent of your profit if you are a sole proprietor (income tax and social security–Medicare taxes) or 30 to 40 percent if you are incorporated. That's a chunk of change! There are many honest deductions that you can take *if* you know about them. Be compelled to develop your financial literacy.

SEW's Suggestions: Questions to Ask the Experts

How do choose an expert? Here are some questions to ask before you hire them.

- *What are your fees and terms of payment?* Do not let a person's profession intimidate you so that you are hesitant to ask an expert his or her fees.
- *Do you have a specialty?* Most experts focus on one or more areas in their industry, and thus are more up to date with the latest information.
- *Did you go to college and/or receive a degree?* Some professions require certain certifications and other professions offer continuous learning programs.
- *What is the best way to get in contact with you: phone? e-mail? regular mail?* It is not too much to expect a same-day response to a phone query from an expert or one of her staff.
- *Do you take emergency calls?* Business emergencies happen at night and on weekends, too.
- *Do you have a couple of clients with whom I can talk?* If your expert cannot give you some names due to privacy concerns, you can still ask other home business owners for feedback or referrals to professionals they respect.
- *Do you consult with other professionals under certain circumstances, and who are they?* It is important you know all who will be involved in helping find a resolution you have with any business problems.
- *Are you a member of any trade or professional organizations?* This information is usually included on most professionals' business cards or promotional materials, but you should ask if you do not see them to make sure they are licensed or qualified according to the regulations of their profession or expertise.
- *If I do not feel we can work together, can I expect any refund of your fees?* If for any reason you do not feel comfortable with this person, or do not think you are being treated with respect, you have the right to choose someone else. Going to an expert is primarily a business arrangement, but you should expect mutual respect and consideration.

INSURANCE AGENT

From your own personal experiences—if you own a vehicle, a home, rent an apartment, or have life insurance—you most likely have an insurance agent (if not several) already. Whether you get insurance through a trade or business group or an independent agent, you want an agent who answers your questions, finds a policy (or policies) that best fits your business needs, and returns your calls. I recently spoke to a woman who canceled a policy because her agent never returned her calls—for several months in a row!

The benefit of having an agent through a local business organization or a local chapter of a trade organization is that you can complain to the head of your organization if you are not satisfied with an agent's service. The adage of "strength in numbers" often works well in helping you get service and the answers you need.

LAWYERS

Whether or not you agree that we have a litigious society, it is a good idea to include a consultation with a lawyer who specializes in home and small business legalities as part of your startup steps (and costs). An attorney can advise you about many legal matters, including forming a business structure; writing and reviewing contracts; and understanding partnership and ownership issues, employee matters (including subcontracting), liability concerns, protection of your business's intellectual property and the future of your business.

You may never imagine needing a lawyer for your business; but having one from the start, even if only to give you peace of mind, is wise. Check with a lawyer referral service—such as the American Bar Associations, www.abanet.org; FindLaw.com; Legal Connections, Inc., www.800wedolaw.com; or USLaw.com—to find a licensed lawyer in your area.

ADDITIONAL EXPERTS

You may also "tap into" the advice of these experts as you start and grow your home business:

Banker

Sooner or later every business will need capital to start up, expand, and/or survive. Over the last few years, bankers have realized that women business owners are a powerful entrepreneurial force and are just as likely as men business owners to pay back their loans (if not more so). Ask for feedback from other women business owners as to the banks that have been their favorites in terms of customer service and loans. Sometimes banks will sponsor financial seminars that you may find helpful in operating your business.

When you do decide on a bank for your business account, introduce yourself to the bank manager and their loan officers. Sometimes they may even help you with your business plan. Check out some of the larger banks' Web sites that have special sections for small businesses, such as Bank One (www.bankone.com/business), Wells Fargo (www.wellsfargo.com/biz), and possibly your own bank.

Business Coach

A professional coach's services include helping individuals and business owners to focus and follow through on their goals. Professional coaches will often also specialize in certain areas, often drawing on their previous work and educational backgrounds. A number of them coach new entrepreneurs. Professional coaches monitor their clients to ensure that they are following through on their daily tasks so they can accomplish what they want to achieve. Coach training programs emphasize that coaches work with their clients in collaborative relationship, a type of partnership. (See chapter 3 for more information.)

Business Counselors

Business counselors can assist you with business planning, loan applications, and referrals to other professionals. The federal government has "Business Information Centers," SCORE (Senior Core of Retired Executives) offices at www.score.org, Small Business Development Centers (SBDCs) at www.sba.gov/SBDC, and Women's Business Development Centers at www.onlinewbc.gov. These centers and offices are located across the U.S., Puerto Rico, and some U.S. territories. In Canada, contact the Canada Business Service Centres, www.cbsc.org/, to register with a business counselor in you province or territory. For the U.S. center locations, call the SBA Answer Desk: (800) 827-5722 (800-U-ASK-SBA); or search their Web sites.

Consultants

Consultants are specialists in their industry or in areas of business—startup, marketing, business plans, computers, education, and many other industries. Most consultants have gained their knowledge through a combination of education, training, and years of experience. You will most likely find you need one when you are unable to solve a problem and need some outside advice to help you find a solution.

Consultants can assist you by offering you new ways and directions for your business, suggesting methods for operating your business more efficiently and keeping your business from stagnating and falling behind your competition.

Financial Advisors

Any person can call him- or herself a financial planner; however, "certified" financial planners have met the educational, ethical, and experience requirements of the Certified Financial Planner Board of Standards. Financial planners are important to help women plan their personal financial goals and to assist with investing and planning for retirement.

Marketing Experts

If potential customers do not know about your business and its products and services, you will not make money. It is as simple as that. What is *not* simple is how you will get that message to these people. That is the importance of marketing. If you are just starting out or have reached a stalemate with your marketing campaigns for an existing business, consider hiring a marketing consultant or agency. Of course, you will want samples of their work and references. One woman who operated a roadside antique and collectibles business saw an immediate increase in profits when the marketing expert she hired suggested she put large, attractive banners outside her shop advertising best-selling items.

The shop owner was amazed at the number of people who stopped in after seeing the banners and told her they drove by daily and never knew she had those items. A marketing expert may be just as helpful to you.

Mentors: Advocates for Business

A mentor is usually a person who has already experienced what you are going through and "takes you under her wing." In this case, an experienced woman business owner guides you along as you develop your business. Some business ownership organizations will assign mentors to new members, and other mentors have developed informal relationships. With the Internet's discussion groups and chats, you might even develop an online mentorship.

Not every mentor relationship will work out, but those that do can be an important part of your success, especially when your mentor prevents you from making startup mistakes. When your business has become successful, you can take your turn encouraging another entrepreneur.

Tax Professionals

Tax professionals can assist you in filing your taxes related to your business if you do not do it yourself. Of the different types of income tax preparers, many focus on specialized fields. An enrolled agent (EA) is one approved by the Internal Revenue Service to represent a taxpayer before the IRS. EAs may work as independent consultants, or they may practice in a firm that includes other tax practitioners. EAs and other tax preparers must follow the IRS's rules and regulations set for them.

Virtual Assistants (VAs)

In the last few years the Internet has seen the growth of a new independent specialist, the virtual assistant. Shane Bowlin, www.ask shane.com, a certified VA, says this:

> A VA is a professional assistant working in partnership with an individual to provide support—without being physically present. They (VAs) are more than just remote secretaries.

They learn their clients' businesses and work closely in helping their clients take their businesses to the next level, becoming more productive and effective.

VAs can assist business owners and professionals in handling correspondence, e-mails, and many other tasks that help a home business owner.

Related Resources

BUSINESS PLANS
Books

Anatomy of a Business Plan: A Step-by-Step Guide to Building a Business and Securing Your Company's Future, 5th ed., by Linda Pinson (Chicago, IL: Kaplan Professional Company, 2001).

Business Plans Made Easy, rev. ed., by Mark Henricks (Irvine, CA: Entrepreneur Media, Inc., 2002).

Your First Business Plan: A Simple Question and Answer Format Designed to Help You Write Your Own Plan, rev. ed. by Joseph Covello, Brian J. Hazelgren (Naperville, IL: Sourcebooks, Inc., 1997).

Software

Automate Your Business Plan by Linda Pinson, 2002, version 10.

Business Plan Pro 2002 by Palo Alto, www.paloalto.com.

BizPlan Builder 8 by Jian, www.jian.com.

Web Sites

www.bplans.com/ — Web site of Palo Alto software company, maker of business, marketing, and Web site planning software.

www.business-plan.com — Web site of Linda Pinson, business plan expert. Lists her book and companion business planning software, "Automate Your Business Plan."

www.jian.com — Web site of Jian, business plan software; includes an online "Business Planning Workshop," www.jian.com/workshop/index.htm.

www.onlinewbc.gov/docs/starting/basics.html — "Business Plan Basics" from Women's Online Business Center.

EDUCATION
Web Sites

Hewlett-Packard, www.hp.com/sbso/advice/index.html, offers free online courses as building Web pages, Photoshop basics, graphic design for non-designers, and more.

Comprehensive Coaching University, www.comprehensivecoachingu.com — Provides coaching and training.

International Coaching Federation, www.coachfederation.org/; (202) 712-9039.

National Association of Business Coaches, www.mynabc.org/; (800) 290-3196.

Books

How to Get a College Degree Via the Internet: The Complete Guide to Getting Your Undergraduate or Graduate Degree from the Comfort of Your Home by Sam Atieh (Roseville, CA: Prima Communications, 1998).

Internet University: Your Guide to Online College Courses by Daniel Quinn Mills (Anaheim, CA: BNI Publications, Inc., 1998).

Home Study Courses

Distance Education and Training Council (DETC), 1601 18th St. NW, Washington, D.C. 20009-2529; (202) 332-1386; www.detc.org — A nonprofit educational association and nationally recognized accrediting agency that provides a listing of accredited home study schools and courses.

Web Sites

Assist University, www.assistu.com.

HOME BUSINESS BASICS
Books: Home-Based and Family

Home But Not Alone: The Work-at-Home Parents' Handbook by Katherine Murray (Indianapolis, IN: Jist Works, 1997).

How to Raise a Family and a Career Under One Roof by Lisa Roberts (Moontownship, PA: Brookhaven Press, 1997).

Mompreneurs: A Practical Step-by-Step Guide to Work-at-Home Success by Ellen H. Parlapiano and Patricia Cobe (New York: Berkley, 1996), www.Mompreneursonlinecom.

The Stay-at-Home Mom's Guide to Making Money: How to Choose the Business That's Right for You Using the Skills and Interests You Already Have, revised 2nd ed., by Liz Folger (Roseville, CA: Prima Communications, 2000), www.BizyMoms.com.

Books: Home Business Dilemmas

Slack: Getting Past Burnout, Busywork, and the Myth of Total Efficiency by Tom DeMarco (New York: Broadway Books, 2001).

The Procrastinator's Guide to Success by Lynne Lively (New York: McGraw-Hill Professional, 2002). Order this e-book through an online bookstore.

The Complete Idiot's Guide to Overcoming Procrastination by Michelle Tullier (New York: Macmillan Publishing, 1999).

Business Plan for the Body: Crunch the Numbers for Successful Weight Loss, Manage Your Metabolism by Eating the Right Way, Invest in the Only Workout You'll Ever Need by Jim Karas (New York: Crown Publishing Group, 2001).

Getting Things Done: The Art of Stress-Free Productivity by David Allen (New York: Viking Penquin, 2001).

You Can Make Money from Your Hobby: Building a Business Doing What You Love by Martha Campbell Pullen, Lilly Walters (Nashville, TN: Broadman and Holman, 1999).

Web Sites

Entrepreneurial Parent, www.en-prent.com.

INSURANCE
Books

The *Confused Consumer's Guide to Choosing a Health Care Plan* by Martin Gottlieb (Concord, NH: Hyperion Press [now Gibson Press], 1998).

Insuring Your Business—What You Need to Know to Get the Best Insurance Coverage for Your Business by Sean Mooney (New York: Insurance Information Institute Press, 1992).

"Protecting Your In-Home Business," brochure by Independent Insurance Agents of America, 127 S. Peyton St., Alexandria, VA 22314. Send an LSAE (long, self-addressed, stamped envelope) for information or check the consumer section of their Web site: www.iiaa.org.

Web Sites

The Agency for Healthcare Research and Quality, www.ahcpr.gov/consumer.

eHealthInsurance, www.ehealthinsurance.com — Rates and quotes to compare health insurance plans.

Health Insurance Assn. of America, www.hiaa.org/consumer — Insurance guides for consumers.

HealthPlanDirectory.com, www.healthplandirectory.com/HealthPlans/Directory — Provides contact information for health insurance plans in your state.

Independent Insurance Agents of America, www.iiaa.org; 127 S. Peyton St., Alexandria, VA 22314. Send an LSAE for information or visit their Web site and read the page entitled "Find an Agent."

Insure.com, www.insure.com/health — Health insurance basics, news, and rate-finder.

Insurance Information Institute, www.iii.org; 110 William St., New York, NY 10038. Its purpose is "to provide accurate and timely information on insurance subjects."

Insurancevalues.com, www.healthinsurance.org — An online health insurance resource for individuals, the self-employed, and small businesses.

InsWeb, www.InsWeb.com — Matches buyers and sellers of individual and Medicare policies.

QuickenInsurance, www.quicken.com/insurance — Information on supplemental health and critical illness insurance, and insurance quotes.

Quotesmith Corp., www.quotesmith.com — An online quote service.

MARKETING

Association

American Marketing Association, www.ama.org; 311 S. Wacker Dr., Ste. 5800, Chicago, IL 60606.

Books

6 Steps to Free Publicity and Dozens of Other Ways to Win Free Media Attention for You or Your Business by Marcia Yudkin (New York: Dutton/Plume, 1994).

101 Ways to Promote Yourself by Raleigh Pinskey (New York: Avon Books, 1997).

Guerrilla Marketing for the Home-Based Business by Jay Conrad Levinson (Boston: Houghton Mifflin Company, 1995).

How to Market a Product for Under $500 by Jeffrey Dobkin (Merion Station, PA: The Danielle Adams Publishing Co., 1996).

Uncommon Marketing Technique by Jeffrey Dobkin (Merion Station, PA: The Danielle Adams Publishing Co., 1998).

Web Sites

www.dobkin.com by Jeffrey Dobkin, "America's Marketer Master." Includes an article/worksheet about how to create a one-page marketing plan.

www.gmarketing.com, "Guerilla Marketing" by Jay Conrad Levinson.

www.onlinewbc.gov — Women's Business Center's online "Marketing Mall" features marketing plan components, plans, outline.

www.yudkin.com/marketing.htm is Marcia Yudkin's "Creative Marketing Solutions."

MENTORING
Book

Mentoring: A Success Guide for Mentors and Protégés by Terri Sjodin and Floyd Wickman (New York: Irwin/McGraw-Hill, 1998).

Federal Program

Women's Network for Entrepreneurial Training Mentoring Program (WNET), www.sba.gov/womeninbusiness/ — Program for helping established women business owners to mentor new women entrepreneurs; (800) 827-5722.

NETWORKING
Books

Home Office Know-How by Jeffery Zbar (Chicago: Dearborn, 1998).

Mastering Home Networking by Mark Hendricks (Alameda, CA: Sybex Inc., 2000); www.sybex.com.

Product

www.intel.com/ — Intel's site with networking products.

Organizations

Headquarters Network, www.hqnet.com.

The Home Phoneline Networking Alliance (Home PNA); www.homepna.org/. A group of computer companies including Compaq, IBM, Intel, Hewlett-Packard, and Tut systems formed to promote phone-line networking.

National Business Incubation Association, www.nbia.org; 20 E. Circle Dr., Suite 190, Athens, OH 45701.

Office Business Center Association, www.officebusinesscenter.com, (800) 237-4741.

Offices2share.com, www.office2share.com; c/o SmallBizRealty, Inc., 1633 Broadway, 23rd Floor, New York, NY 10019.

SETTING UP YOUR OFFICE: TECHNOLOGY AND DESIGN

Books

Business Leasing for Dummies by David G. Mayer (New York: Hungry Minds, Inc., 2001).

Consultants & Consulting Organizations Directory, 24th ed. (Detroit, MI: Gale Research, 2002). This large two-volume reference featuring 400 consulting specialties is most likely found in larger public or college libraries.

Design It Yourself: Logos, Letterheads, and Business Cards: The Non-Designer's Step-by-Step Guide by Chuck Green (Gloucester, MA: Rockport Publishers, 2001).

The Desktop Publisher's Idea Book: One-of-a-Kind Projects, Expert Tips, and Hard-to-Find Sources, 2nd ed., by Chuck Green (New York: Random House Reference, 1997).

Furnishing Your Work Space by Neal Zimmerman (New York: John Wiley & Sons, Inc., 1996).

Home Office Design: Everything You Need to Know about Planning, Organizing, and Furnishing Your Work Space by Neal Zimmerman (New York: John Wiley & Sons, Inc., 1996).

Home Office Life: Making a Space to Work at Home by Lisa Kanarek (Glouster, MA: Rockport Publishers, 2001).

Making Money with Your Computer at Home, 2nd ed., by Paul and Sarah Edwards (New York: Putnam Publishing Group, 1997).

Practical Home Office Solutions by Marilyn Zelinsky Syarto (New York: McGraw-Hill, 1998).

Tips for Your Home Office by Meredith Gould (Pownal, VT: Storey Books, 1998).

Online Publications

www.thaddeus.com/ — publishes *Pocket PC* online magazine, other publications, and catalogs for mobile computing users.

www.hhcmag.com/ — publishes *Handheld Computing Magazine.*

Miscellaneous

For movement-activated, computer anti-theft devices, visit your favorite computer supply store or conduct an Internet search.

For voice recognition software, visit your favorite software store or type in "voice recognition software" into your favorite search engine.

Postage Companies
(for price and service comparisons)

Neopost's Simply Packages, www.simplypostage.com.

Pitney Bowe's PitneyWorks, www.pitneyworks.com.

Stamps.com, www.stamps.com.

U.S. Postal Service, www.usps.gov — General and shipping information and confirmation.

Publications

Better Buys for Business (publisher), www.betterbuys.com, 370 Technology Drive, Malvern, PA 19355. Publishes buyer's guides (print or e-guides) for office equipment. Visit online for publications listing or call (610) 296-4031.

Smart Computing, www.smartcomputing.com; Sandhills Publishing, 131 W. Grand Dr., P.O. Box 85380, Lincoln, NE 68521.

Web Sites

AtYourOffice.com, www.atyouroffice.com — Office supply site, including ergonomic accessories for computers; small business resources.

Business & Institutional Furniture Company, Inc., 611 N. Broadway, Milwaukee, WI 53202-0902; www.nationalbusinessfurniture.com.

BuyerZone, www.buyerzone.com — An Internet purchasing service for the office by Beacon Research Group.

Childproofer's USA, www.childproofing.com. Offers safety products.

www.DesktopPublishing.com offers many pages of helpful tips.

Flexy-Plan Distinctive Office Furniture, 69 W. Ridge Rd., P.O. Box CC, Fairview, PA 16415-0829; www.fyp.com.

HomeOfficeLife.com, www.homeofficelife.com — Web site of Lisa Kanarek, home office expert and author.

www.ideabook.com — Chuck Green's Web site, which includes books, DTP tips, and free info.

IdeaSiteforBusiness.com, www.ideasiteforbusiness.com/org.html — Offers tips on organizing your office.

www.jumpola.com — Also Chuck Green's Web site which includes a large list of links for designers and marketers.

Neutral Posture Ergonomics, Inc., 3903 N. Texas Ave., Bryan, TX 77803; wwwNTRL.com. Offers ergonomic chairs.

Quicken, www.quicken.com/small_business/ — Equipping your office and other information.

Smart Computing, www.smartcomputing.com — Web site of print publications that puts technology into "plain English" for computer users.

Technocopia, Inc., www.technocopia.com — Web sites about technology for consumers. The company also operates The Home Automation Times, www.homeautomationtimes.com/ with a business perspective.

Super Soundproofing, www.soundproofing.org — Information site with soundproofing tips.

U.S. Small Business Administration, www.sba.gov/.

What to Buy for Business, www.whattobuyforbusiness.co.uk — Web site of print (subscription) magazine that reviews the latest office equipment.

STARTUP INFORMATION

Books

The Small Business Start-up Guide: Practical Advice on Selecting, Starting and Operating a Small Business, 3rd ed., by Dr. Robert Sullivan (Great Falls, VA: Information International, 2000).

Software

Adams Streetwise Small Business Startup Software, www.adamsmedia.com/software/sbs/index.asp; (508) 427-7100.

Quicken Small Business Expert, www.quicken.com/small_business/business_solutions/.

Startup Kit

Home-Based Working Moms (HBWM), P.O. Box 500164, Austin, TX 78750. For more information, e-mail: hbwm@hbwm.com.

Web Sites

Financial Planning Association, www.fpanet.org/ — (404) 845-0011.

www.onlinewbc.gov/docs/starting/todo.html — Start-Up To Do List: The Women's Online Business Center.

www.sba.gov/starting/index.html — SBA "Starting Your Business" Web page.

www.bplans.com/sc/ — Free online "Starting Cost Tool" by Palo Alto, maker of business, marketing, and Web site planning software.

YOUR HEALTH
Associations

Home Office Association of America: www.hoaa.com/ (212) 588-9097 or (800) 809-4622.

National Association for the Self-Employed:www.nase.org/ (800) 232-NASE (6273).

Women Incorporated, www.womeninc.org — (310) 815-0975; (800) 930-3993; Offers members an insurance program with multiple insurers and plan options.

Books

Conquering Carpal Tunnel Syndrome and Other Repetitive Strain Injuries by Sharon J. Butler (Oakland, CA: New Harbinger Publications, 1996).

Repetitive Strain Injury by Deborah Quilter and Emil Pascarelli (New York: John Wiley & Sons, 1997).

The Repetitive Strain Injury SourceBook by Sandra Peddie with Craig H. Rosenberg (NTC Publishing Group, 1998).

Equipment

Chairs: Neutral Posture Ergonomics, Inc., www.NTRL.com; 3904 N. Texas Ave., Bryan, TX 77803.

Software

ExerciseBreak, www.hoptechno.com/eb.htm; (952) 931-9376 — Software by Hopkins Technology that helps personal computer users exercise at their desks to avoid repetitive-motion injury.

Web Sites

The Boulevard, www.blvd.com, is a Web site containing information on products, resources, publications, employment opportunities for persons with disabilities and more. Browse their Assistive Online Superstore of "unique and hard-to-find products" in their online catalog or call or write for more information: jjMarketing, 1205 Savoy Street, Suite 101, San Diego, CA 92107; (619) 222-8735 or (800) 833-8735.

CTD News, www.ctdnews.com/ — Major online news source for information for America's information on cumulative trauma disorder (CTDs) injuries and workplace repetitive stress injuries, from carpal tunnel syndrome to low back pain.

Ergoweb, www.ergoweb.com — Ergonomic products, information, and news.

National Institute for Occupational Safety and Health (NIOSH), www.cdc.gov/niosh.

WorkSpaces, www.workspaces.com — Information on ergonomic home office equipment and other home office tips.

CHAPTER FIVE

Legal Considerations

Along with all the decisions in starting a home business, pay attention to the legalities involved. Pleading ignorance will not be accepted as a defense if you are challenged. (*Note:* Chances are you will need to consult a lawyer at some point of your business's operations. To find a lawyer, ask for recommendations from other home or small business owners or from a lawyer referral network See more about choosing a lawyer in chapter 4).

Choosing a Business Name

If you use your own name in your business's name, such as "Smith's Computer Consulting," you do not need to register your business name with your state or appropriate government agency. But if you will be conducting business using a fictitious name, also referred to as "DBA" (doing business as), such as "Commodore Computer Consulting," you will have to register it.

The purpose of this fictitious name registration is to publicly let people know you are the person who is operating this business, and to ensure that you are not using a name already in use or that no one else will use yours. Your state will also let you know whether that name is already registered. You can go to your local courthouse and register the name yourself or you can have your lawyer do it.

If you will do business nationally, you may want to trademark your name by registering it with the U.S. Patent and Trademark Office, www.uspto.gov, General Information Services Division, Crystal Plaza 3, Room 2C02, Washington, D.C. 20231; (703) 308-4357. To ensure that no one else is using that name or mark, you may also want to conduct a trademark search or use an online trademark and copyright service like Thomson & Thomson, www.thomson-thomson.com/, or CCH Corsearch,www.corsearch.com/, to conduct a search for you for a fee. Consult with a lawyer who specializes in intellectual property law.

Choose your name carefully because it will be a constant marketing tool. Here are some considerations in choosing the best name for your business:

- Make it memorable but in good taste or in keeping with the image that you wish your business to portray.
- Your business name should tell potential customers who you are and what advantages they will have by patronizing your business. Names like "Moyer Enterprises" or "XYZ Specialties" do not really describe what service or product you provide or how it will benefit your customers. Peggy's "Canvas Uncommon" aptly describes her custom-made tote bags and products as does professional coach Terri Levine's "Comprehensive Coaching," denoting her professional and personal coaching services.
- Avoid names that are associated with well-known corporations to avoid confusion and even lawsuits.
- Be aware of the first word or any initials you may use at the start of your business name. Certain listings may make finding you in the phone directory difficult for customers.

  For example, businesses started with initials, like "AAAA Cleaning Services" may be hard to find amongst all the other businesses that begin with the letters A, AA, or AAAs, because telephone directories list all the businesses that start with initials first in the alphabetical listing of each letter. A potential customer can easily forget how many A's are in your business's name and give up looking for your telephone number. Or if your last (or first) name is Beau and you make crafts, "Beau's Creations" could be confused with its homonym, "Bow's Creations."

- Use a name that lets prospective customers know your unique benefits, such as "Round-the-Clock Computer Consulting," meaning that you are available for emergency service twenty-four hours a day.

- You can include the geographical location, town, county, and so forth of your potential customers in your name. You could, for example, include such terms as National, Worldwide, Universal, or North American to express the extent of your business market.

- Add a tagline, a short sentence summarizing your services or products, to your business name in five words or less. "Smith Energy, Inc.: Energy Consulting Services" and "Fox Tales: Poetry for All Occasions" have taglines which imply that customers will receive a little extra service.

- Make a list of names you like, then compare them to your competitors' names, and ask others their opinions.

- With desktop publishing software like Microsoft Publisher and business card papers from a local office supply store, create some sample cards with names to "test" people's reactions. Then choose the one with the most favorable responses.

Careful consideration of a name for your business will help you capture the attention of prospective customers, but it is up to you to make your name synonymous with excellent goods and services!

EIN Number

For your business, you will need to obtain a federal tax ID number. In sole proprietorships, this can be your social security number, but many business forms require a federal employer identification number (EIN). This is a nine-digit number that the IRS assigns and uses to identify taxpayers who are required to file various business tax returns. EINs are used by sole proprietors, corporations, partnerships, nonprofit associations, employers, trusts, estates of decedents, government agencies, certain individuals, and other business entities.

To get an EIN, contact your local IRS office by visiting their Web site at www.irs.gov to download the form or by calling (800) 829-1040; or ask your accountant or a local SBA office for the form. For more information, see the IRS publication "Understanding Your EIN" or the "Application for Employer Identification Number," Form SS-4, which you can order by calling (800) 829-1040.

Legal Forms: Sole Proprietorship, Partnership, Corporations

For your home business startup, you will have to choose a legal form or organization.

You should consult with your accountant and attorney when deciding which form is best for your operation. Here are some comparisons you will want to make:

- Compare costs, ease of forming, maintaining, and dissolving.
- Compare the amount of control of the business decisions you and/or partners will have.
- Compare the amount of liability for which you will be responsible.
- Compare the effects each structure may have on your business's image.
- Compare the tax implications of each.
- Compare the objectives you have for your business and how it "fits" with each form.

Here is a brief description of these business entities, along with some pros and cons of each.

SOLE PROPRIETORSHIP

This is the most common form (and the most common with home businesses—at least at the startup phase) because it is the easiest form to establish and maintain. Legally, with this structure, you and your business are one and the same.

Pros: As a sole proprietor, you have complete control, make the major decisions, and receive all the business's income.

Cons: You are responsible for all of the business's obligations and if you are sued, your personal assets are subject to those claims.

PARTNERSHIP

Two or more people form a business ownership together in a general or a limited partnership. A partnership agreement should be drawn up by an attorney.

Pros: This form is easy to set up and the partners can combine their strengths and talents in making the business a success.

Cons: A large percentage of partnerships dissolve because partners may disagree on which direction the business should take, disagree over the division of duties, or have some other conflict. Partners share liability and responsibility.

CORPORATIONS

By law, a corporation is considered to be a unique entity, and separate from its owners. Generally, there are two types, abbreviated C and S. Business owners must apply for a charter from the state in which the corporation will be doing business. The owners are its shareholders who elect a board of directors. With this structure, the corporation becomes an entity unto itself and is separate from your personal life. It must have officers and profits and losses are reported separately. The advantage is that if you incur debts, your personal assets cannot be taken.

Pros: There is a limited liability to the owners, it qualifies for certain tax deductions, and it can raise funds through the sale of stocks.

Cons: This form is more costly, requires more paperwork, and is closely regulated by the state and the IRS.

LIMITED LIABILITY COMPANY (LLC)

Limited liability company is a new form of business structure that is now permissible in some states and combines corporation limited liability features and partnership flexibility. Some states permit individuals to form LLCs.

Pros: Members can be individuals, partnerships, trusts, and corporations, and there is no limit to the number of members.

Cons: It is more costly than a sole proprietorship or a partnership.

You may start with one business form and then change as your business's earnings grow. Do your research and consult with a qualified expert if you have any questions or concerns about your business's legal form.

Get Real! Friends and Partners?

Judith Burnett Schneider, cofounder with partner M. J. Rulnick of The Frantic Woman's Movement, www.franticwoman.com, states:

It's quite easy to start a business with a friend, colleague, or relative, but it's not easy to *stay* in a business partnership. Why? Because it requires as much commitment as a marriage. Two women might be the best of friends—having similar backgrounds, raising their kids accenting the same set of values—but when it comes to business, they might not see eye to eye. And they might not realize this until after they've signed the partnership agreement. So to what are partnership breakups usually attributed? Again, the reasons are often the same as those that cause marriages to end in divorce—time and money. You might believe your time is best spent doing one thing for the business, while your partner believes you would better contribute if you did something else.

Similarly, you might want to direct monies into one aspect of the business, such as advertising or capital, while your partner has other plans for the bank account. In addition, one partner might be quick to take the credit for a great marketing plan after it succeeds—and that same person could shift the blame when a marketing attempt results in a loss. You might think, *We'll just compromise;* but it doesn't always go that smoothly. You both have the same end goal, but your means for getting there might be drastically or even only slightly different. If you do decide to start a business with a partner, it is best to enter a joint venture—in which neither party is personally liable (financially) for the actions of the other.

Get Real! Friends and Partners? *(continued)*

As a step in the process of deciding whether or not to take on a partner, ask yourself the following questions:

1. What are my strengths/weaknesses as far as the business is concerned?
2. What are my partner's strengths/weaknesses related to the business idea?
3. What can my partner bring to the table that I cannot?
4. Am I looking for financial help from a partner that I might be able to get from a small business loan instead?
5. Am I using my partner as a crutch because I'm afraid to go it alone?

By taking the time to answer these questions honestly and thoroughly, you'll be able to see exactly what you're looking for in a partner and whether these are things you would be better off extracting from within.

Here's another exercise concerning partners: Write a list of business-related duties, responsibilities, and tasks that you feel confident handling. Then write a list of what you don't want to handle regarding your business. Ask yourself whether you are entering the partnership so you don't have to take care of those duties that are less appealing to you. (Chances are these responsibilities won't go away, even if you do have a partner.) If so, consider whether you might instead pay professionals to help you in those areas on an "as needed" basis—for example, an accountant, a lawyer, or a publicist.

Contract Concerns

Contracts are binding agreements that may just be agreed upon with a handshake, or put in writing (a better choice). When you are reviewing any business contract, a contract should . . .

- Be an agreement between two businesses, two people, or a business and a person.
- Hold something of value in it for each party (person or business involved).
- Be legal (the transactions must be within the laws).
- Be between acceptable parties—the parties involved must be the right age and of sound mind.

If the business or person with whom you are considering entering a contract does not offer you one, it is best to draw one up yourself, listing the terms that you both agreed to verbally. It can help to clarify what each is expecting from this deal, and prevent any misunderstandings from the verbal agreement.

(*Note:* Always seek legal counsel if you are in doubt about the wording or terms of a business contract!)

A good contract should also stipulate the costs of a project, the payment terms, the number of drafts or revisions that are included (if any) before you begin to charge for the extra work, any extra costs that will be added after so many revisions, and guarantees and/or penalties if one party does or does not meet the contract's terms.

To help prevent lawsuits (either party) and going to court, add a contract clause that stipulates the parties must present any disputes to arbitration.

Here are three other important business contract components:

Disclaimers. You may want to have disclaimers and specific legal contracts for certain business operations to protect you as an independent contractor (or when hiring independent contractors) or for the services or products your business provides.

Non-Compete Clauses. Generally these are clauses that employers ask employees to sign, preventing them from directly competing for the same customers or clients should an employee quit and join a competitor's business, start her own business, or become a free agent. If you signed a non-compete agreement as an employee and then started your own business in the same industry, you may or may not be held liable. This depends on the location of your home business, the length of time since you quit, and the extent of your services. Also, how the courts judge an infraction of a non-compete contract varies from state to state. Business ethics demand that you do not solicit your employer's clients or customers before you quit. It is better to seek customers that your former employer did not serve and design your products and/or services for that "niche." If while you are an employee, you anticipate someday starting your own business, you can always decline to sign such a clause or have it reviewed first by your legal counsel.

Waivers. A waiver in a contract stipulates that you or the other party knowingly relinquishes a right, such as the right to sue if you are injured in the process of performing some contracting work. Be careful what you sign away!

Independent Contractor Issues

It is estimated that more than 20 million self-employed Americans offer their services on a contract basis. If you are one of these independent contractors (ICs)—persons supporting themselves through the delivery of their services and expertise to clients—business experts advise you to understand your IC legal status as it relates to your rights as an IC and IRS guidelines.

WHO IS (AND IS NOT) AN IC?

Independent contractors can exist in any profession, from accountants, doctors, lawyers, and consultants to those providing home care, cleaning, errand, or even construction services to individuals and/or other businesses. If you are an employee of a company, you have certain rights and protections that an IC does not, which is one reason the IRS uses strict criteria in classifying who is and who is not an IC. Plus, there is a big difference in the way an employee and an IC report income taxes and deductions.

These are some of the guidelines that determine an IC status: *(Note:* If you are unsure of whether you are an IC or not, consult with your accountant and a lawyer familiar with independent contractor issues.)

- An IC generally does work for more than one company.
- An IC can terminate a contract with a company as easily as the said company can terminate a contract with the IC.
- An IC generally uses her own tools and equipment.
- An IC generally controls her own hours and pays her own expenses.
- An IC can subcontract portions of a project to other ICs.
- An IC cannot be "fired" like an employee unless she fails to fulfill the terms of the contract.

There are other IRS guidelines, but the issue here is one of "control." As an IC, you control your work and with whom you do business.

Pros of Being an Independent Contractor
- An IC has more freedom in choosing where, when, and for whom to work.
- An IC is often paid more than an employee.
- An IC does not have federal or state taxes withheld—though she is responsible for paying quarterly estimated taxes.
- An IC can deduct business expenses—just as any business owner can.

Cons of Being an Independent Contractor
- Laws to protect employees against racial or age discrimination, and so on do not support claims by ICs, so it is important that you research the background of potential clients to learn how they treat ICs before you sign any contract.
- You may come up against hostile feelings in the company from employees and sometimes their respective labor unions.
- You must pay your own self-employment taxes; your own health, liability, and disability insurances; and other benefits.
- You must constantly market your services so you will have more jobs to produce an income.

PROTECTING YOUR INDEPENDENT CONTRACTOR STATUS

Business experts advise you to protect your IC status by writing a contract (modified for each project for which you are hired). In any contract, they advise you to include the following:

- Stipulation that you will be using your own equipment
- Where the work will take place (depends on the nature of the job)
- The working hours that will be involved to complete the projects
- Which party is (and is not) liable for certain results of the job
- Your fee and who is responsible for the taxes
- That it is your business's responsibility for the method and implementation of performing the work
- Any other conditions that you wish to be "spelled out" in the contract for clarification purposes

Just declaring yourself an IC does not necessarily make it so. Again, if you are unsure of what your status is, consult with those experts who can provide you with the information you need to comply with state and federal guidelines regarding independent contractors.

Discuss any and all of your business contracts with your lawyer "expert," especially to explain any terms that are confusing or legal jargon that is difficult to understand. If you do not like the terms, or something in the contract makes you uneasy, try negotiating. If that does not work, make sure you withdraw before you sign. Never let yourself be rushed into signing any contract and never sign anything unless you understand all your rights and obligations!

Regulations

1. *Name:* If you are working as a freelancer or independent contractor, or if you use your own name in a business, you do not need to register your name. However, if you choose a fictitious name, you will have to register with your county and state as a DBA (doing business as) and publicize it to ensure it is not already in use. You will also want to further check to be sure your name or business name is not already someone's trademark. To find out how

to do a trademark search, visit The U.S. Patent and Trademark Office's Web site at www.uspto.gov or call (703) 308-4357.

2. *Legal Structure:* Most self-employed individuals operate as sole proprietors. This is the most common legal form and is the easiest to establish and maintain. However, understand that you and your assets are also liable in the event of judgments against you. Some states permit individuals to form limited liability companies (LLCs). Other legal forms include partnerships and full corporations.

3. *Zoning:* If you are in doubt whether or not your work is permitted in the area in which you live, contact the office of your local municipality to find out whether any regulations, traffic considerations, or employee considerations are related to your type of work, and whether you will need a business license to work out of your home. Be a good neighbor and avoid complaints by keeping traffic and noise to a minimum.

4. *Licenses:* Depending on your type of work, you may need local, county, state, or federal licensing. If you are researching ideas for a self-employed venture, industry and professional associations will have information about how you can become licensed or certified. Also contact the government office responsible for issuing these regulations for the procedures to get a license or permit.

Labor Laws

As your home business grows, you may need or wish to hire workers to assist you (see also, "Help and Hiring Options" discussed in chapter 8). Before you do, explore such options as partnering with other home business owners, hiring an independent contractor, bartering your goods or services for help, getting someone from a temporary staffing service, hiring family members, or using an intern from a local school or college. If you do decide to hire someone, do it on a trial basis to see whether it will work out for both of you.

When hiring an employee, you, as an employer, must:

- *Follow discrimination laws.* During the interview and hiring process, follow the guidelines that prohibit discrimination against others because of their race, color, religion, sex, and na-

SEW's Suggestions

Check to see whether your state or province has an online resource like that of the state of Pennsylvania (www.paopen4business .state.pa.us/) that allows state residents to register online for tax and business services.

tional origin; their age (40+ years); their disabilities; and their sex as it is relates to equal pay for equal jobs.

- *Make sure you know the difference between who is an employee and who is an independent contractor.* If you incorrectly classify an employee as an IC, you may be fined by the IRS and have to pay taxes.
- *Follow OSHA guidelines.* OSHA, the Occupational Safety & Health Administration, recommends that safe and efficient work spaces for employees should also apply to any employees working out of your home.
- *Follow the proper procedure should you find it necessary to fire an employee.* Provide documentation, time sheets, or other records to substantiate your reasons for letting that employee go; otherwise, you may have to pay unemployment insurance payments or other costs.

If you have never hired (or fired) an employee before, you might check with a lawyer specializing in employment law, or an expert at a local office of SCORE (www.score.org), or a consultant at a Small Business Development Center (www.sba.gov/SBDC). Good employees can contribute much to the success and growth of your home business, and the more familiar you are with employee issues, the less likely you are to become embroiled in a lawsuit.

Zoning Matters

Although more people than ever before have offices in their houses or apartments, not every local government permits actual businesses

---

EXTRA!!: Home & Garden Television (HGTV.com)

If you have access to your local cable television, check out the Home & Garden Television channel. Their programs, such as "Dream Builders," and remodeling shows often feature unique home designing tips and the latest in building trends that can provide you with ideas for planning your home office. For example, one program featured a midwest town that was turning old buildings into remodeled three-storied homes and selling them to attract small business owners, with the buyers' living quarters located above their street-level business space. These included a beauty salon, a chiropractor's office, and similar ventures. It is really reminiscent of years ago in towns and cities when many shop owners lived above their stores. The town is reclaiming its beauty while revitalizing its economy with new businesses.

---

to be run from dwellings in which people live. Magazines such as *Home Office Computing Magazine* have published listings of cities in the United States that are home business "friendly." Do not, however, assume that your area is as receptive to home ventures. Your first step is to know the zoning restrictions that apply where you live. Pick up a copy of your local government's laws and read it thoroughly. If you need a permit or license, find out the specifics then decide whether you can work within the parameters set down.

Most municipalities place restrictions on the types of businesses permitted in residential areas or require operational permits. Some, well aware of the growth of home businesses, have additional regulations; others have no ordinances at all and generally do not object to a home business unless complaints are registered—usually by neighbors.

Zoning restrictions you might face generally deal with:

- whether employees can be hired and work at your house.
- whether retail sales are permitted from your home.

- the amount of shipments or customer traffic to and from your home.
- whether your home business will interfere with your neighbors' lives.

Zoning may be governed by your city, town or borough, township or province, as well as by your county or jurisdiction; or you may be within a homeowner's organization that has written guidelines for operating from your housing complex.

It is best to contact local officials to let them know what business you intend to run. If they object, you can file for a variance or work with other home business owners as a group to make these local laws more "home business friendly." Stress the benefits, especially the taxes a profitable home business could generate (money talks!). If all else fails, move to a less restricted or more home business "friendly" neighborhood!

Licenses

All states and some local agencies have licensing requirements for businesses, as well as the procedures for collecting sales taxes. If you will be doing work or sales in another state, look into their registration and sales tax reporting procedures as well.

For the state or province in which your home is located, visit your local legislator's office for manuals written about conducting business in your state or look in your local library for the book, *Starting and Operating a Business in . . .* (there is one for each state) by Michael D. Jenkins (The Oasis Press); or search your state's Web site for business licensing and operating information (see "State-by-State Information" in the appendix for individual states' Web sites).

Check also with your state and federal regulations regarding your specific business.

Jane Mitchell, who creates specialty cheesecakes, needed to pass an inspection of her kitchen before the state issued a license to bake from her home kitchen. (Some states do not permit *any* commercial cooking from a home kitchen.) Sue Marx, who has operated a home beauty salon for many years, was also required to pass an inspection.

WARNING!!:
Regulations Affecting Your Home Business

LABOR LAWS

Certain businesses involving making or sewing apparel, toys and dolls, infants' garments, jewelry, cooking, and others may require you to have a license to operate or may not be permitted to operate from your home at all by your local or state governments or by the federal government's U.S. Department of Labor (DOL), www.dol.gov. When researching your home business idea, check with current laws put forth by the federal and your state (or province) government as they pertain to your specific business. Many laws were passed to protect employees who work out of their own homes. To be sure of the current laws, consult with a lawyer who specializes in labor laws (she can also assist you in classifying those you hire as either independent contractor or employee).

FDA REGULATIONS

If your business sells food-related products, the U.S. Food and Drug Administration (FDA) has packaging and labeling requirements that are detailed on their Web site: www.fda.gov.

ENVIRONMENTAL REGULATIONS

Depending on your home business, you may need to comply with the U.S. Environmental Protection Agency (EPA)'s regulations. Visit www.epa.gov for publications or information.

Certainly, many home businesses are operating without the knowledge of business officials, but the entrepreneurs who operate them always face the risk of being found out and the subsequent consequences. It is best to be honest in all your operations, thus protecting yourself from penalties while fostering the image of home businesses as legitimate enterprises.

Related Resources

ASSOCIATIONS

National Association of Enrolled Agents (NAEA), www.naea.org; (800) 424-4339. Provides a free referral service.

National Independent Contractors Association, www.independentcontractor.com — "NICA is an alliance made up of independent contractors (ICs)."

BOOKS

The Complete Book of Small Business Legal Forms, 3rd ed., by Daniel Sitarz (Carbondale, IL: Nova Publishing Company, 2001) — Book and CD-ROM.

Consultant & Independent Contractor Agreements, 2nd ed., by Attorney Stephen Fishman (Berkeley, CA: Nolo Press, 2000) — CD-ROM and book.

The Employer's Legal Handbook, 4th ed., by Attorney Fred S. Steingold (Berkeley, CA: Nolo Press, 2000).

The Entrepreneur's Guide to Business Law by Constance E. Bagley, Craig E. Dauchy (Clifton Park, NY: Delmar Thomson Learning, 1997).

Hiring Independent Contractors: The Employer's Legal Guide, 3rd ed., by Attorney Stephen Fishman (Berkeley, CA: Nolo Press, 2000).

How to Create a Noncompete Agreement by attorney Shannon Miehe (Berkeley, CA: Nolo Press, 2002).

Incorporate Your Business: A 50-State Legal Guide to Forming a Corporation by attorney Anthony Mancuso (Berkeley CA: Nolo Press, 2001).

INC. Yourself: How to Profit by Setting up Your Own Corporation, 9th ed., by Judith H. McQuown (New York, NY: Broadway Books, 2001).

Legal Guide for Starting and Running a Small Business, vol. 2 by Fred S. Steingold (Berkeley, CA: Nolo Press, 1999).

Nolo's Quick LLC: All You Need to Know About Limited Liability Companies by attorney Anthony Mancuso (Berkeley CA: Nolo Press, 2000).

The Partnership Book: How to Write a Partnership Agreement, 6th ed., by Attorneys Denis Clifford and Ralph Warner (Berkeley CA: Nolo Press, 2001).

Partnerships: Laws of the United States by Daniel Sitarz (Carbondale, IL: Nova Publishing Co., 1999).

Sole Proprietorships by Daniel Sitarz (Carbondale, IL: Nova Publishing Co., 2000).

Trademark Legal Care for Your Business and Product Name by Kate Mc-Grath, Stephen Elias and Sara Shena (Berkeley, CA: Nolo Press, 1999).

Sexual Harassment on the Job: What It Is & How to Stop It, 4th ed., by attorneys Barbara Kate Repa and William Petrocelli (Berkeley, CA: Nolo Press, 1999).

Working for Yourself: Law & Taxes for Independent Contractors, Freelancers & Consultants, 3rd ed., by attorney Stephen Fishman (Berkeley, CA: Nolo Press, 2000).

LEGAL SOFTWARE

AgreementBuilder, Jian, www.jian.com.

E-Z Business Law Library, www.e-zlegal.com/businesslawlibSOFT.html.

Quicken Business Law Partner by Parsons Technology, www.parsonstech.com.

Smart Attorney Pro by Smart Business Systems (check your favorite computer-software store for availability.

SOFTWARE

Quicken Lawyer 2002 Business Deluxe by Nolo. Includes seven Nolo best-sellers: Legal Guide for Starting & Running a Small Business, Legal Forms for Starting & Running a Small Business, The Employer's Legal Handbook, Domain Names, Tax Savvy for Small Business, How to Write a Business Plan, and Marketing Without Advertising. To order, call (800) 728-3555; or purchase in a major book-, computer software-, or office supply store.

WEB SITES

American Bar Association, www.abanet.org.

The American Institute of Certified Public Accountants, www.aicpa.org; (Main Office) 1211 Avenue of the Americas, New York, NY 10036-8775.

American Woman's Society of Certified Public Accountants, www.awscpa.org; Admin. Offices, 136 S. Keowee St., Dayton, OH 45402; (937) 222-1872.

www.businesslaw.gov — The SBA's site for "Legal and Regulatory Information for America's Small Businesses."

Federal Government Web site for disaster assistance information: www.sba .gov/DISASTER/.

Find Law, www.findlaw.com — Vast resource site about various legal topics; lawyer search; and other related information. Comprehensive legal resources including articles concerning small business; lawyer search and additional information.

IRS Publication # 1779: "Independent Contractor or Employee?" www.irs.gov.

www.nolo.com/ — Web site of legal publisher Nolo Press has an online law dictionary, a Q & A section, information, and books on all types of legal issues, including "Small Business," "Employment Laws," and "Independent Contractors."

www.llcweb.com/ — The Limited Liability Company Web Site provides information about this business form, including a comparison chart of business structures.

USLaw, www.uslaw.com — Legal information resource site, lawyer search.

See articles by Beverley Williams, president of the American Association of Home-Based Businesses, www.aahbb.org, including "Ten Zoning Ordinance Suggestions" and "7 Reasons to Allow Home-Based Businesses to Operate."

Volunteer Lawyers for the Arts, www.vlany.org. Nonprofit provider of low-cost legal services, publications, educational programs, and other legal assistance to the New York metropolitan area's arts community.

CHAPTER SIX

Financing

You may have decided what business (or businesses) to start, but have no idea where you will get the money to finance your venture(s). You are not alone, as entrepreneurs say that raising startup capital was their biggest challenge. Financing your new business venture(s) is one of the biggest obstacles you will face in your startup phase. Adequate financing can either make or break your business's success and future growth. Your first task is to determine the total amount you will need to open and operate your new venture. It bears repeating that writing an effective business plan is crucial. It must reveal two major categories of expenses: one-time startup costs and basic operating expenses, which will help you figure your profit margin.

(*Note:* Business financing is becoming easier and more accessible to home-based entrepreneurs due to the Internet, which is linking business owners and investors and providing other financing. See Related Resources at the end of the chapter for more information.)

Though the statistics show that some 60 percent of all businesses fail within the first two years, the good news is that 95 percent of home businesses succeed the first year, with 85 percent of these still prospering after three years! Many home-based entrepreneurs have met the money challenge with both traditional and creative financing methods. Here are a few of them:

Financial Assessment of Your Home Business

There are a number of reasons why one business succeeds and another one fails. Poor management, inadequate market research, insufficient experience and training, and lack of adequate financing are just a few. Of these, inadequate financing is often the biggest obstacle to overcome in getting a business started. With a new business, you must consider not only the cost of running a business until it begins to bring in revenue, but must add up the one-time fees necessary to establish your business, such as equipment expenditures, legal and accounting fees, and business phone hook-up costs.

ESTIMATING YOUR EXPENSES

You also need to estimate how much money you will need. Good planning can help you determine a realistic amount. Estimate all your startup expenses and then project operating expenses—advertising, postage, supplies, and so forth—for the next six to twelve months. If your business will be the sole means of support of your family, you will have to save enough to cover your living expenses for six months to two years (recommended by business experts) until your business profits can support you and your family. Experts estimate, however, that half of all home-based businesses are started part time and supported by another income (yours or your spouse's) until the initial expenses are met and the business begins to bring in profits that can sustain you.

Before you seek startup or expansion money, determine what type of funding you need. Here are some questions to help you:

- How much money and assets do you have that you can use to start up?
- If you use this money and assets, will you have any money to put aside for living expenses?
- What do you have as collateral if you decide to apply for a bank loan?
- Do you have good personal credit?
- Do you have much personal (or business) debt?
- If you do not qualify for a bank loan, do you have any other financial alternatives (relatives, stock, other)?
- If you find investors for your business, will you feel comfortable giving up some of your control?
- Do you know exactly how much money you need for your initial startup? To sustain your business until it begins to bring in some money?

- Have you consulted with a startup consultant or one of your business "experts"?
- Have you investigated all available financing (not just debt financing)?

Often women are uncomfortable asking for money and would rather use their own financial resources. Lesley Spencer, founder and director of the national association of Home-Based Working Moms (www.HBWM.com), says, "I do not hear a lot of moms looking for startup money. Most are trying to start on a very small budget and possibly have not considered looking for financing."

Business experts are encouraging women not to be afraid to think "long-term" in terms of business goals. Keep this in mind as you seek financing, especially once your business begins to grow. Maybe your business will someday be included in the Working Woman's (Media) America's Top 500 Women-Owned Businesses listed in *Working Woman* magazine (now part of *Working Mother*). According to the June 2001 issue, the top woman-owned business's revenue for 2000 was almost $7 billion dollars and the number 500th business's revenue was over $19 million dollars!

TYPES OF BUSINESS FINANCING

After determining your venture's estimated expenses, decide what type of capital your business needs. Basically, you have three choices: equity, debt, and alternative financing (or a combination of these).

Equity Financing

With this type of financing, an individual, group of investors, or an institution "invests" their money into your company. Usually this type of financing is associated with already established businesses that have a solid record of growth which promises these investors a good return on their money, especially if the business "goes public" or is purchased by a larger corporation. The advantage of this type of money is that it does not have to be repaid, as does a bank loan. The drawback is that in return for their money, investors often ask for some control of your business—something you must be ready to do if you go this route.

For a home business, it is unlikely that a group of investors would want a share of your business. You may want to consider it in the future if your business grows to the point that you need substantial outside money sources to take it to the "next level."

Equity Financing Options

Angel Investors or Angel Groups: These people are small or formal private (wealthy) investor groups that help fund businesses too small to attract professional venture capital. These "angels" do not usually require a large piece of your company in exchange for their money.

One resource is the ACE-Net, The Access ("Angel") to Capital Electronic Network, ace-net.sr.unh.edu, a Web-based service sponsored by the Office of Advocacy, U.S. Small Business Administration (SBA). This organization helps angel investors and small businesses looking for early-stage financing find one another. A fee is charged and companies must register their offering with the appropriate federal and state securities trading agencies as well as submit a small corporate offering registration (SCOR) form for approval to be listed.

Venture Capital (VC): Firms that raise money from other sources to invest in new ventures (currently not a traditional source of funding for home businesses, but the Internet is changing this). "The Venture Capital Industry: An Overview," an article posted on the National Venture Capital Association's site, www.nvca.org, states: "Venture capital is money provided by professionals who invest alongside management in young, rapidly growing companies that have the potential to develop into significant economic contributors."

Statistics show that only a very small percentage of companies receive venture capital, and most of those are for expansion rather than startup activities. Venture capitalists may interview hundreds of applicants before investing in only a few selected companies with favorable investment opportunities. If you think your company would be a good prospect for an equity investment, experts advise you to research and learn the different types of venture capital funds available, especially those invested in companies similar to yours.

Venture capitalists can make up several types of firms:

1. *Private independent firms* that have no affiliations with any other financial institutions.

2. *Affiliate or subsidiary firms* that make investments on behalf of banks, insurance companies, outside investors, the parent firm's clients, or are "direct investors" or "corporate venture investors," subsidiaries of nonfinancial industrial corporations making investments on behalf of the parent itself.

3. *Others,* such as:

   - *"Angel Groups"* (see above)

   - *Government-Affiliated Investment Programs:* These are local, statewide, or federal programs in which venture capital firms may augment their own funds with federal funds and leverage its investment in qualified investee companies.

   - *Small Business Investment Companies (SBICs):* These are venture capital firms licensed by the U.S. Small Business Administration (SBA) to provide either long-term debt or equity financing to qualified small businesses. According to an SBIC fund director, SBIC invests an average of $1.5 million per company (compared to the average investment of $9 million dollars by other VCs), and tends to assist companies located in "grass roots" parts across the U.S.

     Several current SBICs (listed below) are SBA-backed women-owned venture capital companies. Note, however, that these are already established businesses in later stages:

     Capital Across America based in Nashville, Tennessee; www.capitalacrossamerica.org; Whitney Johns Martin, founder.

     Women's Growth Capital Fund, Washington, D.C.; www.womensgrowthcapital.com; Patty Abramson, founder.

Viridian Capital, San Francisco, CA; www.viridian-
capital.com; Willa E. Seldon and Christine B. Cor-
daro, cofounders.

Approaching VCs

Before you approach a venture capital firm, experts also advise that
you . . .

- Consult with an attorney, accountant, and others familiar with
  venture capital arrangements and securities for possible referrals and ongoing advice.
- Avoid wasting valuable management time if your business is
  not a good candidate for venture capital funding. Neglecting
  your daily business's operations may lead to business failure!
  Experts recommend that before you seek venture capital or angel investors, you pursue all other financing options.

Venture capital financing is not essential for your company's
success. Many businesses have prospered without it by using alternative (and often "creative") financing strategies. If you believe
your company has the right combination of a unique idea with a
large-scale market and a high (and rapid) profit potential, however,
then a quest for the ideal venture capital investment might be well
worth your effort.

Debt Financing

Financing of this type involves loans, line of credit, and special loan
programs (such as those offered by the SBA, state and/or city governments, and the like), which usually give you a certain time period to repay your loan with interest.

A Business Plan

Before you borrow any money, though, you have to decide how
much you will need. You can do this by putting together a business
plan. As mentioned previously in this book, a good business plan
is a "strategic" plan for your business's success. It can be a simple
outline or run many pages, but it should tell you how much money

you'll need and what it will be used for, what is your potential market and customers and potential for growth, and what makes your business unique from others, as well as provide a rational and conservative projection of your business's cash flow. Your plan will help you set business goals, define the steps to reach those goals, evaluate your business's progress, and keep you focused on your priorities.

A business plan is almost always required of those seeking a bank loan. See chapter 4 for resources if you need assistance in writing a business plan. The U.S. Small Business Administration's Web site, www.sba.gov, also has an extensive section about business start-ups and what is included in the contents of a good business plan.

Types of Debt Financing Loans

The major types of debt financing loans are:

Term Loans: The type most often used for startups, expansion, and purchasing of equipment, property, or other items. Working capital can often be included in a term loan.

Line of Credit: If an entrepreneur qualifies for this type of loan, she can use it as she needs for short periods of time, repaying and borrowing again as her business financial needs arise.

Specialty Loan Programs: This type of financing primarily pertains to some lines of credit and term loans. These could include city, state, and federal (SBA) loans as well as alternative loan programs such as microloans that are usually offered through a bank. This type of financing is used if the borrower has an insufficient down payment or collateral to back the loan, and is considered a "risk" in her ability to pay back the loan.

WHAT BANKS WANT

Though the good news is that more loans are being given to women business owners, the bad news is that your loan application may still be rejected—not because you are a woman, but because bankers want to feel confident that you and your business are a good investment. Here are some guidelines to help you:

PROFILE: Rochelle B. Balch, RB Balch Associates

Rochelle B. Balch, owner of RB Balch Associates, www.rbbalch
.com, author of *C-E-O & M-O-M: Same Time, Same Place*
    Rochelle Balch founded her computer consulting business in
early 1993 after being downsized out of her job—as a single mom
and with a mortgage to pay. Balch says this:

> Trying to get a line of credit after only about nine months in
> business was tough. The banks kept saying "No!" They only
> wanted businesses already in business for three years. It
> "ticked me off," so I went back and got reeeeeaaalllly pushy.
> I said, "Read my business plan, look at my financials, look at
> my customers, look at my personal financial history, and do
> not make a decision based on what's in your book—make it
> based on my business." It paid off and they gave me a line of
> credit. My point here is that women, those starting off espe-
> cially, need to be a little pushy and a little gutsy and must be
> very self-confident.
>
> In a relatively short time we have received city, state, and
> national recognition and created a three-million-dollar-plus
> home-based business.

Preliminary Steps

1. *Assemble the following (your accountant can assist you):*

   - A business plan—the most important tool for obtaining a loan
   - Your business's cash flow projections
   - Three years' company tax returns (if applicable)
   - A personal financial statement

2. *Do your preliminary research*

   - *Talk to your own financial institution first.* They are famil-
     iar with you and may be able to make some recommenda-
     tions. Ask them to what kinds of businesses they give loans.

- *Talk to other women business owners.* Especially those in your area or your industry who may give you tips, plus some leads on lending institutions with whom they were successful in getting a loan.
- *Check with community business associations.* Ask the chamber of commerce, a home business association, or a women's business organization such as a local chapter of the National Association of Women Business Owners (www.nawbo.org) what microlenders exist in your town. They may also be able to inform you of the existence of "angel" investors—local businesses that invest in other local businesses.
- *Ask your state senator or state representative.* Inquire about special state loan programs for women and minority business owners.
- *Contact your local Small Business Development Centers and/or Women's Business Centers* (www.onlinewbc.gov), which are sponsored by the U.S. Small Business Administration (SBA) for information and availability about SBA LowDoc Loan Programs.

What Lenders Want to See

- *Your contribution:* Your personal pledge of at least 30 percent of what your business needs in terms of tools, equipment, or money
- *Your expertise:* The experience, knowledge, and/or training in your industry
- *Your collateral:* Today there are no unsecured loans. Types and amount of collateral are determined by individual loan programs.
- *Your personal credit history:* If your credit record is blemished, try to clear it before you apply for new credit. Also note that too many inquiries listed on your credit record and/or a record of loan turn-downs can make lenders cautious.
- *Your payback plan:* Consult your accountant.
- *Your honesty:* If you ask for only the money you need (provide written cost estimates) and discuss anything that may jeopardize your loan, your forthrightness will be appreciated.

Preparing to apply for a bank loan will pay off if it results in your getting the money you need and possibly developing a relationship with a lender who can offer you valuable advice on other financial services beneficial to your business.

GOVERNMENT LOANS

The November-December 2000 issue of *Enterprising Women* cited "Economic Prosperity, Women and Access to Credit," a report by the National Women's Business Council (NWBC) and the Milken Institute released in Washington D.C. in October 2000. The report said that though women played a significant role in contributing to the prosperity of the last decade (the nineties) and their access to credit had improved, lending to women still remained inadequate. NWBC hoped the report would make public policy officials and private lending institutions more aware and improve women's access to capital and credit.

Here are resources you might want to investigate for your business funding:

Federal Loans

The Small Business Administration (SBA), the largest source of long-term small business financing in the nation, offers loans such as these:

The 7(a) Loan Guaranty Program: This primary loan program of the SBA guarantees banks major portions of loans made to small businesses, thus enabling banks to provide financing on reasonable terms to small businesses who might not otherwise be able to obtain loans. Your business must meet certain criteria (such as already be operating for a profit) and fall within SBA size standards.

Special Loan Guaranty Programs 7(a): This loan program is governed, for the most part, by the same rules under the 7(a) program, but with some variations.

SBA Low Documentation Loan (LowDoc): One of the most popular of the SBA programs, the LowDoc requires those already deemed qualified by an SBA lender to fill out only a one-page

SBA application form to receive a rapid turnaround approval for loans up to $150,000. Used by business startups and existing businesses that fit the criteria.

SBAExpress: This program makes capital available to businesses seeking loans of up to $150,000 without requiring the lender to use the SBA process.

The 7(M) Microloan: Under this program, the SBA has approved a network of intermediaries to directly provide microloans (from $100 up to $25,000). Small businesses unable to obtain funding through conventional sources or other SBA guaranteed programs should explore this financing option.

Other SBA Loans: The SBA also has loans for assistance to existing small businesses preparing to export products or already exporting. Also ask about FA$TRAK Loans, Microloans, Women and Minority Prequalification Pilot Loan, and Certified Development Company Programs.

To get answers to your specific questions about SBA loans, contact a bank that is an active SBA guaranteed lender or an SBA loan officer.

With the growth of the numbers of the Women's Business Centers across the U.S., along with the already established federal centers located in all fifty states and U.S. territories, available financing information and free or low-cost business counseling is available at the following centers and offices:

U.S. Small Business Administration (SBA), www.sba.gov — Main office, 409 Third St. SW, Washington, D.C. 20416; Call (800) U-ASK-SBA. To contact local SBA offices, call (800) 827-5722. For SBA loan information, visit the following Web sites:

- www.sba.gov/financing/
- www.sba.gov/financing/indexloans.html
- Microloans: www.sba.gov/financing/micro.html

Small Business Development Centers, www.sba.gov/SBDC — Usually located at universities, these centers offer all kinds of business counseling, seminars, and sometimes business conferences.

Small Business Investment Companies (SBIC) — These SBICs are government-affiliated programs that help companies—locally, statewide, or federally—in which venture capital firms may augment their own funds with federal funds and leverage their investment in qualified investee companies, such as venture capital firms licensed by the SBA to provide either long-term debt or equity financing to qualified small businesses.

Generally, SBICs average investments in a company is smaller than other venture capital firms, and apply to already established, revenue-generating businesses.

For more information about SBICs, contact your nearest SBA office or visit www.nasbic.org. (Also see SBICs covered earlier in this chapter).

Office of Women's Business Ownership (OWBO) uses the same address as SBA. It is the only office in the federal government specifically targeted to facilitate the growth and development of women-owned businesses (does not provide direct funding or loan guarantees to women business owners, but does help them achieve financial success through pre-business workshops, management/technical information, and guidance on how to access capital).

Women's Business Development Centers, www.onlinewbc.gov, is a nonprofit organization across the U.S. specifically set up to provide workshops and programs for women entrepreneurs and established women-owned businesses. Its Web site has excellent business startup and management articles, a link to other SBA sites, and a listing of all existing women's business centers.

SCORE (The Service Corps of Retired Executives), www.score.org, is a volunteer management assistance program of the SBA that provides one-on-one counseling, workshops, and seminars. SCORE chapters exist locally throughout the country. Many work in conjunction with local chambers of commerce.

U.S. Department of Agriculture (USDA), Rural Business-Cooperative Service, 12th St. & Independence Ave. SW, Washington, D.C. 20250; Rural Information Center (800)

633-7701 or (301) 504-5547 in the Washington D.C. area and outside the U.S. — Provides information about federal rural development programs. Free information: *A Guide to Funding Resources & Federal Funding Sources for Rural Areas*. (See also your local USDA Cooperative Extension Office in your county, which usually is affiliated with a state university with an office in every U.S. county.)

Certified Development Companies, www.sba.gov/financing/fr-cdc504.html — The 504 Certified Development Company (CDC) Program provides growing businesses with long-term, fixed-rate financing for major fixed assets, such as land and buildings. A Certified Development Company is a nonprofit corporation set up to contribute to the economic development of its community. CDCs work with the SBA and private-sector lenders to provide financing to small businesses. There are about 270 CDCs nationwide. Each CDC covers a specific geographic area.

State Loans

All fifty states have a primary state government agency or office in each state that provides one-stop guidance on financial programs and services offered to small business, including minority/women's opportunities at the state level. Contact the office of your local state senator and/or state representative for referrals and information. Most of these state legislator offices have manuals for small business owners as well as directories of state agencies. (*See also:* "State-by-State Information" in the appendix for a listing of the individual states' Web sites that have links to small business information and agencies in your state.)

Local Government Loans

Besides the federal and state offices in your area, ask your local government if any business funding/support programs exist, and contact your local business groups and associations for any existing entrepreneurship support programs. Some award small business loans to new startup ventures in their area.

Check also to see if your local and/or county government has any funding programs.

Other Financing Resources

Local business groups and associations: These are excellent sources of networking information about lending institutions and existing, community entrepreneurship programs.

Local foundations, colleges, business schools, and other local schools may sponsor business counseling and may also have various programs and continuing education programs to help entrepreneurs.

National associations have chapters all across the U.S. and provide members with information on funding programs in your area and may work in conjunction with banks to provide funding.
Examples include:

- The National Association of Women Business Owners (NAWBO), www.nawbo.org.
- Women Incorporated (WI), www.womeninc.org; www.womeninc.org/nfn/nfn.htm (National Financial Network) — Provides business financing information.
- Banking Programs such as FleetBoston Financial's Small Business Section, "Women's Entrepreneur Connection," which has information about financing a growing business, www.fleet.com.

Foundations: Count-Me-In for Women's Economic Independence, www.count-me-in.org; 22 West 26th Street, Suite 9H New York, NY 10010 — This nonprofit organization raises money from individuals and organizations in order to make small business loans to women across the country.

Borrowing from family: Many people have borrowed from parents or siblings to start their businesses. If you choose this method, make sure you have a contract to ensure you repay your benefactor to prevent hard feelings.

Home equity: Borrowing against home equity is permitted in all states except Texas. Just make sure you pay back the equity or you could lose your home.

Most startup businesses will require you to seek business financing, but paying down some of your personal debt, plus saving to invest in your business, increases your chances for outside funding. Thoroughly research all possible financing resources available to you and then decide which ones will best help your business get the backing it needs to start and succeed.

Alternative Financing Options

In addition to traditional financing methods, a number of popular alternative financing options are available, such as the following:

Sell some personal assets. Do you have any antiques, jewelry, stocks, cars, or other items of value that you really do not need? Sell them for needed funds.

Borrow from insurance policies, IRAs, pension plans, stocks, and securities. Check with your insurance agent or your certified financial planner if you are considering borrowing from your mutual funds or retirement account. Before you borrow, though, make sure you are aware of the pay-back terms and any penalties.

Look for contests. Some business associations and/or nonprofit foundations also help with loans or give cash awards. Check entrepreneurial publications like *Home Business Magazine* and *Entrepreneur* magazine for announcements and advertisers' ads for business contests. And in your public library's reference section, you can research the large directory, *Gale's Awards, Honors, Prizes,* which lists 20,000 sources.

Corporate sponsors. If you are creating new products and technology, you may be able to find a larger company that offers money or access to a distribution network in exchange for licensing rights to new products.

Credit cards: A few years ago, over half of all women used credit cards to finance new businesses because they had fewer financial resources than exist for women today. Credit cards are still good for fast cash, but look for ones with the lowest interest rates and pay off the balance before rates increase; otherwise your business could get into too much debt.

Early inheritance: Check with your accountant or tax specialist to see how much money can lawfully be given to you.

Factoring: Factoring of accounts receivable (money owed to you by customers) are sold to a third party—a factor—which pays you a percentage of your invoices. This is an expensive option.

Internet. Entrepreneurs are now using the Internet to find information on funding and investors. Visit not only the government Web sites listed previously but also those listed in the Web Sites Resources section to follow.

Partner financing: Partnerships can assist expansion and growth, but have a signed contract to designate responsibilities and payments.

Part-time job/moonlighting: Over three-quarters of all home ventures are started part time. Most of these earnings are put back into the business to meet its capital needs. Work at a part-time job for extra cash. This is also a good way to get experience in an industry in which you may be starting a business. Running a home business part time will also give you time to "test" your products and/or services with your customers; allow you to put the money earned back into the business to purchase equipment upgrades, or pay off debts incurred. A part-time venture will give you time to learn the basics of entrepreneurship and time for you to experience "balancing" your business concerns with your family and personal needs.

Suppliers, Customers. Trade credit if your suppliers will agree to accept payment in 90 days instead of 30 days. If your customers make advance payments, you have some leeway to pay and some cash to use. Just make sure you make your payments as agreed upon and deliver the "goods" as expected to your customers.

Keep your expenses down. For example, negotiate with your bank for less costly services tailored to your business's financial situation; look for mail-order bargains for supplies; and learn how to do some of your business's tasks yourself. Once you have obtained financing, concentrate on your marketing plan for continued growth and profits. Set up a business budget, scrutinize every purchase, and you may never need to seek financing again.

Financial Planning

Having the funding you need to start up and operate your home business is only part of ensuring your business success. You will have to develop an ongoing "cash flow plan" that will sustain your business through slow periods. (How to develop a cash flow plan will be discussed in chapter 8, Managing and Maintaining a Profitable Home Business.) Even when your business is bringing in brisk profits, you have no guarantee that you will not face bankruptcy should you fail to maintain the balance between profits and expenses. That is why it is very important that you consult with your business's experts—your lawyer for contracts, your accountant for your taxes and record keeping, and your financial planner for helping you set both personal and business goals.

Use a financial plan that you form with your advisors as you would your business plan to do a periodic "checkup" to make sure that your business is staying out of debt and increasing profits. Check these financial areas on a regular basis:

- *Business's budget:* Review this.
- *Sales reports:* Go over these carefully.
- *Pricing policy:* Be sure your products and/or services are priced competitively.
- *Target market:* Watch to see if you are getting your target customers' business.
- *Advertising budget:* Check to see if you are getting the most response for your advertising dollars.
- *Bookkeeping system:* See that you follow your system faithfully.
- *Monthly bank statement:* Make sure it "balances."
- *Monthly tax deposits:* Set aside money for your taxes.
- *Cash-flow needs:* Project what you'll need.
- *Future growth:* Set aside money for expansion, growth.

Make it a habit to evaluate your business's financial status on a regular basis so you will not be in a financial "crisis" should a slowdown or unexpected change occur.

Grants

Many women ask about grants to start their businesses. Grants are not as readily available as some sources would have you believe. The SBA does not offer grants to individuals, and only offers a limited number to support nonprofit organizations, lending institutions, and state and local governments, who in turn pass the grants along to qualified entrepreneurs.

For example, the SBA's grant program to the Women's Business centers has been essential in these centers, in turn, helping many women all across the U.S. to start new businesses and grow current ones. These centers provide business training, counseling, and other assistance (not funding, but how to get funding) to women business owners and women who want to start businesses.

Check, too, with your state office of economic development to see what support programs they have for small businesses.

Bartering

Instead of cash, many new and current entrepreneurs barter their goods and/or services for items and other services that they cannot afford or to save cash. Patricia Gallagher, author of two child-care business books, created Team of Angels, www.teamofangelshelpme.com, a product of angel pins with inspirational messages two years ago, after her husband was seriously injured. In her marketing efforts for her pins, Gallagher, mother of four children and marketing expert, has bartered her pins for hotel accommodations for her family's vacation and for her attendance at a healing conference. She recently approached an advertising publication that is distributed monthly, offering to provide a testimonial in return for a free ad. They accepted.

Before entering into the barter economy, analyze your services and products and your buying and spending practices to see if they fit with what is available through the barter exchange. If you join a barter exchange, you can receive a member list and a description of what they offer, making it easier for you to "match" your offerings with what you can use. Barter exchanges charge a transaction fee and some initial or other fees. Make sure, though, that you do not overtrade, because you still need cash to operate. The Internet has enabled even more people to trade as the number of online trading services grow. Bartering can help market your business while getting goods and services you need for your business now instead of later.

Related Resources

ASSOCIATIONS

Please Note: Associations and their staff do not "match" companies seeking financing with venture capitalists. Doing your own research about venture capital companies that interest you and approaching them directly with your ideas is recommended.

Forum for Women Entrepreneurs, www.fwe.org — "An organization cofounded by Denise Brosseau, whose mission is to provide access to funding and connections to fellow entrepreneurs." It co-sponsored the first all-women venture-capital forum in January 2000: Springboard 2000, www.springboard2000.org, which gave twenty-five women-owned firms the chance to present their business plans to investors.

International Reciprocal Trade Assn. (IRTA), www.irta.com; 140 Metro Park, Rochester, NY 14623.

The National Venture Capital Association, www.nvca.org — Educational and networking opportunities for people who wish to learn more about equity investment.

The National Association of Trade Exchanges, www.nate.org; 8836 Tyler Rd., Mentor, OH 44060.

BOOKS

Angel Investing: Matching Startup Funds with Startup Companies—a Guide for Entrepreneurs and Individual Investors by Mark Van Osnabrugge, Robert J. Robinson (New York: Jossey-Bass, Inc. Publishers, 2000).

Bootstrapper's Success Secrets: 151 Tactics for Building Your Business on a Shoestring Budget by Kimberly Stanséll (Franklin Lakes, NJ: Career Press, 1997); (800) CAREER-1.

Complete Guide to Getting a Grant: How to Turn Your Ideas into Dollars, rev. ed., by Laurie Blum (New York: John Wiley & Sons, 1996).

Fail-Proof Your Business: Beat the Odds and Be Successful by Paul E. Adams (Los Angeles: Adams-Hall Publishing, 1999).

Finding Money: The Business Guide to Financing by Kate Kister, Tom Harnish (New York: John Wiley & Sons, 1995).

Finances & Taxes for the Home-Based Business by Bryane and Charles P. Lickson (Menlo Park, CA: Crisp Publications, 1997).

Free Money from the Federal Government for Small Business & Entrepreneurs, 4th ed., by Laurie Blum (New York: John Wiley & Sons, 1995).

Free Money from Uncle Sam to Start Your Own Business (or Expand the One You Have) by William Alarid, Gus Berle (Santa Maria, CA: Puma Publishing Co, 1997).

Fundamentals of Venture Capital by Joseph W. Bartlett (New York: Madison Books, Inc., 1999).

Government Giveaways for Entrepreneurs III, 5th ed., by Matthew Lesko and Andrew Naprawa (Kensington, MD: Information U.S.A., Inc.).

How to Find Money Online: An Internet-Based Capital Guide for Entrepreneurs by Alan Joch (New York: McGraw-Hill, 2001).

Launching Your Home-Based Business: How to Successfully Plan, Finance, & Grow Your New Venture by David H. Bangs and Andi Axman (Chicago: Dearborn Trade, Chicago, 1997).

Pratt's Guide to Venture Capital Sources, 2001, by Securities Data Publishing, New York. Check for the latest edition in your public or local college library's reference section.

The SBA Loan Book: How to Get a Small Business Loan, Even with Poor Credit, Weak Collateral, and No Experience by Charles H. Green (Holbrook, MA: Adams Media Corporation, 1999).

Start-Up Financing: An Entrepreneur's Guide to Financing a New or Growing Business by William J. Stolze (Franklin Lakes, NJ: Career Press, 1997).

FREE INFORMATION

"Access to Credit: A Guide for Lenders and Women Owners of Small Businesses," Federal Reserve Bank of Chicago, Public Information, P.O. Box 834, Chicago, IL 60604. A free, 41-page guide offering advice to entrepreneurs and bankers.

"The Credit Process: A Guide for Small Business Owners." A free 26-page workbook offering guidance to entrepreneurs seeking first-time financing. Order from the Federal Reserve Bank, Public Information Dept., 33 Liberty St., New York, NY 10045.

"The Small Business Financial Resource Guide: Sources of Assistance for Small and Growing Businesses," www.nfibonline.com or www.mastercardintl.com/business/smallbiz/sbfrg/ — MasterCard International and The National Federation of Independent Business. A free (you pay $5.95 postage and handling) 150-page book discussing various funding options and sources: Write to 53 Century Blvd., #300, Nashville, TN 37214.

PUBLICATIONS

Grants on Disc, from Gale Research — Check your local library or a college library near you or call (800) 877-GALE for this a regularly updated library reference guide providing electronic access to information on 260,00 grants per year.

SBA Publications, www.pueblo.gsa.gov — For 50 cents, order a copy of the SBA's *Resource Directory for Small Business Management,* which contains a listing of publications on small business startup and management such as "Financing for Small Business" or "Business Plan for Home-Based Business." Order from SBA Publications, P.O. Box 46521, Denver, CO 80201-46521.

SOFTWARE

"Federal Money Retriever" — Order from IDI Magic Technologies Corp., P.O. Box 97655 Las Vegas, NV 89193.

WEB SITES

America's Business Funding Directory, www.businessfinance.com.

Capital Across America, www.capitalacrossamerica.org.

The Catalog of Federal Domestic Assistance (annual), www.gsa.gov/fdac — Lists awarded federal grants for each year.

Financing for Women, www.financingforwomen.com.

FinanceHub: Venture capital on the Web, www.financehub.com — Includes articles and a database of investors with links to venture firms.

www.insiderreports.com/ — Information on home business financing and credit.

Live Capital.com, www.livecapital.com — Internet-based loan center, including SBA-backed loans.

www.microenterpriseworks.org — Organizations list that provide microloans.

Online Women's Business Center, www.onlinewbc.gov — See their "Financing Your Business" section.

StartUpbiz.com, www.startupbiz.com — Includes a number of relevant links to investment capital sources and to leading VC firms.

www.toolkit.cch.com/ — Business Owner's Toolkit lists great books, including the financing book, *Small Business Financing,* and articles on business.

Venture Capital Resource Library, www.vfinance.com — Bookstore, glossary of terms, news.

Women Angels.net, www.womenangels.net — An all-female angel fund.

CHAPTER SEVEN

Open for Business

Marketing a home business presents more of a challenge than a shop or storefront business, because you have to let potential customers know that (1) your business exists, (2) you are open for business, and (3) you have a product or service that will be beneficial to them. Besides finding money to start a business, many women say marketing is the next most difficult problem they face in starting up. This statement is supported by Lesley Spencer, founder of the group, Home-Based Working Moms, www.HBWM.com.

When asked, "What do you see as one of the biggest problems for a woman and/or mother in operating a business out of her home with her family and loved ones?" Spencer responded, "The biggest problem I hear from most moms is finding customers and marketing their businesses. So many of these moms are great at their particular business or skill but not necessarily good at bringing in clients and customers."

This chapter will provide you with some marketing, advertising, and promotional ideas to assist you in finding the best marketing solution to your marketing problem.

Creating and Implementing a Marketing Plan

Marketing strategies often consist of the following components that you can apply to each method you use:

221

MARKETING COMPONENTS

- *Objectives:* Determine whom your best buyers (potential customers) are as shown to you by your market research and how you are going to connect with them.

- *Invitations:* Just how powerful "permission marketing" can be is apparent to Web site owners who include an "opt-in" section, inviting visitors to enter their e-mail address to receive more information on products or services, receive regular notices, or be placed on an e-zine mailing list. In direct mailings, recipients can return postcards or use coupons for a discount.

- *Connection:* After you have received the first initial responses from your invitations, then you will have to put forth your best follow-up methods to build a relationship with your potential customers to keep their interest and confidence so that they are ready to buy your product or service.

- *Follow-Up:* Once a customer buys from you, never let them go (unless they tell you to). Send mailings with discounts for faithful customers. One appliance dealer in a small town always sets aside the first day of any sale for loyal customers to whom he sends personal invitations. Of course, he and his sons were known for his fast and excellent repair service, so he had many customers.

Using these tactics does not always lead to sales, but it will help you to improve your marketing strategies.

To implement marketing strategies you need a plan, which was discussed in a previous chapter. Here are tips to review:

MARKETING PLAN TIPS

1. *First (and most important), take the time to make a plan!* Just because you are a small home business does not mean you cannot plan *BIG* in your marketing strategy! All those big businesses started small, but they took time to plan when they were still little businesses. Write your marketing methods and plan (and prioritize) your strategy.

2. *Review your plan.* Make sure your plan is concise, considers your mission, emphasizes what you bring to your customers, and targets your strongest niche.

3. *Implement your plan!* Put your marketing strategies into action.
4. *Keep your plan going!* Keep your old customers, strive for new ones, and always keep "an eye" turned to your customers.

Marketing Mistakes to Avoid

You will make many mistakes as you start up and run your home business, but marketing mistakes can be costly. Here are a few (of many) to avoid:

- *Marketing to people who do not want or need your product or service.* Once you have defined a target market, your research should have also told you what they read, watch on television, and listen to on radio; which places they frequent; and other pertinent details. Direct your marketing efforts to those specific areas instead of trying to reach every person and hoping a percentage will respond.
- *Not motivating your potential customers to respond in some way.* Make sure your marketing and ad campaigns are written to encourage customers to call, return a postcard, or visit your Web site.
- *Trying too many marketing strategies too fast.* Yes, you need a trial-and-error period until you discover the most effective marketing methods. Go slowly at first, concentrating and tracking the responses with each method. When you find one that works well, do not abandon it completely for a fad.
- *Not studying what really works in marketing or consulting with a marketing expert.* Your marketing can be clever, creative, and humorous, but if it does not bring results, then it is just entertainment.

Marketing is not "hit and miss." It is a science with specific causes and effects. Study it well and use its rules to bring in the best results for your home business.

Mission Statement

Remember your mission statement as you plan your marketing methods. For example, if your mission as a computer consultant is

Money$aving Tip: Creating a Marketing Budget

Marketing activities can quickly drain your money from
your business, but wise budgeting can get you more promotions per dollar. Here are some tips to create the best
marketing budget for your business:

1. *Draw up a long-term budget, emphasizing short-term
   goals.* Review your business plans and your goals and plan
   your marketing efforts around those.
2. *Test your marketing strategies.* Spread your marketing dollars
   on different activities to see which ones are most effective.
3. *Remember that keeping a customer costs less than acquiring
   a new one.* Remind your current customers why your products and services benefit them more than your competitors'.
4. *Balance your marketing expenditures.* Budget more money
   for launching a new marketing effort and less for a continuous one.
5. *Give each marketing activity some time so you can see the
   effects.* Results of marketing tactics often require some time
   to pay off.
6. *Never stop looking for creative and low-cost opportunities
   to market your business.* Read your daily paper and listen
   to local news. You never know when you can tie in your
   market or product with an ongoing event. The more creative your marketing tactic, the more it will be remembered.
   A good book offering some unusual marketing ideas is *Off-
   the-Wall Marketing Ideas: Jumpstart Your Sales Without
   Busting Your Budget* by Nancy Michaels and Debbie J. Kar-
   powicz (Holbrook, MA: Adams Media Corp., 1999).

Marketing is an investment in your home and small business, so spend wisely, and as your business needs it.

---

to help new home and small business owners choose and set up the
best computer and system for their venture, you will concentrate
your marketing and advertising to reach those beginning entrepreneurs. You will also emphasize how your expertise will save them

time and money as you make your recommendations to the computers and software that will fit their budgets, and how you will save them headaches and time as you set up their systems.

A mission statement will help you concentrate on your goals and keep you from diverging in too many directions. Your mission statement will say what you want your business to do; include a description of your products and services and of the people most likely to use them; and, of course, it is understood that your mission is to make money!

Memorize your mission statement so that when someone asks, "What does your business do?" you will have a comeback and a greater chance to make another sale or gain another customer. What is your business's mission statement?

LOGOS AND SLOGANS

We are all familiar with large companies' logos and slogans, such as identifiable marks on sportswear or jingles that we or our children can sing. You might also want to create a recognizable identity. Stephanie Lavigne, chief creative officer of Stelo, LLC (www .stelocreative.com), a company that specializes in creating logos and corporate identities, says this:

> In today's competitive marketplace, a professional image goes a long way. A great logo is important in any business, but for the person with a home-based business, it is essential for success. It projects trust, professionalism, and knowledge in your field.

Angelo Skouras, president of Stelo, LLC, the slogan of which is, "We'll make you look like a genius," says this:

> The primary purpose of your company is to make sales and earn a living. A professionally designed image should do just that. The small price you'll pay to get a corporate identity that oozes professionalism and ultimately sells your service or product will give you a return on your investment a thousand-fold. However, don't be fooled by cheap design. Corporations spend millions of dollars creating their identity and brand, and it shows. Choose your designer wisely and don't be afraid to ask questions. If they couldn't be bothered with addressing your

concerns, look for someone else. In the end, you'll have an image you'll be proud of that will stay with you for years to come.

Design a logo and slogan that will become identifiable with your business's name. Display them on all your business cards and promotional materials; on magnetic vehicle and lawn or sidewalk signs; as well as on T-shirts, flyers, and other items that you distribute.

If you are creative, you can create a logo yourself or hire an artist, graphic designer, or desktop publisher to design one for you. Dover Publications, Inc. (www.doverpublications.com) 31 E. 2nd St., Mineola, NY 11050, publishes a number of copyright-free design and business clip art books. Write for a catalog. As mentioned earlier, Chuck Green's book, *Design It Yourself* is a good resource for tips on designing a logo, letterhead, or business card. Once you decide on a logo, you may want to consider conducting a trademark search and then registering it. For more information, contact the U.S. Patent & Trademark Office, www.uspto.gov/; General Services Div., U.S. Patent & Trademark Office, Crystal Plaza 3, Rm 2C02, Washington, D.C. 20231; or read *Trademark: Legal Care for Your Business & Product Name*, 5th ed., by attorney Stephen R. Elias (Berkeley, CA: Nolo Press, 2001).

You can also use copyright-free images (according to the company's "usage policy") from the software and Web sites of companies like ArtToday, Inc., www.artoday.com.

Image and name recognition are important to help your home business succeed, but do not forget to keep your main focus on what you are offering customers and quality service.

Advertising

Advertising is the part of marketing that you use to introduce your product or services to others. Unlike publicity, you control what your ads state and when and where they are placed in order to reach your target customers.

AFFORDABLE ADVERTISING AND LOW-COST PROMOTIONS

If you have a limited budget for your advertising, you can use a number of low-cost but effective alternatives:

Promotional Materials

These include your business stationery, newsletters, brochures and pamphlets, flyers, business cards, and other printed items. Make sure your materials are proofread for errors and typos, grab your audience's attention, highlight the benefits of your products or services, and illustrate and amplify the message you wish to convey. Do not let your graphics and illustrations overpower your information. You can have your desktop publishing expert help you design your materials or use one of the popular desktop publishing programs that come already installed on your computer or more sophisticated software, depending on the complexity of your design and your computer skills.

Promotional products such as pens, magnets (I have my plumber's and my auto shop's on my refrigerator for emergencies!), calculators, mouse pads, hats, T-shirts, and other items with your contact information are ways for you to get new or repeat business and are also good as giveaways and holiday gifts. If interested, contact a promotional products company or consultant in your area; visit the Promotional Products Association International Web site, www.ppai.org/; or write to 3125 Skyway Circle North, Irving, TX 75038-3526.

Four inexpensive but effective advertising materials to promote your business are:

- *Bookmarks:* Patricia Gallagher designed 50,000 bookmarks to hand out for free to help promote her angel pins.
- *Brochures:* Have a simple, uncluttered design and an "eye-catching" headline; provide relevant information such as ordering information (and cut-off form); a show schedule if you exhibit at trade shows or exhibitions; an invitation to visit your Web site or to call you; and again, include your contact information.
- *Business Cards: Design stand-out business cards (Victoria* magazine issues highlight women's unique business cards). Hand them out to everyone you meet. Ask relatives and friends to do the same.
- *Post Cards:* These direct-mail pieces are inexpensive and get very good customer responses. One professional organizer sent

out post cards in December with practical holiday season organizing tips along with her seasonal greeting message. Or you
can use one of the Internet businesses that can send (not spamming) uniquely designed electronic post cards to your customer
e-mail list.

Try to make all the many materials you have or will produce
for your business "fit" together and reflect your business's professionalism and best image.

Endorsements and Testimonials

Endorsements and testimonials by your customers can be effective
in your ads, but they must be factual, not exaggerated. You must
have the permission of the person giving the testimonial and are required to keep copies on file for inspection upon request. The FTC
also says, "Expert endorsements must be based on appropriate tests
or evaluations done by persons with expertise in the field."

Testimonials can lend credibility to your product or service; just
be sure that you and the person providing the testimonial or endorsement are credible and respected or your business's reputation
could be in jeopardy.

CO-OP AND SPONSORSHIP ADVERTISING

Co-Op Advertising: To double your advertising resources, you can
organize with local, non-competing businesses to help promote
one another. For example, an owner of a historic restaurant gives
his diners after-dinner chocolates made in the image of his restaurant, which are produced by a local woman's chocolate factory.
The restaurant windows are decorated with lace curtains from
another local woman's country store who placed a small card-
board display holding her brochures and business cards on each
restaurant window sill, stating who donated the curtains.

You can also place larger ads together by splitting the costs
with co-op advertising. Several home business owners did this
in their local paper's annual business section and received some
very good responses.

If you are selling items from a larger company, you might
approach them to see whether they have budgeted money for

co-op advertising for their distributors. If you do make such an arrangement, make sure you furnish proof—copies, tear sheets—that your ads were published so these companies will be willing to help you with future co-op ads.

Sponsorships: Sponsoring a community athletic team, an annual student scholarship, runners (or walkers) for a fund-raising event, and other nonprofit groups or special individuals can set you apart from your competition while providing a valuable showcase for your services or products. In one local community's Little League ballparks, each business sponsor has a large sign hung on the backfield fence in view of all the spectators for the entire baseball and softball season.

Any sponsorship in which you participate should be suited for your business and provide you, if possible, with exclusivity in your type of business. Use your sponsorship to lead into related advertising opportunities and publicity.

INTERNET

The Department of Commerce (www.doc.gov) said that the total U.S. retail e-commerce sales for 2001 were estimated at $32.6 billion, up almost 20 percent from 2000, and International Data Corporation (IDC) (www.idc.com), a principal source of technology intelligence, said that it expected worldwide e-commerce spending to surpass $1 trillion in 2002.

Whether or not you have a Web site, you cannot afford to pass up the many marketing and advertising opportunities the Internet can offer your home business. To mention a few: e-mail ads, e-mail newsletters and e-zines, search engine listings (free and paid listings), online networking, reciprocal linking, writing articles, hosting online chats, and many more. (For further information, see my book, *HerVenture.com: Your Guide to Expanding Your Small or Home Business to the Internet—Easily and Profitably,* 2000.)

See the Profiles to follow to learn how two entrepreneurial women have used the Internet to promote their home-based businesses.

With the Internet, no one can tell whether you are working out of an office building or a home office, and you can reach customers around the world. Even home businesses whose main customers are

PROFILE: Debbie Williams, organizing coach

"A Virtual Expo"
Debbie Williams, an organizing coach and founder of the online organizing site, Organizedtimes.com, and author of *Home Management 101: A Guide for Busy Parents* (Champion Press, 2000) states:

> After attending a one-day women's conference online in 1998, I was inspired to create my own virtual event to bring "the best of the best" to my online readers. Each year I recruit talented experts in the time management, parenting, and home decor field, and enjoy expanding my online network to include their work. Experts contribute articles which serve as content for their Virtual Speech, donate their time teaching an interactive TeleClass (a seminar using a simple conference call on the telephone), and graciously donate door prizes. It's all free of charge, and there's no babysitting or dressing up involved—just an Internet connection. It's a lot of fun and a great way to get organized from the comfort of your own home!

in their local area use the Internet to highlight their services and communicate with customers.

TRUTH IN ADVERTISING

No matter where you place your ads—whether online and off—you must follow regulations.

According to the Federal Trade Commission (FTC):

- Business ads must be truthful and non-deceptive.
- Advertisers must have evidence to back up their claims.
- Advertisements cannot be unfair.

The FTC further states that additional laws apply to ads for specialized products like consumer leases, credit, 900-telephone numbers, and products sold through mail-order or telephone sales. And

---

PROFILE: Debra S. Haas, Haas Policy Consulting, Inc.

"A Virtual Resume"
Debra S. Haas, president, Haas Policy Consulting, Inc., www.haas
policy.com, states:

> I use my Web site as a "virtual resume." I don't sell a service
> or product directly over the Internet—my business, which is
> consulting tailored to the needs of a client, doesn't lend itself
> to that. Rather, I suggest that interested potential clients look
> at my site as a source of information about the types of prod-
> ucts and services that my business can provide. Recently, I had
> a prospective client, an executive director of an organization,
> ask for something her board could look at before they offered
> me a contract. The Web site was perfect because it provided
> them with instant access to information about me, as well as
> links to some of my other clients. Additionally, I feel that the
> Web site enhances my credibility and makes me "look" truly
> professional to the outside world, even though I am a small,
> home-based business.

---

every state has consumer protection laws that govern ads running
in that state.

Contest Regulations: According to the Fair Business Practices Act
(FBPA), you must follow certain guidelines for online contests;
and the Federal Trade Commission also states that sweepstakes-
type promotions that require a purchase by participants are illegal in the United States. Other agencies, including the United
States Postal Service (USPS) and the Federal Communications
Commission (FCC), also enforce federal laws governing contests
and prize promotions. And each state has laws that may require
promoters to make disclosures, seek licensing, or post a bond.
Since state laws vary, check with the attorney general's office in
the state(s) in which you plan to advertise.

Labeling: Food products, clothing, and certain other products must be labeled to certain laws and regulations. Contact the FTC in Washington, or one of its regional offices for the exact rules you must follow.

ADVERTISING COPYWRITING ESSENTIALS

Whether you are writing an ad for print, online, or for a direct mailing piece, you should include certain elements to ensure an excellent (customer) response rate. Here are five important ones:

- *An attention-getting headline* . . . to compel the reader to read more.
- *Exactly what you are selling and some of the best benefits* . . . so readers can clearly picture what they are being offered.
- *Contact information:* phone number, Web site address, and other details . . . so the reader can get in touch with you.
- *Some sort of action* . . . such as "Call," "Visit" (your Web site), "Send" (back a detached post card).
- *A standout-guarantee* . . . which must be visible to the reader so she knows you stand behind your product or service.

If you are not skilled at writing, look for a freelance copywriter or an advertising agency that specializes in home and small businesses to assist you in composing your ad pieces. You do not want to waste money on poorly written ads that bring little response. It is also a good idea to code your ads so you can track the response rates.

ADDITIONAL PROMOTIONAL METHODS

Here are some additional ways to bring attention to you and your home business:

Presentations

Whether you do or do not like getting up in front of people to conduct a presentation, it is almost assured that sometime along your way as an entrepreneur, you will be asked to speak to an organization, class, or other group. Whether giving a presentation gives you the "shakes" or you look forward to it, this is an excellent way to

Warning!! Advertising

The Federal Trade Commission (FTC), www.ftc.gov, prohibits misleading statements in business ads. The FTC has a "Business Guidance" section on its Web site with publications in text or for downloading (www.ftc.gov/ftc/business-menu.htm) that presents its regulations on advertising claims, endorsements, telemarketing, mail and telephone orders, and many other topics concerning business. The FTC also regularly posts the latest scams to which both consumers and business fall victim. Visit the FTC Web site to read the information or write to the Federal Trade Commission, 600 Pennsylvania Ave. NW, Washington, D.C. 20580.

stand out in your community and industry. You might want to explore these avenues to present yourself and promote your business.

Seminars: Many successful businesspersons, authors, and experts start giving seminars as promotions for their books, training programs, and businesses, then go on to discover that the seminars are not only good ways to sell their products and services, but also profitable in themselves. This may be an option for you as your business grows.

If your business becomes successful, others will want to know your "secrets" for success. Taking public speaking courses and attending and participating as a guest presenter at entrepreneur conferences and seminars is a good way to prepare yourself for organizing and conducting a seminar.

Teaching: Many high schools, community colleges, and community centers welcome instructors. If you enjoy sharing your experience with others, you may want to approach the director of the programs. Usually a prospective instructor submits an outline and a course description. You will usually be paid so much an hour, but if you include in your course the price of a handout,

PROFILE: Susan Anderson, M.Ed., certified massage therapist
and Reiki instructor

After being a special education teacher for twenty years, Susan Anderson retired to become a certified massage therapist and Reiki instructor. Her business has been growing slowly, but steadily, as she
constantly studies in her field. Using her teaching background, she
is now an instructor at several adult evening schools that she says
have helped her garner new customers while bringing her recognition in her community. She also sends out a print newsletter to her
regular clients and to new ones. Anderson says she would like to
contact retirement communities to see their residents could benefit
from her services.

special tools, or other related items, you can earn more money.
One adult evening school included courses taught by people
with home businesses: a personal fitness trainer, an herb
grower, a skilled basket artisan, a professional photographer,
and a lawyer.

Speaking: Community groups, industry trade organizations, and
large corporations are often looking for speakers. At first, you
may do some free speaking for nonprofit associations; but as a
rule, you should ask for some compensation. If you find you
have a gift for speaking, you can parlay your speeches into
tapes, books, and CDs, and also join the National Speakers Association. Otherwise, speaking is a good way to garner publicity for you and your home business.

Here are tips for speaking effectively:

- Know your audience and prepare your talk targeted with their
  interests in mind and use anecdotes to which they can relate.
- The more eye contact you make with your audience, the more
  they will feel you are speaking directly to them.

SEW's SUGGESTIONS: Don't Let Others Intimidate You

Rochelle Balch, www.rochellebalch.com, is a professional speaker, consultant, and author of *Brag Your Way to Success* and *CEO & MOM*. She says she has generated $17 million from the home-based computer consulting business she started in 1993. How? "With great quality resources, of course, and through extensive self-promotion," says Balch. She provides this tip from her e-newsletter, *Brag Your Way to Success* (bragnews-request@rbbalch.com):

> The first time you start promoting yourself, you may get funny looks. Others may still think that "bragging" and self-promoting are being too self-indulgent, too obnoxious. Wrong. If *you* don't promote *you*, who will?
>
> Be secure in what you do; maintain your confidence. Make sure you have a solid base; that is, feel good about yourself. When you are confident in what you do, it's harder to let others allow you to become intimidated or feel inadequate. You're good; believe it and project the image. Don't let others intimidate you!

- Speak clearly and with varied inflection in your voice instead of droning along and putting your audience to sleep.
- Think about creative elements—such as quotes, visuals, charts, videos, and computer software (PowerPoint)—that you can use to emphasize your message and make your talk more lively and interesting.
- End with a suggested action you would like your audience to take. For example, if your talk is about how to do "cold-calling" sales, urge them to go home and make ten calls or visits to prospective clients.

Signs

Depending on your zoning, you may or may not be permitted to have a business sign outside on your house. If you do work at

Smile!

Debbie Williams, founder of Organizedtimes.com, tells this story:

> The funniest thing that happened to me ended up being an ice breaker for a first-time presentation. I was on my way to give a short speech to a group of stay-at-home moms, with my son in tow. It was the first time I had spoken since launching my organizing business, and after being out of the working environment for several years, I was a bit nervous. But I was sure I had everything organized: Speech, handouts, and even a door prize (organizing book) were all neatly contained in my leather briefcase, tossed into the backseat of the car with my son. After I dropped my toddler off at the nursery, I was confident and ready for a fun and upbeat presentation. Only one thing stopped me: During our commute to the meeting, my active son had played with the lock on my briefcase and it was locked tight! My husband (unbeknownst to me) had changed the combination when he borrowed my briefcase, and was unavailable in a meeting of his own! So much for being organized . . .
>
> Luckily I knew the material, and the meeting planner (a friend of mine) had copied the handouts beforehand. We quickly came up with a Plan B, a fun mixer for the women to do as they arrived. And a wonderful woman volunteered to crack the combination when she heard of my predicament. I don't know—maybe she really was motivated by that door prize, or just liked a challenge, because for ten minutes she tried every combination imaginable to open that briefcase.

Smile! *(continued)*

So, as I was jotting down an outline for my speech, and the meeting planner was lightheartedly sharing our news with the gathering group, I was prepared to just make the most of an embarrassing situation and plow full steam ahead. At least I had the handouts, right?

But immediately after the opening prayer, the lady jumped up with an "I got it! I got it open!" and everyone applauded! So, what could have been a fiasco simply reassured my audience that I, too, am human and that life happens, regardless of how well you think you plan for it. And as a professional organizer delivering a time management speech to a group of veteran moms, that message was crucial!

---

clients' homes painting or wallpapering, for example, you might ask your client if you could put a temporary sign outside their home so neighbors and passersby can take note. Magnetic vehicle signs are also popular. Patricia Gallagher (with the angel pins) recently bought a white van and is considering having clouds and angels painted on it as she does another cross-country tour with her four children!

Telemarketing

You may not have considered calling prospects for business (or cold-calling, as it is termed). Calling from a list of people who have shown an interest in your product or services is better. You can gather such lists at trade shows or demonstrations, through returned post cards from your mailers, and even via your Web site. (*Note:* Check the FTC regulations on telemarketing if you decide to do it as a regular part of your business.)

Azriela Jaffe, author of *Starting from No: Ten Strategies to Overcome Your Fear of Rejection and Succeed in Business*

(Chicago, IL: Dearborn Trade, 1999), offers these tips for over-coming the fear of making sales calls to prospective customers:

> Figure out whether it's scarier for you to prospect strangers or people you know. Most people are more frightened of one or the other. Then, concentrate your efforts on the kind of sales that doesn't push your deepest panic buttons, until you are strong enough to handle the kind of sales that gives you the creeps and makes you not want to get out of bed in the morning. Build on success and improve your self-confidence over time before tackling your hardest prospects.

Some other cold-calling tips come from Kim Essenmacher, www.ld.net/?lowtelerates.com, who is an independent agent for Cognigen, a global provider of discount telecom services. She says: "Have a written script before you that you can refer to and modify for each call. If you are having a bad day, stay off the phone! And be prepared for many 'hang-ups.'" She encourages those who are reluctant to try calling by saying, "When you avoid what you fear, then you accept failure before you accept success."

Essenmacher is also editor and publisher of a free, semi-monthly e-newsletter for entrepreneurs, *BizPreneur News* (bizpreneurnews-subscribe@yahoogroups.com).

Trade Shows, Expos

Trade shows, expos, and women's business conferences are good places to not only present workshops, but excellent opportunities to network with other women entrepreneurs. Check with your in-dustry association or business ownership organization for dates and locations at which you may be able to exhibit and promote your business. You may be able to barter table space if you offer to con-duct a workshop or talk.

Videos

If you have success at your business, you may consider parlaying your profits into having an instructional video made to sell along with your services or products. To cut down on costs, you may want to see if a local college's video students or class would be will-ing to make one for you. Videos are also good to send to television producers who might just invite you onto a local cable television show. One woman did this and ended up having her own weekly show about raising and using herbs.

Word-of-Mouth

Many home-based businesses receive more business from referrals from satisfied customers and from their entrepreneurial network. You can encourage the number of referrals by offering incentives—such as a discount coupon or a month's free service—as do many Internet service providers. One car dealer pays $100 to previous customers every time one of their referrals results in a sale. Remember, though, bad service or experiences often spread "faster" than good ones—it's just the nature of people—so make every contact with a customer a good one.

Writing

Consider writing to promote your home business. Jeffrey Dobkin wrote an article for the newsletter, *Book Marketing Update* (John Kremer, editor-in-chief and author of *1001 Ways to Market Your Books*), saying that after four years of steadily mailing out his self-syndicated articles to a list of publications that reach his audience of small business owners and direct-marketing professionals, he has seen this marketing method result in over $400,000 worth of books sold. Your articles may not bring such dramatic results, but writing articles, a newsletter, or books and e-books, help to establish you as an "expert." Oftentimes, home-based professionals will pay to publish a small column of tips or a Q & A for their local paper's readership. If you are not a good writer, you can hire a local ghostwriter.

Yellow Pages, Women's Yellow Pages

Many prospective customers will still turn to local telephone directories' advertising pages. Having an ad in these pages can be expensive, but worthwhile if it brings you business. An ad in such a directory also gives permanency to your business. In some regions of the U.S., women's "Yellow Pages" directories, such as The National Association of Women's Yellow Pages (www.womensyellowpages.org), are distributed throughout the area. For more information about a Women's Yellow Page listing, visit their Web site or call (800) 869-1203.

Do not be afraid to consult with a marketing expert or agency that serves home and small businesses. Their expertise can save you many dollars, as they can advise you where to get the best results for your advertising dollars and/or suggest additional low-cost advertising ideas you never knew existed.

Public Relations

Public relations (PR) involves activities that promote positive messages and images about your product and services to the public. As mentioned previously, with advertising you control the placement of your ads and promotions; with PR, the media is in control of your announcements and news about your business. A publicity "hit" is when you get positive coverage in the media as a result of your efforts.

Media Contacts

How do you find media contacts to get you coverage? Create a publicity plan and you will know who the best contacts are and where they are. Here are some tips.

- Aim to get publicity in media that reaches your target customers.
- Familiarize yourself with the media—get copies of the newspaper, listen to the radio, and watch the programs so you can avoid sending PR materials to media that is not a match with your business.
- Compile a database of each specific media, including contact people, addresses, telephone and fax numbers.
- Talk to the editors (when they are not on deadline) who receive the releases and press kits and ask them their preferences in receiving submissions for their review—via mail? fax? e-mail?
- Put together a press kit for each of these editors.
- Ask for editorial calendars, schedules of programming and regular features, and dates of special editions so you can slant your news releases accordingly.
- If you can afford it, take ads out in publications that are sent to national media like the *Radio, TV, & Interview Report*

(www.ritr.com) published by Bradley Communications Corp., P.O. Box 1206, Lansdowne, PA 19050-8206. Or look for a local PR firm or freelance professional that handles small and home business promotions.

Do not forget to ask other home and small business owners for their favorite media contacts.

Press Releases

For Peggi Clauhs and her mother, Winnie McClennan, submitting a press release about the opening of their home-based cooking school resulted in a major feature in a large city newspaper that brought customers from all over the area. Editors know what they want and do not want in a press release. Here are some quick tips to get your home business's press release published:

• Include the most important information in the first paragraphs—who? what? where? when? why?—because editors cut from the bottom up.
• Make it interesting, credible, and newsworthy. Include quotations and statistics from experts, agencies, and/or industry organizations. Add testimonials if they contribute to the release's value.
• Concentrate on the news story, not advertising.
• Make your headline clearly state why this news is important to your readers. *Note:* The headline or lead will often be the determining factor whether or not your press release will be published or broadcast—it will have to "hook" the media contact and audience into paying attention to it. Wait until you have finished writing the release, then jot down several headlines until you believe you have the one that best captures your press release's slant and purpose.
• An accompanying photo will also enhance your chances of getting your press release published.

Once you write a few, you can use your best one as a "template" for your future press releases.

Press Kits/Packages

What goes into a press kit or package? A press kit's purpose is to increase awareness about your business and its services and/or products and provide exposure and visibility for your business. A typical one could consist of a white notebook/folder with two pockets on the inside; your business cards and brochure; a press release announcing the launching of your business; a color photo and a black-and-white photo of yourself; a background or bio sheet about you and the story about your business; a sales flyer about your products or services; testimonial sheets and any endorsements by famous or familiar people.

Ask other entrepreneurs for samples of their press kits so you can get some good ideas for yours. Be creative and let your kit reflect the image and purpose of your business.

Media Interviews

When you finally do get some responses from reporters, editors, writers, producers, and other media personnel for interviews, follow these suggestions to create a good impression:

- Have a list of questions and answers that you have composed in the event they should need it for your interview. It will save them time and make them appear knowledgeable.
- Ask the interviewer if you can have a copy of the publication, audio- or videotape of your interview.
- Offer to send readers, listeners, and viewers some free information or to visit your Web site so you can garner new prospective customers.
- Always be sure you send a follow-up thank-you note after your interview.
- Offer them leads for other sources should they ever need a subject to interview.

If you are professional, positive, and honest in your interviews, chances are the interviewer will be contacting you again when they need more information related to your business, and that means more publicity for your and your home business.

Time Management and Organization

Did you receive the e-mail (one of those thousands of "Internet Lit" messages passed on by family and friends which seldom credit the writer) that read like this: "There is a bank that credits your account each morning with $86,400. It carries over no balance from day to day. Every evening deletes whatever part of the balance you failed to use during the day. What would you do? Draw out *all of it*, of course!!!! Each of us has such a bank. Its name is TIME. Every morning, it credits you with 86,400 seconds. Every night it writes off, as lost . . ."

It is true, we are all given the same number of seconds, minutes, and hours each day, and how we manage them depends on what we accomplish and what makes our lives meaningful.

Add a home business into our already-hectic lives, and we can quickly find ourselves overwhelmed and out of time. Ami White, who owns two online stores, Sweeter Celebrations (www.sweeter-celebrations.com), a home-based party supply business, and My Sonflower, a country gift store, says this:

> The most difficult aspect of working for myself is the challenges of doing "everything" by myself. When questions or problems arise, you have yourself to turn to. Being the owner, operator, secretary, packer, shipper, bookkeeper, maintenance, etcetera, is real challenging but at the same time rewarding. Owning your own business all the responsibility falls on you.

CREATE A TIME MANAGEMENT PLAN

In starting a home business, many women draw up a business plan, a financial plan, a marketing plan, and a life plan; but they forget to plan for the *time* it takes to implement all these plans! Here are some tips for finding the time management system that works best for you:

- Review your business's primary goals and your life's goals daily! If you write them down, experts say you are more likely to accomplish those goals.
- Create monthly, weekly, and daily "to-do" lists, starting with the most important items first. Make sure your lists include

activities that take you closer to each of your goals. You can monitor both your business goals and personal goals if you simply divide your "to-do" list sheets in half—one side for personal/family tasks and one side for business tasks.

- Discipline yourself to focus on your tasks and set deadlines to them; but schedule in time off, too.
- Use technology, daily planners, and any other devices that save you time.
- Each week, review your progress and re-evaluate your plans. Reward yourself in small ways for what you have accomplished.
- Do not forget to involve the input—favorable and unfavorable—from those with whom you live.

An ideal time management plan is an individual plan that prioritizes your activities so you will accomplish the goals you've set for yourself and your business, while helping to relieve your stress and giving you more time for family and friends.

Eliminate Time Wasters

Wasting time when you work at home is so common. You will find yourself constantly battling distractions and going off in "tangents" instead of doing what you set out to do for the day.

Juli Shulem, author of *Home-Based Business Mom,* gives these tips:

- *Keep all work in the designated office area at all times —* *no exceptions.* It takes self-discipline to keep work from getting past the threshold of the office door.
- *Set specific work hours.* It is also important to set aside time to do the important tasks and be with children.
- *Work at times when distractions will be at a minimum.* This is especially crucial and is often accomplished by working very early in the morning or late at night.

Packy Boukis, home business owner of Only You Wedding and Event Consulting (www.clevelandwedding.com/), says, "Not having a 'plan of action' is a great time waster," and that you should plan for your business "with the same organized and well-thought-out plan and enthusiasm as if you were suddenly given two tickets for a 'free' destination of your choice" and had to get ready for this trip.

Dr. Robert Sullivan, small business expert and author of *The Small Business Start-Up Guide* (www.isquare.com), adds his input:

In my opinion, the biggest time waster is the telephone. The best thing that a business can do is to make maximum use of e-mail. It's also a good idea to force yourself to keep telephone conversations as short as possible. With a little self-discipline, this becomes easy to do without offending anyone." And remember that old axiom: "The optimum number of people in any meeting is zero." And (as you already know) a successful entrepreneur must be a "one-man (or woman) show."

To avoid wasting time, learn what your own worst personal time waster is and eliminate it. Other home business experts recommend that you set apart blocks of time to carry out specific tasks. For example, block out a specific day and/or hour(s) to run business errands and assign yourself as many as you can do into that designated time period in order to save time and gas money.

True, life has its unexpected small, and sometimes serious, emergencies that destroy your good intentions of getting activities accomplished. That's life! Just get back on track as soon as possible after a setback and keep going forward, controlling as many time-wasters as you can.

Being aware of how you use your time can help you be more productive and organized, thus increasing your business's profits, while possibly even freeing up more time to spend with those people who are most important to you.

Networking: Leads and Referrals

Networking is the exchange of information and leads between business owners and associates with the purpose of encouraging referrals and helping to promote one another's businesses.

Networking Sources

Where and with whom can you network? Here are some suggestions:

Associations: Home-based business associations, women's and men's business ownership organizations, and industry and even informal associations are all sources that provide networking opportunities. A good source to find an industry association related to your home business is to look in the *Encyclopedia of Associations* (Gale Research), available in the reference section of most libraries. These associations usually do not have business startup information; however, the Web sites of those associations often list publications for sale that you may find helpful in your venture.

Not all associations will fit you and your business. If you consider joining, attend an open meeting as a guest so you can judge whether or not this group will work for you. Often local chambers of commerce have "business card exchange meetings," at which you will have the opportunity to not only meet the members but also to hand out your cards.

Internet: With all the business, Web business, mothers' business, and industry-sponsored Web sites, you could spend twenty-four hours a day on the Internet, chatting with other entrepreneurial women. A large (portal) Web site like the women's site iVillage.com, for example, has a number of business-related message boards and regular chats where visitors can ask questions and interact with other site visitors. A smaller Web site, such as BizyMoms.com, also has regular real-time chats with business experts and women who own and operate specific businesses.

And of course, e-mail discussion groups, and one-on-one networking is very good. Do be cautious, however, of e-mail overload—receiving more messages than you could possibly respond to. In other words, be careful what groups you join.

Other: You have business expos, conferences, trade shows, and special events that are also places to connect with other women in business. Always, always carry plenty of business cards wherever you go, and hand out two at a time—one for the person you just met and one for them to give to someone else.

EFFECTIVE NETWORKERS

Kim Essenmacher, editor and publisher of *Bizpreneur News,* an e-newsletter or e-zine that comes out twice per month, loves networking and helping make the connections among entrepreneurs.

She says, "Successful networkers look for opportunities to connect with others. They do not wait for others to come to them."

Here are some additional characteristics of "successful networkers":

- They tell you their name, their business's name, and what they do.
- They ask you, first, what you do and ask you questions to really understand your business.
- They are always ready to help you in a crisis.
- They stand tall and speak with confidence.
- They stand out from others. For example, one woman whose family business makes canvas awnings had a multicolored business suit made from canvas that she wore to networking events.
- They provide you with a description of the customers that their business serves, so you can refer the "perfect" customer to them.

Surely, you can add to these characteristics from observing business owners who made an impression with you. One more: If you promise to give a lead contact information later, remember to follow up as soon as possible. Networking is a win-win relationship when it works.

Ethics, Etiquette, Image, and Professionalism

Most of us are familiar with the familiar sayings, "First impressions are important;" "Your actions speak louder than your words;" "Put your best foot forward," and other similar phrases about how our behavior is observed and judged by others, especially those who are meeting us the first time. This holds true, too, of a business owner and her venture. How you operate your business and conduct yourself with those in your industry, your customers, the media, and in the community you live will be scrutinized, whether you like it or not.

Thus, you will want to be aware of the policies you set for your business concerning its ethics, etiquette, image, and professionalism to ensure you and your business are perceived positively by those you serve and network with. If you do not value how you conduct business, neither will any present or potential customers.

If you are unsure of how to improve you and/or your business's overall image, you might want to consult with a professional image consultant. Image consultants can help improve a person's personal appearance, speech, and manners; while some specialize in improving the overall image of a business itself by improving public relations. Visit the Web site of the Association of Image Consultants, International, for a referral at www.aici.org.

BUSINESS ETHICS

Business ethics are a reflection of your own morals and beliefs and how you conduct yourself in those "gray areas" of what is right and what is wrong. It is an issue of what you consider or do not consider to be "honest" practices. Think about these sample scenarios:

- If you are going to be late with the deadline of a project, do you claim a relative just died, or do you contact the client and let her know you miscalculated and ask if you can work out an extension date?
- Do you "bad-mouth" your competitors to your customers, or do you stress the benefits of your products and services to your customers?
- Do you take responsibility for your mistakes, or do you blame them on other reasons?
- Do you promise more and deliver less?

Being true to yourself and your values will help you choose the right decision when you face a business dilemma. To paraphrase someone wise, "If you never tell a lie, then you will not have to remember who you told it to and who you did not!" Lose your credibility with your customers, and your business's reputation may suffer irreparable damage at the expense of customers and profits.

BUSINESS ETIQUETTE

Business etiquette is concerned with your behavior and communications toward your customers and business associates. If your business goes global, then cultural differences will demand behaviors appropriate to the customs of the country with which you are dealing. Just as you should display proper etiquette when you entertain or meet new people, you will enhance your business by exhibiting certain manners. Here are some examples:

- Developing a positive relationship through courteous and prompt service with your customers will encourage their repeat business.
- Replying to business e-mail within 24 hours shows courtesy.
- In the business "world" especially, treat men and women equally.
- Follow up with thank-you notes for service or assistance.

There are many other rules. In general, however, business etiquette parallels proper behavior in everyday life. It basically comes down to having respect for others and being treated as you wish to be treated (in other words, follow The Golden Rule).

BUSINESS IMAGE

Your business's image is a reflection of the products and services you produce. For example, the clowning duo "Whoopsie & Daisy," partners in the business Educational Clowning, display a dramatically different business image from that of a Web site designer. Whoopsie & Daisy's business cards have a bright yellow background featuring their happy and funny faces, whereas the Web designer's card has an illustration of a computer with her contact information written in standard script.

What makes the difference in your business's image? Your customers! Whoopsie & Daisy's customers are schools and children. The Web designer's customers are home and small businesses. You should fit your business image to your customers' age, sex, marital status, location, occupation, education, interests, and background.

Another difference is your business's positioning in your industry. This depends on how your business compares with your competitors' in terms of pricing, style, quality, exclusivity, and service.

Take time to analyze *what* your business is offering and to *whom* you offer it to create the right image in the minds of your target customers. If you have trouble deciding what your image is, ask for feedback from other entrepreneurs or seek the advice of a small/home business consultant.

BUSINESS PROFESSIONALISM

No matter how small or casual your business is, or that you operate it from home, you must operate it with professionalism if you want to be taken seriously and respected by your customers, other business owners, and those in your industry.

Factors in operating a business with professionalism include:

- Having "regular" business hours so clients and business associates know when they can best reach you. Susan Abrams, author of *The New Success Rules for Women* (www.newsuccess rules.com) says:

  > Invest in a separate telephone line and voice mail (not an answering machine) for your business. That way, only you or your associates pick up the business calls and your clients won't end up speaking to your spouse, friends, or children. Thus, you will present yourself in a professional manner, and you'll get all your messages.

- Promptly return business-related calls and/or e-mails and letters.
- Present polished promotional materials. Use business cards, brochures, and stationery with your correct business contact information (and no typos) that help promote the image you wish your business to portray to potential customers.
- Treat customers and business associates with respect, courtesy, and appreciation.
- Strive to be honest in your dealings with customers and other business owners.
- Conduct yourself in a manner that establishes you as a respected expert in your field.
- Follow a fair set of standards and ethics in how you conduct your business.

Being a professional does not mean you have to have a college degree. It is being true to your word and offering the best you have to your customers.

Related Resources

BOOKS

303 Marketing Tips Guaranteed to Boost Your Business, edited by Rieva Lesonsky (Irvine, CA: Entrepreneur Media, 1999).

Be Your Own Mentor: Strategies from Top Women on the Secrets of Success by Sheila Wellington, Betty Spence, Catalyst Inc. (New York: Random House, 2001).

Brag Your Way to Success: The Guidebook to Self-Promotion by Rochelle B. Balch (Glendale, AZ: RB Balch & Associates, Inc., 2001).

Buff and Polish: A Practical Guide to Enhance Your Professional Image and Communication Style by Kathryn J. Volin (Minneapolis, MN: Pentagon Publishing, 1999).

Business Etiquette in Brief: The Competitive Edge for Today's Professional by Ann Marie Sabath (Holbrook, MA: Adams Media, 1993).

Business Etiquette: 101 Ways to Conduct Business with Charm and Savvy, 2nd ed., by Ann Marie Sabath (Franklin Lakes, NJ: Career Press, 2002).

Business Etiquette Professionalism by M. Kay duPont (Menlo Park, CA: Crisp Publications, Inc., 1998).

Design It Yourself: Logos, Letterheads, and Business Cards by Chuck Green (Glouster, MA: Rockport Publishers, 2001).

Endless Referrals: Network Your Everyday Contacts into Sales, New and Updated Edition by Bob Burg (New York: McGraw-Hill, 1998).

Gale's Directory of Publications and Broadcast Media (Detroit, MI: Gale Research) — Lists most trade magazines.

Grassroots Marketing: Getting Noticed in a Noisy World by Shel Horowitz (White River Junction, VT: Chelsea Green Publishing, 2000); www.chelseagreen.com.

Guerilla Marketing Online Weapons: 100 Low-Cost, High-Impact Weapons for Online Profits and Prosperity by Jay Conrad Levinson, Charles Rubin (Boston: Houghton Mifflin, 1996).

Guerrilla Trade Show Selling by Conrad Levinson, Mark S.S. Smith, Orvel Ray Wilson (New York: John Wiley and Sons, 1997); www.wiley.com.

Home Based Business Mom: A Practical Guide to Time Management and Organization for the Working Woman by Juli Shulem (Santa Barbara, CA: Newhoff Publishing, 1998).

Home Management: A Guide for Busy Parents by Debbie Williams (Vancouver, WA: Champion Press, Ltd., 2001). Also offers an excellent resource section of organizing products.

Marketing for the Home-Based Business by Jeffrey P. Davidson (Holbrook, MA: Adams Media Corp., 1999).

Secrets of Savvy Networking: How to Make the Best Connections for Business and Personal Success, 1st ed., vol. 1 by Susan RoAne (New York: Warner, 1993).

Start-Up Marketing: An Entrepreneur's Guide to Launching Advertising, Marketing, & Promoting Your Business by Philip Nulman (Franklin Lakes, NJ: Career Press, 1996).

Teaming Up: The Small Business Guide to Collaborating with Others to Boost Your Earnings and Expand Your Horizon by Paul and Sarah Edwards (New York: Putnam Publishing Group, 1997).

Uncommon Marketing Techniques by Jeffrey Dobkin (Merion Station, PA: Danielle-Adams Publishing, 1998).

PUBLICATION, PROMOTION (ADVERTISE FOR A FEE)

BizStarz Quarterly (www.BizStarz.com), BizStarz, Inc., 910 Florin Rd., Ste. 200, Sacramento, CA 94831. Entrepreneurs pay to have their businesses featured. They submit photos and stories about their businesses and themselves that can be used for free by interested media.

TRADE ASSOCIATIONS

American Advertising Federation, www.aaf.org; 1101 Vermont Ave. NW, #500, Washington D.C. 20005-6306.

American Marketing Association, www.ama.org; 250 S. Wacker Dr., #200, Chicago, IL 60606.

Direct Marketing Association, www.the-dma.org; 1120 Ave. of the Americas, 13th Floor, New York, NY 10036.

WEB SITES

Bacon's MediaSource Software, www.baconsinfo.com.

www.dobkin.com — Tips by marketing expert Jeffrey Dobkin.

www.thebusywoman.com/ — Susie Glennan's The Busy Woman's Daily Planner. Offers time-saving tips and products.

www.EtiquetteSource.com — An online resource of videos, books, and online tips about business and consumer etiquette, a.k.a. Manners International.

www.gebbieinc.com, Gebbie Press — PR data resource of newspapers, magazines, and radio and TV stations on disks, mailing labels; online site lists these media's Web sites.

www.getmediacoverage.com/, Get Media Coverage — Broadcast journalists will write and send out your press release to target media for a price; check Web site for current prices.

www.GetOrganizedNow.com — Web site of Maria Gracia, professional organizer, speaker, and author of *Finally Organized, Finally Free!* Offers tips, ideas, and articles.

"How to Get More Done with Less Time and Effort: A Streamlined Time Management Course," audio program by Marty Foley, seminar speaker and author, available through www.profitinfo.com/catalog.

www.ideabook.com — Chuck Green's desktop publishing Web site with design tips.

www.netrageous.com/pr/, NETrageous, Inc. — Free zine, *Paul's Publicity Pointers.*

www.prfirms.org — Council of Public Relations Firms

www.PublicityHound.com — Articles and special reports.

www.prsa.org, Public Relations Society of America.

www.rhondaonline.com/index.asp — Online Web site of Rhonda Abrams, small business columnist and author of several books in her Successful Business Series. Newsletter and tips.

www.tscentral.com — Search here for trade shows.

Women's Business Center Online's "Marketing Mall," www.onlinewbc .gov/docs/market/ — Helpful articles about marketing, advertising, and publicity.

www.yudkin.com — Web site of Marcia Yudkin, marketing expert and author of *Six Steps to Free Publicity: And Dozens of Other Ways to Win Free Attention for You or Your Business.*

CHAPTER EIGHT

Managing and Maintaining a Profitable Home Business

Starting up is just the beginning of having a profitable home business. Learning how to manage, maintain, and hopefully develop it will be the real test to see if you and your business survive the growing pains. The overall success rate for home businesses, however, is better than other small businesses because a home business can be started on a shoestring budget and on a part-time basis. Even when a home business does not work out, many women who had a "taste" of being their own boss will just go ahead and start another one.

Polly, a grandmother of three children had three part-time businesses—custom quilted jackets, painted sweatshirts, and potpourri products—which made money, but not enough for her to do full time. Then she taught herself how to make soap, and she now makes it for gifts as a full-time business. If you ask Polly, she will say those former businesses were not a waste of time because she learned about marketing, selling, and all the other aspects of running a business—which helped her find success with her handmade soaps.

Jennifer Basye Sander, founder of the women's wealth-building and motivational Web site "Goals & Jewels" (www.goalsandjewels.com), says this:

The great thing about building your own business from home is that you can directly profit from your own hard work and ability to spot a need, rather than having the fruits of your creativity go towards a company bottom line while you are stuck with a salary. You think of a great idea—and you get to cash in as the great idea catches on. If you think of a great idea while working for someone else, they get the majority of the financial rewards while you get a pat on the back.

Resources for Home Businesses

Working alone does not mean you are alone. As was discussed previously about combating isolation (see chapter 4), resources for home-based entrepreneurs and small businesses are literally all around you—in your state or province, in your country, and now, with the Internet, throughout the world! And the good news is that these resources are available to just about anyone and are usually low-cost or even free. Successful entrepreneurs share two characteristics: perseverance and inquisitiveness. If you have these, you can find almost all the information you need to keep your business going and even more.

LOCAL RESOURCES

Your local government or municipality can supply you with manuals on zoning, permits, and any licenses you need to conduct business in your community.

Local public and college libraries, supported by either public or private funding, contain a wealth of information for your business. Most public libraries are now connected to one another in a city- or county-wide system, sometimes even statewide and all use a common computer system. Community colleges in your county may also be encompassed in the same system. This enables you to request a book from another library via inter-library loan. If there are four-year colleges or universities in your area, you can do research there and may also be able to take out books.

Here is a sampling of what you will discover at the library:

- *Publications and Periodicals:* You'll find consumer and business magazines (home, small, and large business) and local and national newspapers such as the *Wall Street Journal* and *The New York Times.*

- *Books:* Business books are usually found in the 300 and 600 sections (according to the Dewey Decimal System). Books on specific businesses may be listed by their subject matter. Also check to see if your library system has the "Books in Print" database, which enables you to look up almost any book on any subject that is in print.

- *Reference Section:* Larger libraries have specialized reference librarians who will even help you answer questions. Some libraries will also have special reference sections for business.

  Here are just a few of the many, many sources available to help you find business information:

  Community: Telephone directories, local business listings, local ordinance books, etc.

  State: Directories of state offices, colleges, grants, etc.

  Federal: References containing government agency offices and contact information, etc.

  Business Reference Annuals: *Business Information Desk Reference: Where to Find Answers to Business Questions* (Macmillan, New York); *Gale Reference Books* (Detroit, MI; Gale Research, annuals), www.gale.com/gale.html — Includes business plans, associations, broadcast media, and much more. *Ward's Business Directory of U.S. Private and Public Companies* — Directory of existing firms.

  Industry Surveys: *Standard & Poor's; Thomas Register of American Manufacturers* (Thomas Register, www.thomas register.com)

- *Special Sections:* These include:

  Reading documents on microfilm, microfiche

  Locating articles in the library via another computer system.

Exploring vertical files, which are collections of pamphlets, articles on certain subjects, etc.

Accessing booklets and pamphlets (free for the taking) such as tax booklets forms, community organizations, college and high school adult evening course schedules and applications.

Accessing SBA documents and pamphlets detailing governmental programs and information for startup businesses and loans. (Some libraries are designated as a depository for SBA materials.)

- *Programs:* Many libraries have community rooms where various speakers and organizations conduct presentations and meetings. Get a copy of the library's schedule because you never know what expert or group you might encounter that could be of assistance to your business. You might find an opportunity to give a talk on your expertise and at the same time develop good public relations for your business.

- *Computer and Internet Access:* Many libraries offer access to the Internet for those who do not have it at home. Expect to have to sign up in advance because of the demand.

- *Commercial Online Databases:* Libraries frequently have these databases available:

    American Business Disc that has the address, telephone numbers, and contact names of thousands of U.S. businesses.

    Commerce Business Daily that lists the procurement needs of U.S. government agencies.

    National Trade Data Bank that has lists of U.S. government databases on U.S. domestic and international trade and exporting.

    Lexis/Nexus, www.lexis-nexis.com — Lexis pertains to law and court cases; Nexis contains business articles and reports.

- *Other:* Here are two examples of library sections accessible on the Internet:

Library Spot, www.libraryspot.com — Extensive Web site of research resources.

Internet Public Library, www.ipl.org — University of Michigan's Web site of business information.

STATE

Chambers of Commerce: Provide startup kits, information about state legislation affecting small business, and numerous publications for entrepreneurs.

Offices of Local Legislators: Provide startup business manuals, listing of agencies that direct small business matters, support women entrepreneurs, and contacts for possible state contracts.

(*Note:* See appendix for a listing of states' Web sites that can "connect" you with this same information.)

OFFICES OF THE FEDERAL GOVERNMENT

These include SBA centers and Business Information Centers that offer technological and on-site business counseling. Here is a sampling:

Business Information Centers (BICs). One-stop locations for information, education, and training designed to help entrepreneurs start, operate, and grow their businesses with free, on-site counseling, training courses, workshops and other business resources. To find a BIC in your area, contact the local SBA office or call the Small Business Answer Desk at (800) U-ASK-SBA.

Office of Women's Business Ownership, www.sba.gov/womenin business/; (202) 205-6673.

SCORE offices, www.score.org; (800) 634-0245. These involve retired businesspersons who volunteer their time for business counseling.

Small Business Development Centers (SBDCs), www.sba.gov/SBDC — These work in conjunction with universities to provide business counseling and services. They are located in over forty-six states, the District of Columbia, Puerto Rico, and the Virgin

Islands. Look in your telephone directory (white pages) under "Small Business Development Center."

Women's Business Centers, www.onlinewbc.gov; (202) 205-6673. These new federally funded women's business centers offer various startup business programs and guidance. Call or visit their online site to find the center nearest you.

Federal Government Online

Here are some additional Web sites for U.S. government offices pertaining to small business:

Internal Revenue Service, www.irs.ustreas.gov. Help for small businesses.

Minority Business Development Agency, www.mbda.gov; (202) 482-0404; assists minority and women business owners in accessing markets, capital, management and technical assistance, and education and training. Visit their Web site for information, helpful articles, and more.

The Small Business Innovation Research Program, www.sba.gov/ sbir/ — Gives small-business firms the opportunity to compete for financial awards to conduct research and development.

The U.S. Business Advisor, www.business.gov — Provides businesses with one-stop access to federal government information, services, and transactions.

U.S. Equal Employment Opportunity Commission, www.eeoc.gov; (202) 663-4900. Deals with anti-discrimination laws; focuses on small and mid-sized businesses which may lack the resources to implement effective anti-discrimination measures.

U.S. Patent and Trademark Office, www.uspto.gov; (703) 305-4357. Information about registering patents, trademarks, copyrights, domain name registrations, business guides, and more.

OTHER
Cooperative Extension Services

Every county in the U.S. has a Cooperative State, Research, Education Extension Services office, sponsored by the U.S. Department of Agriculture (USDA). These offices work in affiliation with state universities, and in some states, they sponsor courses and programs for home business owners. Contact your local office (in the white or blue pages of your telephone directory), or visit the USDA Web site (www.reeusda.gov), which provides links to cooperative extensions.

Business Incubators

Incubators are establishments in your community that "house" small, and often former home-based businesses, that are in a growth transition. These small businesses are guided in their growth by business experts, and all use the same support staff. Some incubators specialize in just one type of business such as food or technology businesses. (See chapter 11, "Planning the Future for Yourself and Your Business," for more information.)

PRICING AND PROFITS

Deciding what to charge for one's services and/or products is a dilemma many home business owners face. They are afraid if they charge too much, prospective customers will patronize their competitors; but if they charge too little, they many not be able to meet their businesses' expenses, let alone make a profit. Here are some guidelines to assist you in arriving at the best prices for your home business services and/or products:

DETERMINING YOUR PRICES

Four factors are involved in determining pricing.

Cost-Based Pricing: With this type of pricing, you take the breakeven point at which you established the "floor" for your price and set your prices based on financial goals. You can add a certain percentage to create a profit, as with adding on to a wholesale price. This is the most popular form of pricing, but is not very flexible in its ability to react to changes in demand or competition.

Competition-Based Pricing: With this type of pricing, you compare your products and services with prices of competitors and either raise or lower them in comparison. A mistake that new entrepreneurs make is that they often think they must charge less than their customers. If you emphasize the benefits of your products and services and how they make your business stand out from others, you can actually charge more.

Region-Based Pricing: You can charge more for your products and services according to the area. One builder of housing developments, for example, charges almost double for houses located closer to two large cities and routes than for the same houses built in a less desirable location. Your preliminary market research can help you determine which population can best afford and is willing to pay your prices.

Value-Based Pricing: As mentioned previously, ask yourself (and potential customers) what value your product and/or service is to others. If it is unique and in demand, you can charge more than you think, because you fulfill your customers' needs or desires. Be aware, though, the value of your business's offerings can be enhanced by the reputation of the quality of your goods and services—to a point. You can price yourself right out of the market, so be aware of your potential customers' perceptions and opinions of your prices.

PERFORMING A BREAK-EVEN ANALYSIS

You will need to perform a break-even analysis—the point at which the revenues of your business equal its expenses. Most home and small business books contain "formulas" for determining a break-even analysis as well as those for determining formulas. These can provide you with some understanding. If you find it confusing, consult with your accountant for determining your business's break-even analysis. The SBA's pamphlet, "Business Plan for Small Service Firms," gives this formula to find the break-even point:

Break-even point (in sales dollars) equals: Total fixed costs, plus the
total variable costs times the corresponding sales volume.

Example: If fixed costs equal $9,000, and variable costs equal $700
for every $1000 in sales, with $40,000 in sales volume, the formula
would look like this:

$9,000 + ($700 × 40 [$40,000 ÷ $1,000]) = $37,000 — your
break-even point in sales dollars.

With the break-even point, you can determine a service price
for each job by using a formula such as this:

material/supply costs + labor (your time) + overhead
+ the percentage of profit you want to make = your price.

Overhead costs include all expenses other than materials used
and your labor. If your business is your sole income, do not forget
to include costs such as health insurance, social security, taxes, loan
payments, and so forth in your overhead calculations. Also do not
forget to charge for your time and/or labor.

Pricing Your Product

If your business produces a product, you have to include the following costs in determining your price: production, shipping, a percentage of your overhead (fixed and variable operating expenses),
plus your profit percentage.

If you are selling your products wholesale—quantities and what
a retailer will pay so she can add her price (adding on at least 100
percent more of your wholesale price), you have to include in your
wholesale prices the following:

- *Fixed costs:* Rent, utilities, and other costs that do not apply directly
  to the product but that you need for your business's operation
- *Variable costs:* Materials and labor
- *Other costs:* Those that are neither fixed nor variable, such as
  business travel expenses, trade or wholesale show fees, and
  other one-time costs.
- *Profit:* What you expect to make per item

You can ask for higher prices compared to competitors' similar
products by using distinctive presentation techniques—such as

colorful wrapping and packaging, unique labels, or more expensive materials. Your markup has to cover your overhead costs plus your preferred profit. In your business, have a selection of low and higher-priced items to attract all kinds of buyers until you see which ones are your best sellers.

Pricing Your Services

Pricing of services can be more difficult to determine than pricing of products because you—your activities and performance, knowledge, and expertise—are the business.

Generally, you will charge a total of three to four times the annual salary goal you wish to earn (the average annual salary that you would be paid by an employer) because you are now self-employed and will have to include in your prices the costs of benefits, taxes, social security, and other fees; plus you should be compensated for the work you do in marketing and operating your business.

You can get some idea of hourly billable rates from recommended industry standards and/or from how your prices compare with similar experts or businesses. With your hourly billing rate, you can estimate charges per hour, per day, flat rates, or per project fees.

Remember, some customers may be frightened away if you quote your rate at $130/hour (others may expect it!) and be more receptive if you quote a price for an entire project. Others may prefer to pay you by the hour. You will have to operate your business for a period of time while keeping a close record of your preparation and actual work time, plus any incurred expenses and your business's expenses to really determine the best prices for your services. If you have any questions, consult with your accountant or a business consultant to help you figure the best prices to charge for your home business.

Estimating Projects

When you start advertising your business and you begin to get your first calls, you may feel panicky when they ask you to give an estimate or bid on a project. These suggestions may help you:

- Check with industry standard pricing books or manuals or your trade association to see if they have any pricing guides to help you in your estimation.

SEW's SUGGESTIONS: Don't Start "The Clock" Running Too Soon

Janet Attard, author of *The Home Office and Small Business Answer Book*, founder of BusinessKnowHow.com, and owner of Attard Communications, Inc., which has been providing editorial content and community development services to the online world since 1988 (www.businessknowhow.com; www.careerknowhow.com), says this:

> I've often found that sharing a little bit of knowledge for free has led to contracts and long-lasting relationships. In one case, one person took about a half hour of my time asking how to do something, then gave my name to another person in his organization, who proceeded to take up about another half hour of time. I was a little annoyed when I got off the phone with the second individual, and chided myself for not stating upfront that I'd be glad to help if they paid my consulting fee. But then a couple of weeks later I got another call from the company, this time asking me to prepare a quote for a project they were getting ready to launch. So, as it turned out, the hour I spent answering questions initially resulted in a contract that was expanded and extended several times, ultimately bringing in more than a quarter of a million dollars in revenue.

- Never give an immediate answer. Take the time to compute all the costs of supplies, materials, your time (and any assistants' hours), and always overestimate your completion time to allow for "life emergencies" (children's sickness, technology breakdowns, and so on).
- Meet with your client to get as many specific details about what they want or do not want. Make careful notations and even tape your conversation (with their permission) to make sure you get all the details correct.
- Write up your estimation and go over it with your client and customer and negotiate such factors as who uses what

equipment, and who pays extra costs should something unexpected happen.
- Write up a contract and have your lawyer review it if you are unsure of the terms.

After each project or job is completed, write up an evaluation of it and things learned so you will have a record for future projects. You will improve in figuring profitable estimates, the longer you are in business. In other words, the more jobs and projects you do, the better you will become at estimating your time and the costs involved.

PREPARING INVOICES

You can buy generic invoices at office supply stores or have them printed with your business name and logo; or better yet, you can buy software that customizes and fits your billing needs. Before you buy any invoicing software, read your trade publications for their specific recommendations, ask other home business owners which ones they prefer, and get demo copies of the ones that interest you so you can try them out.

KNOWING YOUR CASH FLOW

Cash flow pertains to money coming into your business due to revenues and money going out to pay expenses. Obviously, you want more money coming in than going out! Performing ongoing record keeping will help you know if your business is making or losing money.

Jan Zobel, EA, author of *Minding Her Own Business: The Self-Employed Woman's Guide to Taxes and Recordkeeping,* says this:

> Although we tend to think of record keeping as something we're doing to help us in the event of an IRS audit, your records can tell you a great deal about your business: Which are the slow months? (Would this be a good time to take a vacation?) Which are the months in which you have the most expenses? Will you have enough income or savings to cover those expenses? Are you charging enough for your services to cover the expenses you have? How does this year's income

compare to last year's at this time? Instead of resenting the time you spend keeping records, consider this a way of running your business better (as well as a way of saving taxes).

You will need to estimate your average monthly net (after taxes) income, and then project it over the next twelve months so you can have a more accurate average of what you earn. This is important if you have a seasonal business or if your earnings fluctuate. In your first months of your business startup, you will have to monitor what you charge, your ongoing business expenses, the number of customers you have and whether you are getting new ones, and the time it takes your customers to pay you. All these factors affect the amount of money going in and out of your business.

MANAGING YOUR CASH FLOW

As you operate your home business, you will want to manage your cash flow to ensure your business will continue to thrive. That means also coping with erratic monies and expenditures and the ups and downs of business cycles. If you should have a bigger demand for your business products and services than you can handle, you may want to raise your prices.

The following suggestions can help you boost your cash flow:

- *Increase your collections.* Encourage clients to pay sooner by offering discounts on their bills if they pay by a certain date.
- *Put your business on a "budget."* Decrease expenses when you can do so without hurting the quality of your product or service.
- *Track your advertising.* See which ads are bringing in the most new customers. Try a new promotion that is more creative than costly.
- *Reuse and recycle.* See if you can get your printer and copier cartridges refilled instead of replacing them; use flyers and unrelated correspondence that are printed on only one side for scrap paper or to photocopy information for your own files.
- *Monitor your inventory.* Move poor-selling items by offering them at discount prices.

Your cash flow statement is a monetary guide to help you keep aware of your business's financial position and can make you aware of when you will need to budget for potential cash flow shortages. It is the indicator to help you control your business's expenditures and pricing to ensure you will have a successful (and profitable) business.

OFFERING DISCOUNTS

If clients or customers balk at your prices, you either need to lower them and search for ways to lower your costs, or to find ways to add desirability and value to your product or service that will justify your higher price to potential customers. Customers sometimes equate lower prices with cheapness or poor quality or service. As discussed previously, instead of lowering your prices, offer special sales or incentives to loyal customers.

With your prices, remember why you are in business. Cristi Cristich, founder of Cristek Interconnects, Inc., president of the California chapter of the National Association of Women Business Owners (NAWBO) says this:

> Regardless of why you started your business—whether "to make money," "to do something for the greater good," or "to improve the flexibility and quality of life and that of my family"—the bottom line is still the "bottom line." If you don't budget a sufficient salary for yourself *and* design your plan to make a reasonable profit, you won't be able to sustain the business and do all those well-meaning things for very long. Many women think that since they didn't get into business to make a lot of money, "profit" is a dirty word. Women who want to make a positive impact on the world must learn to embrace profit as the most essential part of achieving the "greater good." A profitable business provides women the ability to realize their dreams . . . whatever they are!

The price determination suggestions presented here are for information purposes only. To determine the ideal prices for your service or products, consult with your financial and marketing experts, follow industry guidelines, and adjust according to your customers' responses.

Record Keeping
and Taxes

Doing your business's books is seldom a favorite task of home business owners. Sue Anderson taught school for over twenty years before becoming a certified massage therapist and Reiki instructor. Anderson said one of her most difficult adjustments in working for herself is handling the business aspect of self-employment. "I had no formal business training before starting my venture, so I'm learning as I go, the necessary bookkeeping basics and marketing strategies. It's difficult, but I absolutely love the massage and Reiki and how it is helping my clients. I believe I made the right decision, and my business is growing slowly, but surely."

However routine, record keeping is very important because it helps you to monitor your business and alerts you to any problems that should be brought to your attention.

TAXES

Along with paying local and state taxes and registering your business properly (including a tax ID number and a sales and use number for sales tax from the IRS and your state), you will have to pay the IRS a quarterly estimate of your federal taxes as well as a self-employment tax to cover social security and Medicare. Of course, your accountant and/or a tax specialist can assist you in knowing what taxes to pay and when.

The Internal Revenue Service (IRS) online, www.irs.gov/smallbiz/index.htm, has a helpful section, "Small Business and Self-Employed Community," for small business owners and self-employed individuals that provides specific industry/profession information and links to other helpful sites. At the IRS site, you can also download multiple small business and self-employment forms and publications that relate specifically to self-employment and home business tax matters, such as "Business Use of Your Home" (publication 587); "Your Business Tax Kit: Starting a Business & Keeping Records" (publication 583); and others. You can also phone the IRS for a free "Small Business Tax Kit" at (800) 829-3676, and request forms by calling (800) TAX-FORM.

SEW's Suggestions: Record Keeping and Saving on Your Taxes

Here is some good advice from Jan Zobel, author of *Minding Her Own Business: The Self-Employed Woman's Guide to Taxes and Record keeping*:

Most taxpayers are forever in search of the "secret" deduction that will allow them to pay much less tax. As a tax professional, I can tell you what that secret is: good record keeping. While it's true that tax planning can have an impact on the amount of taxes you pay, you can greatly reduce your tax liability by something as simple as keeping good records. That doesn't necessarily mean that you must use a sophisticated bookkeeping system or a computerized accounting program; it means that you get receipts for everything you might be able to deduct, you keep all your receipts in one place, and you know where to find them when it comes time to do your taxes. It means that in the mind-set of thinking of yourself as a business owner, you think about every expense you have and wonder, "Is there any way this can be deducted as a business expense?"

If the answer is yes, make sure that you have the proper documentation (such as receipts and/or canceled checks) that would allow you to deduct it on your tax return. If you use a car or truck in your business, you keep track not only of the total miles you drive for the year but, more importantly, the number of business miles you drive. Although these are not exciting tips for reducing your taxes, this is truly where the tax savings are.

Here's an example of how good record keeping can help you save taxes. Let's say you drive 1,000 miles for your business. If you haven't kept records of your business mileage, you can't take any deduction. However, if you do have records (even a notation in your appointment book serves as a record), you can deduct 36.5 cents for each business mile you drove. That 36.5 cents × 1,000 miles equals a $365 tax deduction. If you are in the 27 percent tax bracket, a $365 deduction saves you $99 in federal income tax. You also will save $52 in self-employment (social security) tax. Additionally, if your state has an income tax, you'll save even more by having kept the records that allow this deduction.

From the IRS Web site, you can also order one free copy of their annual "Small Business Resource Guide, CD-ROM," which provides tax information, forms, publications, business resources, and essential startup information for new small businesses. You can order online at www.irs.gov/bus_info/sm_bus/smbus-cd.html or by calling (800) 829-3676. Ask for IRS Publication 3207 when ordering your free copy.

Judith Dacey, CPA, president of Small Business Resources, Inc. (www.easyas123.com) in Orlando, Florida, concludes:

> In addition, learning how to keep records and read your financial statements is critical if you are to keep your business profitable. In your personal life, you know if you successfully purchased and maintained your car by its operating performance and breakdown record. You know if you successfully raised your child by the values instilled, school record, character developed, and hugs received. In business, the books are your measurement of success and the first bellwether of impending problems.

Customers

Customers and businesses are connected in that there is a mutual need: Customers need businesses that supply various products and services, and businesses need customers to even have a business. However, if you do not treat your customers well, they really do not need you and your business and they will go elsewhere.

Barbara Mainhart, an independent marketing communications professional with twenty years of experience, says this:

> Always treat each client as the most important client; make it personal. He or she has gone outside the existing organization to find a resource or talent that's not currently available. So in addition to doing the work, you must always reassure the client that he or she made a good decision. Their reputation is on the line and their decision may be questioned by others. Your client's success is your success.

Establishing Customer Policies

Customers generally do not care whether you work from your home or an office building, as long as you supply the products and/or services they need in a timely manner, and that you back up your work or product. From the start, you should have established customer policies. Here are some considerations:

Put your customer policies in writing. If you are a designer or writer, state in your brochure and contracts how many revisions you will do.

Put guarantees and agreements in writing. When providing a guarantee for a product or service, write the details in the sales agreement and your promotional products.

Put your rates in print. Have your rates listed so there are no surprises.

Basically, people do not like any "surprises," so let them know your policies in advance. It will not stop them from complaining, but it will help you to establish guidelines for them.

Practicing Customer Basics

Every business should follow certain customer principles. Here are the five important ones:

1. **You set the example.** If you do the best you can in supplying the best service, you "set the bar" high and that will often have happy customers referring new customers to you.
2. **Listen to your customers.** Solicit feedback with questionnaires, surveys, phone calls. Welcome even negative (but not abusive!) comments, because it will help you know what you are doing right and what areas in which you need to improve.
3. **Thank your customers.** Do this verbally, with special sales, rewards programs, little "extras," and nice surprises that show them you value their patronage.
4. **Keep "connected."** Keep in touch with customers through letters, newsletters, and e-mail (not unsolicited) so you do not lose them to your competitors.

It's basic: Treat your customers as you would like to be treated!

ACCEPTING CREDIT CARDS

Many customers prefer the convenience of paying by credit card. If you wish to get their business—especially if you have a mail-order company—you will need to be able to accept credit card payments. With the continued growth of home businesses (including those that advertise their businesses on the Internet), more banks are granting credit card vendor status to these home-based ventures, especially one that has existed for several years and has a good sales and financial record.

If a bank accepts you, expect to pay them a commission percentage for each transaction. You will probably be charged a monthly support or rental fee for equipment. It is very important that you take time to compare the companies' rates and stipulations or it can be a very costly proposition for you!

Talk to other home business owners who have vendor status to see with whom they have accounts. If you are turned down by one bank, try others. If none will accept you, ask your bank to recommend an independent service organization (ISO) who will match you with a bank that meets your needs. The disadvantage is that it may cost you much more to go through an ISO than to deal with your local bank. Check also with the bank with whom any ISO claims that they do business to make sure they are legitimate!

Some industry and business associates work with major credit card processing service companies to provide their members with the benefit of having credit card vendor status. Check with the business associations to which you belong or others in your industry that provide this benefit.

Avoiding Costly Mistakes

We all fail, but this is all part of our "learning curve." As one woman entrepreneur said, "A mistake is only bad if we fail to learn from it. In starting a home business, all the tasks can soon overwhelm you."

Cheryl Demas, owner of *WAHM* (www.wahm.com), an online magazine for work-at-home-moms, says this:

> The thing I always emphasize is that we have to realize that we can't possibly "do it all." Don't try to be superwoman. Taking care of a home and family is a full-time job in itself. If

you add a home business to the mix, something's got to give. Determine your priorities and decide what you can either do without or hire someone else to do.

Here are some costly mistakes you will want to try to avoid:

Underestimating your startup costs: Go over your projected needs with an accountant and do not forget that it takes time for your business to sustain itself and your needs.

Thinking like an employee instead of an owner: As the owner, you have the entire fiscal responsibility to all aspects of your business and have to budget accordingly.

Not monitoring your cash flow: As mentioned previously, you need to know at all times the financial status of your business so you can adjust your prices, your marketing efforts, and your expenses.

Not listening to your customers: Know your customers' needs and when their interests are changing with trends so you can still serve them.

Growing too fast: A slow, gradual growth is better than too fast. When one crafter received an order from a catalog house for Christmas, she asked every friend and family member she could get to help her in the making of her items. The next year, she was better prepared.

You will make mistakes as an entrepreneur, but if you have your network of business associates and experts established, at least you will have people to help you out.

Product-Oriented Business

Not everyone who works from home has a service. If you create and make a product, one at a time or many at a time, here are some production tips:

Production Tips
- *Plan your production well in advance.* As was discussed previously, use a calendar to mark off nonworking days.

SEW's Suggestions

Deanne Bryce, owner of Leader Strength (www.leaderstrength .com), a training development company shares this tip:

> This is a reminder to not take yourself and your failures too seriously. Failure is part of the process of learning a new profession. Let's face it: Running a business from your home is a whole new profession even if you are like me, still doing the same kind of work (corporate training). Early in my visits with networking leads, I met with a woman who needed contract trainers. I was so nervous that I got my fees all messed up. When I stated my fees, I stated a ridiculously low rate—a sure sign of an amateur. I was so embarrassed I never followed up and neither did she. In my mind I figured I'd never hear from her again. I was wrong. About a year later she called after she accepted a new position. She was looking for information on leadership and thought of me. Since then we've had several great networking conversations.

- *Remember your family.* If you have a family, you will want to have a life with them, so do not forget to include them in your schedule, even during your busiest times.
- *Set up your work area for maximum efficiency to save time and steps.*
- *Monitor your inventory and your bookkeeping.* Have your record keeping software or system set up so you can do so.
- *Build up inventory in your slow times.* Use help from family and friends if they offer, or use the services of workshops for persons with disabilities to save you packaging time.
- *Monitor your sales.* Determine which products sell best and which ones do not, and find out why in both cases.
- *Calculate the costs of making a product and its profits.*
- *Re-evaluate your production periodically.* Do it yourself or consult with an efficiency expert to make the most of your production time.

Extra!! Product Barcode

A barcode, a UPC-A, is used for marking USA retail products. You do not have to have a barcode on your products, but resellers and distributors may require you have one if you sell many items. They use the barcode for inventory and sales records; its purpose is to identify a manufacturer and other information. The UPC-A Code and the assignment of manufacturer ID numbers is controlled in the U.S.A. by the Uniform Code Council (UCC), www.uccouncil.org/; 7887 Washington Village Dr., #300, Dayton, OH 45459; (937) 435-3870. Contact them for an application form. Fees start at $500 for companies whose sales are less than $2 million.

You can also check with the Barcode Software Center, a company that makes labeling software and hardware, by calling (847) 866-7940 or visiting their Web site: www.makebarcode.com/.

LIABILITY

If someone is injured as the result of using your product, you could be held responsible. Reduce your risks by analyzing your product for any and all possible hazards and make sure your products adhere to any standards set by law. Talk to an insurance agent who specializes in insuring products for some input, because product liability rates vary greatly from state to state and according to the product and just who is the intended customer. An attorney may also be able to give you some advice as how to best protect yourself.

FINDING SUPPLIERS AND DISTRIBUTORS

Finding the supplies you need to make an item is not always easy; it's especially difficult to find suppliers that will deal with smaller businesses. Then once you make your product, you will want to look for distributors. How do you find them? Here are some tips:

- Get referrals from business associates you trust.
- Exhibit at or attend trade shows to make contacts.
- Check out the *Thomas Register of Manufacturers,* either at your local library or online: www.thomasregister.com.
- To get distributors to want to sell your product, create a demand among consumers with ads, articles, sample giveaways, and other marketing avenues.

WHOLESALE PRICING

When selling for a wholesale price, your product is sold to a retailer who typically will put a 100 percent markup on your wholesale price to sell to the public. One crafter who sells her crafts mainly through wholesale craft shows says, "I look at one of my items and ask myself, 'What would I pay for this?' Then I half that price because shops will usually add 100 percent onto the price, and see if I can make a profit at that wholesale price."

Business experts recommend a minimum wholesale price be the total of your fixed costs (percentage of your rent/mortgage, utilities, and your salary), your variable costs (the materials and your labor), and your profit percentage. You can then evaluate your customers' responses to your prices to see if they need to be raised or lowered (or production expenses lowered).

The right price is the one that makes you an equitable profit and is acceptable and fair to your customer.

Business Credit and Debt

If your business hits busy times or rapid growth, you can apply to your local bank for a line of credit, including a credit guaranteed by the SBA. This is a certain amount that you can borrow for a short period of time, then repay it, then borrow it again. You apply for it like any bank loan and your application will be based on the same criteria as if you were seeking a lump sum of money. Check with your local banks for their interest rates, fees, and credit loan options. Usually you are given checks for this type of loan that you use to write the amount you need (up to your limit).

If your application for business credit is rejected, you can request in writing the reason for the rejection from the creditor, who must provide you with the specific reason within 30 days of your request.

HANDLING BUSINESS DEBT

If you are in a cash-crunch caused by business expenses, maxed-out credit cards, and your living expenses, here are some tips to stay solvent:

- Cut up all your credit cards except one for business and one for personal use, and stop borrowing on them until you can pay off more of your other debts.
- Look for ways to increase your sales with new marketing methods, sideline services, and other new ways to appeal to both old and new potential customers.
- Look for help from your lenders, who may give you an extension on payments.
- Consult with your financial advisor or planner.
- Use any extra cash to start paying down your debt.

Monitor your business expenses constantly and look for "creative" ways both to save and make money.

Help and Hiring Options

If you need help fast for a rush on your services or your products or maybe some business evaluation, who are you going to call? The options of hiring family, friends, and your spouse; virtual assistants; and independent contractors were discussed in previous chapters. Here are some additional options to find the help you need:

Business Support Services: What used to be described as secretarial services is now referred to as business support services. They can provide everything from transcription and research assistance to desktop publishing or professional writing services. Check locally first for a service or contact The Association of Business Support Services, International Inc. (www.abssi.org).

College Business Classes: Sometimes college business classes will help you with a marketing plan or you can find an intern to assist you or even a student in Web design to assist you in planning an Internet Web site.

Seniors: Many senior citizens may be looking to supplement their retirement income. If they worked in your industry, they can add their valuable work experiences to their skills. Talk to directors of senior citizen centers.

Centers for Persons with Physical and/or Mental Disabilities: Ask whether shelters, workshops, or rehabilitation facilities can recommend some of their clients to assist you in various projects.

Partnering with Other Small Business Owners: Often two independent contractors or home-based business owners can work together on a project or collaborative effort.

Barbara Mainhart, who often works with a graphic designer on her communications projects, states:

> We both have our own businesses, so we are invested in making them a success. I can rely on top-notch professional service from my affiliation with the designer; and she can rely on me to manage, research, create the program, and provide all copy and to liaise with the client. In effect, we are equals. I relish not having to check up on a partner. I don't have time for it. This, of course, is completely unlike a subcontracting job where triple-checking is the only option to ensure a good job.

Not all partnering or "strategic alliances" work out, because such a relationship requires complementary skills and must be beneficial to both parties.

Management of your business is a constant job, but with your business experts and networking contacts and your hard work, you can take a startup home business to a money-making and satisfying venture.

Related Resources

ASSOCIATIONS

Customer Care Institute, www.customercare.com; 17 Dean Overlook NW, Atlanta, GA 30318. Offers information research.

International Customer Service Association, www.icsa.com; 401 North Michigan Avenue, Chicago, IL 60611. Provides networking opportunities and certification.

(The following associations provide credit card vendor status for qualified members. Also see "Associations" under Resources in appendix for addresses.)

The National Association of Women Business Owners, www.nawbo.org.

The Small Office Home Office Association (SOHOA), www.SOHOA.com.

Women Incorporated, www.womeninc.org — Provides Business Card Credit Program for its members through Bancard Systems, Inc.

Also check with the associations in your industry to see if they offer merchant vendor status to their members.

BOOKS

Calming Upset Customers, rev. ed., by Rebecca Morgan (Menlo Park, CA: Crisp Publications, 1996).

The Complete Guide to Getting and Keeping Visa/Master Card Status by Pearl Sax and Larry Schwartz (National Association of Credit Card Merchants, updated annually). To order, call (561) 737-8700.

Creating Demand: Move the Masses to Buy Your Product, Service, or Idea by Richard Ott (Richmond, VA: Symmetric Systems, Inc., 1999).

Customers for Keeps: 8 Powerful Strategies to Turn Customers into Friends and Keep Them Forever by Lois K. Geller (Holbrook, MA: Adams Media Corp., 2001).

Customers for Life: How to Turn That One-Time Buyer into a Lifetime Customer, rev. ed., by Carl Sewell and Paul B. Brown (New York: Pocket Books, 1998).

Customer Service for Dummies by Karen Leland, Keith Bailey (Foster City, CA: IDG Books).

Fail-Proof Your Business: Beat the Odds and Be Successful by Paul E. Adams (Los Angeles: Adams-Hall Books, 1999).

Finances & Taxes for the Home-Based Business by Bryane and Charles P. Lickson (Menlo Park, CA: Crisp, 1997).

Find and Keep Customers for Your Small Business by Joanne Y. Cleaver (Torrance, CA: CHH, Inc. 1999).

How to Get, Keep, and Use Visa, MasterCard and American Express Credit Card Merchant Status to Earn Millions: Even If You Work at Home, Operate a Mail-Order Business or Are Just Starting a New Company (Inter-World Corporation, 1992). ISBN: 1-880199-95-5.

J. K. Lasser's Taxes Made Easy for Your Home-Based Businesses by Gary W. Carter (New York: John Wiley & Sons, 2000).

Knock Your Socks off Answers: Solving Customer Nightmares and Soothing Nightmare Customers by Kristin Anderson, Ron Zemle (New York: Amacon, 1995).

Master Directory of Bank Credit Card Programs (Gordon Press, 1992); $255.95; ISBN: 0-8490-5353-6.

The Power of Two: How Companies of All Sizes Can Build Alliance Networks That Generate Business Opportunities by John K. Conlon, Melissa Giovagnoli (New York: Jossey-Bass, Inc., 1998).

The Self-Employed Woman's Guide to Taxes and Recordkeeping, 3rd ed., by Jan Zobel (Holbrook, MA: Adams Media).

Simplified Small Business Accounting, 2nd ed., by Daniel Sitarz (Carbondale, IL: Nova Publishing, 1999).

The Small Business Troubleshooter: 152 Solutions to the Problems Faced by Every Growing Company, 2nd ed., by Robert Fritz (Bloomington, IN: Unlimited Publishing LLC., 2000).

Strategy and Tactics of Pricing: A Guide to Profitable Decision Making, 3rd ed., by Thomas T. Nagle, Reed K. Holden (Upper Saddle River, NJ: Prentice Hall PTR, 2002).

Teaming up: The Small Business Guide to Collaborating with Others to Boost Your Earnings and Expand Your Horizons by Paul Edwards, Rick Benzel, Sarah Edwards (New York: The Putnam Publishing Group, 1997).

Up Your Cash Flow by Harvey A. Goldstein (Granville Publications Software). Book and software: $139. To order, call (800) 873-7789.

The Women's Business Resource Guide: A National Directory of More than 800 Programs, Resources, and Organizations to Help Women Start or

Expand a Business, 2nd ed., by Barbara Littman (Lincolnwood, IL: NTC Publishing, 1996).

SOFTWARE

MyAdvancedInvoices & Estimates by MySoftware Company, ww.mysoftware.com; (800) 325-3508 — For estimating.

Microsoft Publisher by Microsoft, www.microsoft.com/publisher; (800) 426-9400.

MyInvoices by MySoftware Company, www.mysoftware.com.

M.Y.O.B., www.myob.com; (800) 322-MYOB — Accounting software.

Peachtree, www.peachtree.com; (800) 247-3224 — Accounting software.

Quickbooks by Intuit, www.intuit.com; (800) 446-8848.

Timeslips by Sage U.S. Inc., www.timeslips.com.

TurboTax Home & Business for Windows www.quicken.com — For sole proprietors.

WEB SITES

Biz Office, www.bizoffice.com — Look in this site's "SHBBL Library" under "C" for articles on "Customer Aftercare" and "Customer Relations."

Charge.Com, www.charge.com, specializes among firms that specialize in small and home-based operations that do business online. Call (800) 7MERCHANT [(800) 706-3724].

Electronic Clearing House, www.echo-inc.com; (800) 233-0406; 28001 Dorothy Dr., Agoura Hills, CA 91301.

SOHO Guidebook: Pricing Your Product, www.toolkit.cch.com/text/p03_5200.asp.

Women's Online Business Center's "Business Basics: 'The Finance Center,'" www.onlinewbc.gov/docs/finance — Articles and formulas to help you understand basic financial statements, cash flow, and other financial factors to help you monitor your business management.

ADDITIONAL RESOURCES

BIG E-Z Bookkeeping Company, www.bigez.com/; 37637 5 Mile Road, #217, Livonia, MI 48154-1543 — Bookkeeping books and software.

Government and Foreign Contracts and Assistance

Because government offices and agencies at all levels contract with large and small businesses for many types of products and services, it is important that you investigate to see if these opportunities are a potential market for your business. Often a certain amount of paperwork is involved in the process of seeking government contracts, including having your business "certified" at the state level to qualify you to bid on some of these job opportunities. Fortunately, there are government workers, especially at the state and federal levels, who can assist you in learning how to qualify, find, and bid successfully for such contracts with potentially profitable results.

Local

Cities, towns, townships, boroughs, counties, provinces, and territories all put out bids for various jobs to be performed at their buildings or in their jurisdictions. Jobs or projects these local government employees cannot do are usually put out for bid and published in local newspapers.

To understand how the bidding and procurement process operates, visit these offices and get a listing of what products or services they put out to bid and detailing procedures for submitting bids for contract awards. Attend the public meetings of these local government agencies to see how the meetings are conducted. To get some recommendations, talk to other business owners and/or members of business associations, such as women's business groups and chambers of commerce, who have dealt with these governments and can help guide you in the bidding process.

Of course, make sure you are registered legally as a business and have the insurances and licenses required for your business.

State

All states and territories also award contracts to qualified businesses. When you visit or contact the following offices, ask whether any special programs are available to support women's businesses. Each state varies in its offerings and programs. Here are some common sources for state procurement information:

State Senators' and Representatives' Offices: Ask for free booklets or pamphlets, plus the legislator or staff members will be glad to assist you with information.

State Departments of Commerce: Most have small business assistance centers.

Bureaus of Women Business Development: These are usually established with the department of commerce and can provide financial and procurement assistance information, sponsor business training programs, and publish and distribute resource directories and other publications. They are also advocates for women's businesses that sometimes have problems.

State Chamber of Commerce: These offices have the latest information about recent legislation affecting small business owners. Many have manuals, worksheets, and videos of startup information, and often sponsor seminars.

State Departments of Revenue (State Tax Agency): These departments have the latest information about your state income tax and sales taxes, and can answer your questions.

State Conferences: If you think your business has a statewide market, see what state publications and newspapers reach your target market and advertise in those, or attend state-sponsored entrepreneurial conferences.

SCORE Offices, Small Business Development Centers and Women Business Development Centers: These offices, which are run through the SBA, also work in conjunction with state agencies to help entrepreneurs. The SBDCs are listed in your telephone directory's white pages, and a listing of the Women's Business Centers' locations can be found on the Internet at www.online wbc.gov.

Also see the "State-by-State Information" section in the appendix, which lists the states' Web sites for additional procurement information.

Federal Small Business Assistance

Dr. Robert Sullivan, founder of the business Web site, "The Small Business Advisor," says on his site, "The United States government is the world's largest purchaser of goods and services to the tune of over $225 *billion* dollars annually, and . . . the majority of purchases are for $5,000 or less."

The federal government is the largest buyer in the world. To help make sure disadvantaged, small, and women-owned businesses qualify for a percentage of these contracts, most federal government agencies provide information and programs to help these businesses qualify. Programs and staff are available to provide counseling and assistance at local offices of SBA, SBDCs, and Women Business Development Centers are located across the country.

Dr. Sullivan, who is also the author of *United States Government, New Customer,* also says, "The federal government has numerous programs and set-asides in place to assist women-owned businesses and the best source of women-owned business information can be found at www.WomenBiz.gov. The first step for a women-owned business in selling to the federal government business is to register with PRO-Net. This is the government's contractor registry for small businesses. By registering in PRO-Net, your women-owned business is instantly accessible to every federal government contracting officer." You are encouraged to self-certify your business as a woman-owned small business (WOSM) in the SBA's PRO-Net database and may register your business online at www.pro-net.sba.gov/pro-net/register.html. Here is some additional information.

- As suggested by Dr. Sullivan, go to www.WomenBiz.gov, "The Gateway for Women-Owned Businesses Selling to the Government." This Web site covers five specific stages for women to go through as they explore selling to the government.
- At WomenBiz.gov, you can register your business with the three major federal government contractor databases: PRO-Net, Central Contractor Registration (CCR), and Electronic Posting System (EPS).
- Read the SBA Guide, "Selling to the Federal Government," on the Women's Online Business Center. This is a step-by-step guide about federal contracting. To read the complete guide online, go to the Web site: www.onlinewbc.gov/government_contracting.html.
- The SBA recently has added a new office, "Contracting Assistance for Women Business Owners." At its Web site (www.sba.gov/GC/indexprograms-cawbo.html), it provides information and answers questions about the federal certification programs. (800) U-ASK-SBA or (800) 827-5722
- www.GovCommerce.net is another Web site for federal contracting.
- Also visit or call the nearest Small Business Development Center, www.sba.gov/SBDC, nearest to you and ask for the person in charge of the "Government Marketing Assistance Program." This person can assist you in certifying your business (as minority and/or women-owned), registering your business in the "BidMatch" for finding all levels of government opportunities, and completing other contracting procedures.

Contracting with local governments may take some time until you learn about all the procedures, but the profit potential in contracting is worth the effort.

Foreign Contracts

Whether you own an established or new business or are contemplating starting a business, you may consider entering your goods and/or services into the global market. Advancements of technology and Internet connections, plus an increase in trade relations among countries, are helping small businesses to find markets the world over. Because exporting helps create new jobs and improves a country's balance of trade, most governments offer a number of free or low-cost comprehensive information and support services to promote and assist businesses in their exporting ventures.

Customs offices, some federal small business development centers, and different international trade organizations within individual countries give out helpful information on importing. Government support for importing matters is more likely when the country has joint ventures with businesses located in other countries.

PRELIMINARY CONSIDERATIONS FOR AN INTERNATIONAL BUSINESS PLAN

Whether you live in the U.S., Canada, or another country, both Canada and U.S. international trade experts offer these suggestions for what you should consider *before* you begin an international trade venture:

- *Do preliminary product research.* Research to find out whether you have the right product. If your competitor is selling a similar product overseas, perhaps you can too.
- *Research the market.* See if there is a market for your product or services in the countries to which you are interested in selling. Will your product require translations in that country's language?
- *Determine your costs.* If market research results show potential foreign markets, you then have to determine your extra trade costs, and ask yourself whether you can still sell your product(s) at a profit.
- *Study the trade process.* A very important part of mastering the trade process is learning what is required to complete the international transaction.

(*Note:* Cross-border movement of business persons is governed by chapter 16 of the NAFTA. For customs information relating to NAFTA, visit the NAFTA Web site at www.nafta-customs.org.)

EXPORTING ASSISTANCE (U.S.)

First-time exporters are urged to investigate the following:

Local: Check with your nearest chamber of commerce, city or town offices, or your county's economic development arm to see what trade offices or councils may exist. Search for non-competing businesses in your area involved in exporting to ask for referrals for assistance and tips to help you avoid mistakes they might have made.

State: Check with the U.S. state in which you live to see whether they have an office for international trade assistance or an export network.

Federal: You can access any of several Department of Commerce resources. Although the Trade Information Center is an export promotion office, it can direct importers to their local customs office for information on U.S. duties and taxes.

Please note that the agent-distributor service, while explained by the Trade Information Center (TIC), is ordered through the USEACs and EACs. The TIC provides potential exporters with the contact information for their local USEACs and EACs so that they can obtain information on the agent-distributor service there. You can access information through the U.S. Export Assistance Centers (USEAC), part of the Small Business Administration's Office of International Trade at www.sba.gov/OIT/txt/export/index.html. Almost one hundred of these centers/offices are located throughout the United States to serve firms that are ready to export and need to identify potential foreign markets, or current exporters in search of new markets. These offices can also provide information about The Export Working Capital Program (EWCP) that provides pre- and post-export working capital financing for export sales to qualifying business. The Web site URL that is listed above begins with the section, "New-to-Export Small Business" and provides important links concerning international trade.

No matter what the size of your business, international trade can be beneficial in many ways to your venture, your customers, and your country. With statistics showing an increasing number of small businesses finding overseas markets each year, you cannot afford to ignore expanding global opportunities for your business that will surely open up as we enter into the next century.

Related Resources

BOOKS

Latest editions of *Starting and Operating a Business in* . . . (there is one for each state) by Michael D. Jenkins (Grants Pass, OR: The Oasis Press). Check to see if free books are available, such as *Starting a Small Business in Pennsylvania*. Do not forget to visit your local library, which may have these books and manuals.

The Small Business Start-Up Guide: Practical Advice on Selecting, Starting and Operating a Small Business, 3rd rev. ed., by Robert Sullivan (Great Falls, VA: Information International, 2000). Look for the section entitled "State Specific Information."

United States Government—New Customer! A Step-by-Step Guide for Selling Your Product or Service to Uncle Sam by Robert Sullivan (Great Falls, VA: Information International, 1997).

E-NEWSLETTERS

BidRadar, www.bidradar.com is a contract market e-newsletter (monthly subscription fee) listing bids from federal, state, local and municipal governments.

GovCon, www.govcon.com is an information source for the government contracting industry; free newsletter, publications.

EXPO

U.S. General Services Administration — Sponsors annual expos featuring representatives from all major federal agencies and some commercial businesses where small business owners interested in doing business for the government and other companies can introduce themselves and their products and services. For more information, visit www.expo.gsa.gov/.

ORGANIZATIONS

Small Business Advisor, www.isquare.com — Includes an information section about doing business with the federal government, including a helpful question-and-answer section.

SBA Government Contracting Glossary of Terms: www.sba.gov/GC/index-glossary.html.

The Women's Business Center Online, "Government Contracting," www.onlinewbc.gov/government_contracting.html — Links to additional Web sites.

Women's Business Enterprise National Council (WBENC), 1120 Connecticut Avenue NW, Suite 950, Washington, D.C. 20036. This nonprofit organization works with U.S. women's business organizations to provide access to a national standard of certification and provides information on certified women's businesses to purchasing managers through an Internet database, WBENCLink, which can be accessed at www.wbenc.org.

WEB SITES

The International Trade Administration, www.ita.doc.gov — offers news and information, links and more about international trade, exporting and importing.

The International Trade Center, www.tradeinfo.doc.gov — Provides answers to export questions; also can call 1-800-USA TRADE; and also related export information can be found at the U.S. Government Export Portal www.export.gov/.

STAT-USA, www.stat-usa.gov/ — This is an Economics & Statistics Administration Agency (U.S. Dept. of Commerce) that offers U.S. government economic, business, and international trade information on a subscription basis. *Note:* Free access to this information is available through federal depository libraries throughout the U.S. (or contact your local SBDC office to see whether it subscribes).

United States International Trade Commission, www.usitc.gov/ — Includes independent federal agency providing news, publications, trade resources, and miscellaneous trade information generated by the Commission.

CHAPTER TEN

Going Online

The Census Bureau (www.census.gov) of the Department of Commerce (www.doc.gov) stated that the total U.S. retail e-commerce sales for 2001 were estimated at $32.6 billion, an increase of 19.3 percent from 2000. By some estimates, as of 2002, 85 percent of small firms are doing business over the Internet. And according to an SBA survey, small businesses that use the Internet for business purposes generate nearly 30 percent more revenues than those that do not. Even though some of the biggest and best known of the "dot.com" businesses closed down in 2000 and 2001, many of the smaller online businesses and home businesses with Web sites are still operating—even without the big venture capital bucks!

Patricia Cobe and Ellen Parlapiano, authors of *Mompreneurs Online* (www.mompreneursonline.com), say this:

> Since the publication of our first *Mompreneurs* book in 1996, we've watched the Internet revolutionize the way home-based moms work. Moms are using the Web to research, launch, and market their home businesses, as well as to network with clients, customers, other professionals in their field, and each other. Now more than ever, moms want better work/family balance in their lives—whether it's through launching a home-based business or linking up with companies offering flexible employment opportunities. The Internet makes it easier to achieve that balance.

PROFILE: Amy von Kaenel, founder of GenerationMom.com

Amy von Kaenel, B.A., MBA, founder of GenerationMom.com, calls herself an "accidental entrepreneur" when she started her Web site after the birth of her son. Her site caters to working moms looking for both family-friendly professions and household support. She says:

> I created GenerationMom to be a supportal for moms based on my belief that technology can play a key role in helping moms balance work and home. It's incredibly empowering to click on a mouse, then have your groceries magically appear at your doorstep. The same result can take several days' worth of nagging most husbands—and it doesn't cause marital tension. More empowering, however, is the ability to source and perform a job that is structured to respect both a woman's talent and dedication to family. GenerationMom's flexible jobs and consulting channels are the most heavily traveled. Domestic delivery is also popular as it can literally condense a day of running errands into an hour click-and-browse session.

Virtual Help for Your Home Business

Here are just a few of the many ways the Internet can help your home business:

- *A Web Site:* Costs can range from nothing—just having a few pages with your Internet service provider (ISP) to paying thousands of dollars to have someone design and host your Web site.
- *Business Web Site:* Take your time and determine the objective of your Web site. You should have ongoing information on your site—a reason for potential customers to come back.
- *Research:* Even without a Web site, the Internet offers endless market and business research opportunities.

PROFILE: Kim Essenmacher, editor, Bizpreneur News

Kim Essenmacher, the editor of *Bizpreneur News,* an e-newsletter or e-zine that comes out twice per month. Essenmacher started her online newsletter in conjunction with an entrepreneurial newsgroup, but she is now presently publishing just her e-zine. To get content, she asks authors for free tips, which they send her. She says she started the e-zine as a free resource to help others grow their businesses and to establish herself as an "accountable" (legitimate) business person in her community. Kim says, "It's a tool that opens the 'networking' door. I tell people that I publish an online e-zine that helps entrepreneurs and they ask to see a copy of it."

To subscribe, send an e-mail to: bizpreneurnews-subscribe @yahoogroups.com.

- *Business Ideas:* Searching for some home business ideas? Check out Liz Folger's site at www.bizymoms.com and Georganne Fiumara's Mother's Home Business Network at www.homeworkingmom.com. Fiumara also has a Web site for women in business, those who want to find at-home computer jobs or freelance or telecommuting jobs online, those wishing to start an online business and additional related information.
- *Source of Startup Information:* These sites have a wealth of information: The Small Business Association's Online Women's Business Center, www.onlinewbc.gov; The Business Owner's Toolkit, toolkit.cch.com.
- *Source of Financing Info:* Look for funding information at the following sites (and many others!):

Small Business Association, www.sba.gov/financing/ — Online section with information on *all* the financing programs.

Business Owner's Toolkit, www.toolkit.cch.com/ — Great books, including financing book, *Small Business Financing* and articles on business.

- *Networking Opportunities:* You can share information and find solutions to business problems by connecting with other home business owners through Web rings, chats, message boards, home business newsgroups, and at women's business sites such as these (just a few of many!):

  iVillage.com — One of the largest women's sites and also has forums discussing work-at-home issues; creating a Web page, and more.

  WholeWomen, www.wholewomen.com — Listing of women-owned businesses — Site founded by Deb Nyberg that is home to over 8,000 women in business.

  Mom's Network Exchange, www.momsnetwork.com. Offers a free Moms Network 2002 Business Directory & Resource Guide; free Home Business Matchmaker Service; and helpful information for mothers in a home business.

  The Women's Forum, www.womensforum.com — An entrepreneurial site whose mission is ". . . to provide the women's online community with the tools, resources, and relationships they need to succeed." Has over 100 women partners' sites as members.

- *Advertising and Marketing:* You can market your business with a Web site and submissions to search engines (free and for pay); e-mails, e-zines, and e-newsletters; articles and other ways to announce and promote your off- or online home business. (Also see methods below.)

- *E-mail:* The Internet literally opens the entire world for you and your business with its unlimited marketing and contact opportunities! (Also see details below.)

Internet Business Guidelines

Whether you are planning an Internet-based business or using the Internet for your home business, going online requires planning and set goals as with any venture. You can almost think of it as an "on-line, sideline" business (unless, of course, you are planning to go exclusively with a business operating on the Web). Here are some business guidelines:

PROFILE: Debbie Williams, author of *Home Management 101*

Another example of using the Internet for both marketing and networking with your business is Debbie Williams, author of *Home Management 101* and founder of OrganizedU.com. She says:

> I was in between jobs raising a toddler when I launched my professional organizing business from home. However, I shared the challenges that many of my colleagues faced in that my marketing and networking time was limited to part time at best. Unable to make sales calls, attend local professional association meetings, or the usual networking forums, I had to create my own marketing and networking efforts, or "internetworking" online. It's worked for me, and even as my business and working hours grow, I've already formed such a strong alliance online that it's made real-time leads almost effortless.

INTERNET BUSINESS PLAN

Questions: When you plan your Web site, ask yourself:

- What is the purpose of my site?
- What will be my commitment in terms of money and time?
- Who will help me?
- What kind of technology will I need?

Startup Costs: The basic cost components of your Web site will be:

- Your Equipment and Technology: This includes hardware, equipment, software applications, backup, and UPS protection devices.
- Experts' Fees: This includes Web designer, graphic designer, marketer, lawyer fees for trademark search and other legalities.
- Advertising and Promotional Fees.

You can start with the basics for your Web site to keep costs down and enlarge it as your business grows.

SEW's Suggestions

Shannan Hearne-Fortner, president of SuccessPromotions.com, on "Building Your eBusiness Better"

The most important thing to do in today's Internet marketplace is to get your own domain/URL. Don't rely on a self-replicated site like you find with affiliate programs or a page resting on the parent company's domain. It is too hard to attain high search engine rankings. And without them, you cannot get traffic to build a thriving business. You wouldn't put your brick and mortar store at the end of a never-traveled dead-end street. Don't do this with your home business either. Free pages at sites like angelfire.com are okay, but ideally a wholly owned domain is much better. It gives you a much more professional image.

Once you get traffic to your Web site, it is imperative that you have visitors bookmarking your site and joining your e-mailing list. You can attract them to do this with contests or the promise of e-mailed specials and discounts. Your site has to be easy to navigate. Your order form has to be easy to find and use.

Make sure that your Web site is clean and crisp. Floating images and cute sounds are nice, but not particularly professional looking. Content is key, too. If you want to get ranked well in the search engines, you have to put lots of appropriate keywords in both your text and your meta tags. For more Internet marketing information, you can subscribe to my free Internet marketing newsletter by sending any e-mail to: shearne-marketing-subscribe@yahoogroups.com.

Low-Cost Marketing

The advantage of using the Internet for marketing purposes is that it only requires a connection to the Internet for you to start promoting your home business. Here are a few low-cost marketing ideas:

- Take advantage of free submission on search engines.
- Participate in online chats and message boards. (Again, you have to follow protocol and not solicit business.)
- Participate in e-mail discussion groups. Through moderators and/or asking one another for help, you can be involved with others who have common interests by expressing your ideas or responding to posted questions that will have your business' signature file with your business's site, and other information in it.
- Send *invited, not unsolicited e-mail* ("spamming"), such as e-zine advertising, publishing, and discussion group participation.
- Include a business *signature* (a tagline at the end of your e-mail message) to all your customer e-mails. You can create differently worded signatures, depending on to whom you are sending it. You can add a slogan, your business's contact information, the title of a publication, the URL of your Web site, and all kinds of messages that your customers will read.
- (Without a Web site) Market your business by offering to host a newsgroup, online forum, message board, or chat session that will help to position yourself as an industry leader. You could also ask managers at other sites that your potential customers visit whether they would like to post your articles or edited chat transcript.
- Use the free publishing opportunities such as e-zines and e-newsletters at Yahoo! to stay "connected" with your customers.
- Purchase low-cost classified ads in other people's e-zines.

SECURE ORDERING

If you plan to take credit card payments, you will want a Web hosting service that provides a secure server. This will protect the directory on your site that is to receive customer-sent data that should be private. Some Web hosts include the use of a secure server in their monthly fees, while others charge extra. Buying statistics demonstrate that online customers are more likely to buy online if they can use their credit cards.

Business E-Mail

With millions of Americans having e-mail addresses today and the projections in the next five years that this number will be equaled and surpassed, a home or small business owner cannot afford to ignore e-commerce if they want to succeed with the online marketing of their ventures. The question, then, is *how* an entrepreneur can best use business e-mail for the most effective (and legitimate) results for her business. Here are some guidelines, tips, and helpful resources to help you tap into this Internet marketing medium:

Business E-Mail Use Tips

- *Avoid "spamming."* Follow, business "Netiquette," or the "rules of ethical Internet conduct" on sending business e-mails to potential customers. Sending unsolicited e-mail to persons who do not want commercial messages—spamming—can cause repercussions, such as the possible loss of credibility to your business, and possibly even resulting in your receiving "flames," which are nasty return e-mails from persons who are angry at having their e-mail privacy invaded.
- *Make sure you use the BCC (blind carbon copy) feature with any e-mail program you install.* This blocks from sight other persons' e-mail addresses, so that no one's e-mail privacy will be violated.
- *Use e-zines and e-newsletters.* Depending on your e-mail program and ISP and the number of persons on your e-mail list, you can send it out yourself, or use a listserver service like Skyweyr's Skylist (www.skylist.net) that forwards your newsletter to every subscriber on your list.
- *Conduct online market research.* As with an off-line marketing plan, before you do any advertising or direct mailing (or e-mailing), you will have to do market research to find online, prospective buyers who will actually welcome and invite your business-related e-mails. With *careful* wording to selected online newsgroups, you can offer free information to those readers who request it and get valuable feedback as to what potential customers are looking for in services and/or products.

Marketing Your Web Site

As discussed previously, marketing is ongoing; this is also true when you have a Web site for your business. How do you get visitors to your Web site amongst the millions of sites on the Internet? Here are some popular methods.

- *Banners:* Though they can be annoying to visitors, you might want to try this once to see if you get any responses.

- *E-mailing press releases:* Instead of spending money for postage, you can e-mail your press releases directly to media contact persons or take advantage of services such as the following, which e-mail your release for you (for a fee): www .businesswire.com, www.newsbureau.com, or /www.press-releases.net.

- *For-pay search engines:* Use services like Submit It! Online to announce your Web presence to search engines so you can be listed on their sites: www.submit-it.com ($59) or www.site owner.com

- *Direct e-mail marketing:* With your target market in mind, you can use your e-mail to get to them directly in the following ways:

  E-mail newsletters or e-zines. By publishing an online newsletter or e-zine, you can keep those customers who want to be on your mailing list up to date with industry tips as well as announcing your services and/or products. You can pay a company to send your list or you can use free e-mail programs like Qualcomm's Endora, www.eudora.com, or Pegasus Mail by David Harris, www.pmail.com.

  Rent "op in" e-mail lists. You can rent e-mail addresses of people who have okayed e-mail on certain subjects. It is advised, though, before you rent these lists to make sure the companies are legitimate with lists of persons who will not be angry in receiving your e-mail messages. Internet marketing experts, though, say the best list is the one you have compiled yourself through asking potential customers to join it!

Purchase e-zine advertising. E-commerce experts say this type of advertising may be even better than banner advertising as far as being cost-effective and the number of persons that can be reached. Before you pay for this advertising, make sure these ads are going to persons who are within your potential target market.

Use an autoresponder. These are e-mail addresses configured to automatically respond to information request. Place these on your Web site, in your classified ads, and other places. Web host will then provide you with a list of e-mail addresses that contacted your autoresponder.

Affiliate Programs

You can make money by being an *affiliate* (sometimes called an associate) by placing a graphic link or logo from another commercial Web site. You then get paid every time someone clicks on that commercial advertiser's link to go to their Web site. A popular user of this is the online bookstore, Amazon.com. This works best if the affiliate you have on your Web site is related to your business—a sort of online strategic partnering.

Catering to a Global Market

With the potential of the Internet to reach customers around the world, you may want to consider planning to service international customers, depending on your product and/or service. Considerations for international trade include language barriers, international shipping and customs regulations, and credit card verifications. A good book on this topic is *Internet Resources and Service for International Business* by Lewis-Guodo (Westport, CT: Oryx Press, 1998).

Related Resources

BOOKS

The Art of Self-Promotion (www.selfpromotiononline.com) by Ilise Benun (Cincinnati, OH: North Light Books, 2001).

Complete Guide to Internet Publicity by Steve O'Keefe (New York: John Wiley & Sons, Inc., 2002).

Cybergrrl: A Woman's Guide to the World Wide Web by Aliza Pilar Sherman (New York: Random House, 1998); Two others by Aliza Pilar Sherman: *Cybergrrl at Work: Tips and Inspiration for the Professional You* (New York: Berkley Publishing Group, 2001); and *Powertools for Women in Business: 10 Ways to Succeed in Life and Work* (Irvine, CA: Entrepreneur Press, 2001).

HerVenture.com: Your Guide to Expanding Your Small or Home Business to the Internet—Easily and Profitably by Priscilla Y. Huff (Roseville: Prima Communications, 2000).

How to Get Your Business on the Web: A Legal Guide to E-Commerce by Fred Steingold (Berkeley, CA: Nolo Press, 2002).

How to Write a .COM Business Plan: The Internet Entrepreneur's Guide to Everything You Need to Know about Business Plans and Financing Options by Joanne Eglash (New York: McGraw-Hill Professional, 2000).

Internet Law and Business Book by J. Dianne Brinson, Mark F. Radcliffe (Palo Alto, CA: Ladera Press, 2000).

Internet Messaging: From the Desktop to the Enterprise by Marshall Rose, David Strom (New York: Simon & Schuster Trade, 1998).

Mompreneurs Online: Using the Internet to Build Work@Home Success by Patricia Cobe and Ellen Parlapiano (New York: Perigee, 2001).

Planning Your Internet Marketing Strategy: A Doctor Ebiz Guide by Dr. Ralph F. Wilson (New York: John Wiley & Sons, 2001); www.wilsonweb.com/webmarket.

WEB SITES

www.bizweb2000.com/articles.htm — Web site by Jim Daniels, also author of *Inside Internet Marketing,* "which will teach you how to generate Web site traffic." Also offers *BizWeb E-Gazette* Internet marketing tips.

www.DrNunley.com — Web site of Dr. Kevin Nunley, Internet marketing expert (also has the site, www.BizGuru.com, with low-cost advertising strategies, etc., for "home biz workers").

www.edirect.com — Edirect Web site, a free subscription-based e-mail service.

www.everythingemail.net/emailtips.html — E-mail tips, glossary, and other relevant information.

Net Future Institute, www.netfutureinstitute.com — Research information, internet surveys. Founded by Chuck Martin, author of *Net Future* (New

York: McGraw-Hill Company, 1999) and *Max-e-Marketing in the Net Future* (New York, McGraw-Hill Company, 2001).

www.poorrichard.com — Web site information and examples of free and low-cost Web site utilities presented by Peter Kent, author of *Poor Richard's Web Site: Geek-Free, Commonsense Advice on Building a Low-Cost Web Site.*

www.sba.gov/classroom/courses.html — A six-course learning program, sponsored by the SBA and Cisco Systems, Inc., "Internet Essentials for Growing Businesses," to help small businesses that want to enter or expand into the e-commerce market.

CHAPTER ELEVEN

Planning the Future for Yourself and Your Business

S ometimes starting a home business is the easy part; the hard part is managing its growth and planning which direction to take it. Jane Mitchell, who makes a variety of cheesecakes and desserts in her business, Sweet Endings, toned her business down, even though her desserts were in demand. "I had to cut back, at least for now. I have teenage twins who both have their driving permits on top of all the other activities in which they are involved!"

As with Jane, the demands of your life and your business have to balance—at least somewhat. But, again, having a home business gives you that opportunity to pace your business so there will not be too many conflicts. Like Jane, who intends to expand her business when her twins go to college, you, too, can expand your business when your life is at a more manageable pace.

However, if you wish to grow your business, here is a tip from Diana Pemberton-Sikes, a former accountant and owner of several success-oriented Web sites, including www.NiftyBusinessideas.com; www.FashionForRealWomen.com; and www.FashionJobReview.com:

> When you start to consider expanding your business, make a game plan and break it down into "doable" pieces. While your ultimate goal may be to offer or do A through E, start with A, then go to B, then go to C, then to D, then to E. Check yourself after each step.

Trying to do too much too soon is not only overwhelming, but it can be risky. Build a solid foundation one step at a time, and alter or modify your plans as needed. Don't "bite off more than you can chew," as the saying goes. Plan for growth . . . instead of reacting to it.

Staying in Touch with Customers

Even if you have to cut back on your business's output, do not forget your faithful customers.

Denise O'Berry, small business expert and consultant (www .WhatsPossible.com), says:

> When I ask small business owners what action they are taking to keep in touch with current customers, the answer is normally "We don't." They're missing a gold mine of opportunities to make easier sales and create a loyal following of customers that will return time and again.

If you do not let your customers forget you, you will have a good base from which to launch "Phase II" of your business when you are ready to grow and expand.

Monitoring Trends and Future Trends

Whether you cut back on your business's output or "step it up," a big factor in whether a business survives or not is how well it keeps up with current trends and prepares for future ones. You can keep up by reading trade and general business publications, soliciting your customers' feedback on a regular basis, and listening to what futurists like Hazel Henderson, Faith Popcorn, Gerald Celente, Chuck Martin, and others known for their business foresight are saying about business trends now and later.

Home businesses have changed from twenty years ago and will be different twenty years from now. Stacy and Richard Henderson, publishers/editors of *Home Business Magazine* for nine years, have seen these changes, as they have grown their publication while balancing a home life with five children.

In answer to the question, "How has the home business 'scene' changed from when you first began *HBM* to the present day?" Stacy Henderson says this:

At the time of the magazine's founding in 1994, the home business "scene" was only beginning to emerge as a major economic marketplace and demographic force. Up until the early '90s, home businesses were primarily small micro-businesses such as mail-order endeavors, small business opportunities, network marketing opportunities, small services businesses, craft assembly, and those operated by professionals such as writers and small-time consultants.

After the early 1990s, however, the home business scene changed as the workplace began to revolutionize. Personal computers became affordable and powerful enough to operate a home business. Office equipment that greatly increased productivity became affordable, including fax machines, small copiers, scanners, and cellular phones.

The home business scene has also changed due to the Internet and e-mail dramatically improving communication and information management capabilities. In the mid '90s, millions of downsized-out corporate professionals began to use this technology to work independently as consultants, which has increased the quality and productivity of the home business sector.

Today's more positive outlook toward the home business scene has expanded telecommuting opportunities for those working for corporations. Corporate managers are more open to offering such opportunities, and corporate workers are more frequently proposing telecommuting to their managers.

No matter whether the economy is good or poor, the number of home businesses continues to grow and does not look like it will slow down any time soon.

Selling or Stopping Your Business

Should you come to the point that you wish to sell or stop your business, you may want to consider several factors. One of these is the value of your business. The selling value of a one-person service or small product business is typically lower than the value of a larger business. Business experts recommend you work on establishing a business on its own before you think of selling it for profit. If you have a partner, she may offer to buy out your share. Plan ahead if you are entertaining the thought of selling your business to reap the best benefits from such a sale.

You may have mixed feelings in selling or stopping your business, as did Aliza Pilar Sherman, author (*Cybergrrl* and *Power Tools for Women*), technology expert, and founder of several Internet Web sites, including RVgirl (www.rvgirl.com). Sherman says:

> When I started an Internet consulting company from my home in 1995, the "early days," I only wanted to be able to pay my bills. Cybergrrl, Inc. was my "baby," born of my ideas and my love of the Internet.
>
> By the time I realized we had to move into an office space, I was getting anxious. My "baby" was becoming a restless toddler and was consuming all of my money. When the business began to attract attention, I was torn. On the one hand, we were getting more clients, which is great for any business. On the other hand, I felt as if I was losing control and being forced into an administrative and management role, something I had never expected.
>
> Eventually, I think I held on too tightly, mostly out of fear of growth and change, and probably prevented my business from reaching its full potential. By the time I was ready to let it go and grow, the entire market had changed and it was no longer as attractive to investors or potential buyers as it once was.
>
> I learned that I had put too much of the wrong kind of emotion into the process of building a business. You have to have passion and fire, but always remember that your business is not YOU.

Dealing with Family Business Issues

Families have always worked together in joint-owned businesses throughout our country's history. Theirs is a unique situation with

its own set of problems and also always facing "who is going to in-
herit the family business." A good publication that covers these issues is *Family Business Magazine*. Visit its Web site (www.family
businessmagazine.com) for more information.

Growing Through a Business Incubator

If your home business has been operating a year or more and, by all
your projected cash flow estimates and financial forecasts, it appears
your home is getting *too small* for your business, then you might
want to consider applying to a business incubator as the next step in
growing your business. Business incubators consist primarily of two
types: "mixed-use"—those serving a diversity of businesses—and in
recent years new "niche" incubators that have been formed, such
as "kitchen" incubators for small food-related businesses, and
e-business "hatcheries" like the Women's Technology Cluster
(WTC), www.womenstechcluster.org, that have been formed to support growth and find funding for women technology entrepreneurs..

In order to qualify to be included in a business incubator, you
must fill out an application and submit a business plan and fulfill
other requirements. The usual term of involvement for a business is
around three years, when you will be expected to move on. Contact
the National Business Incubation Association for a list of member
incubators.

Retirement: Issues, Options, Planning

An important factor many new entrepreneurs often overlook is
planning for their retirement. New business owners tell themselves
they will formulate a financial plan when their business's profits
become substantial. However, they may not realize that most retirement planning experts estimate that each of us will need
around 60 to 80 percent of our present annual income to support
every one of our retirement years! Fortunately, movements like the

recent legislation, the Taxpayer Relief Act of 1997, and a 1998 joint campaign by the former National Association of Women Business Owners (NAWBO; now the Center for Women's Business Research) and the Department of Labor to educate women entrepreneurs about retirement savings plans are encouraging more women business owners to establish retirement plans. Why else should a small business owner or self-employed woman set aside money for retirement? Once you have committed to starting a savings retirement plan, where do you go next?

- First, consult with a financial adviser before you select any plan. Ask your accountant, another woman business owner, your banker, or members of a business association to which you may belong for names of qualified advisers they recommend. These experts advise you how best to use your retirement funds and how you should withdraw that money. (Take advantage of IRAs even if you have a 401(k) plan where you work. The savings can add up.)
- Next, take a realistic look into the future to estimate the amount you will need to maintain your expected standard of living and then set your goals accordingly. Make sure you diversify your retirement money to balance the ups and downs of investing.

With these figures in hand, you will be better able to choose the best plan for you.

Working with Disabilities

The SBA says that many people with disabilities and chronic health conditions are starting businesses at twice the rate of people who do not have physical or mental challenges.

Improvement in technology and equipment, passage of laws like the American Disabilities Act of 1990, and more awareness of the needs of differently-abled persons have helped give impetus to this movement.

If you or a loved one has a disability, you may be eligible for funding or counseling to get you started in a home venture. Contact your nearest Small Business Development Center (www.sba.gov/SBDC) for information on available programs sponsored by the federal government and also the state in which you live. Below are some resources to assist you.

Redefining Self-Employment

Diana Pemberton-Sikes, a former accountant and owner of several success-oriented Web sites—including www.NiftyBusinessideas .com; www.FashionForRealWomen.com; and www.FashionJob Review.com—sums up women entrepreneurs very well with this statement:

> I believe women are constantly redefining what's acceptable in small and home-based businesses. From flexible schedules to telecommuting, women are finding ways to "get the job done" in response to the other pressures in their life. They're making money when it's convenient for them, not when someone else says they should be doing it. I think you'll continue to see a lot more of this in years to come as the number of home-based businesses skyrockets and work-at-home moms gain more legitimacy.

May you, too, join this exciting movement of self-employed women operating profitable and satisfying home or small businesses while enjoying those you care about most!!

Related Resources

ASSOCIATION

National Business Incubation Association, 20 E. Circle Drive, Suite 190 Athens, OH 45701-3571; (740) 593 4331 ; e-mail: info@nbia.org; Web site: www.nbia.org.

BOOKS

No More Job Interviews: Self-Employment Strategies for People with Disabilities by Alice Weiss Doyel (St. Augustine, FL: Training Resource Network, Inc., 2000).

Unlikely Entrepreneurs: A Complete Guide to Business Start-ups for People with Disabilities and Chronic Health Conditions by Roseanne Herzog (North Peak Publishing, 1999).

EXPO

Abilities EXPO, www.abilitiesexpo.com — Sponsors expos featuring assisted living products and services in designate U.S. states.

TECHNOLOGY

AbleLink Technologies: www.ablelinktech.com.

Dynavox Systems LLC, www.dynavoxsys.com, 2100 Wharton Street, Suite 400, Pittsburgh, PA 15203; speech output devices and technology.

TREND EXPERTS

Gerald Celente of The Trends Research Institute: www.TrendsResearch.com.

Faith Popcorn, author of *Clicking:* www.BrainReserve.com.

Hazel Henderson, independent futurist, lecturer, and author of *Globalization:* www.HazelHenderson.com.

Chuck Martin, chairman of Net Future Institute and author of *Net Future:* www.NetFutureInstitute.com.

WEB SITES

Bold Business Consultants, www.bold-owners.com/ — Resources, consulting services, about entrepreneurship for people with disabilities. Web site provides other helpful information and links.

The Boulevard, www.blvd.com — A disability resource site containing information on products, resources, publications, employment opportunities more.

The Cure Network, Inc., www.cure.org — Nonprofit organization, training programs.

www.dol.gov/dol/odep/, Office of Disability Employment Policy — Web site provides link to The Small Business and Self-Employment Service (SBSES), part of the U.S. DOL's Office of Disability Employment Policy, which provides information, counseling, and referrals about self-employment and small business ownership opportunities for people with disabilities.

www.onlinewbc.gov/women_with_disabilities.html — Women's Business Online section offering "Women with Disabilities," an illustrated guide of how businesses can make services accessible for people with disabilities. This site also includes information about tax credits and deductions that may be used to offset specific costs. Find this resource and more at: www.sba.gov/ada/.

www.ssa.gov, Social Security Adminstration — Information about Social Security's disability programs.

www.va.gov — U.S. Department of Veteran Affairs. The VA offers loan programs to qualified veterans.

World Institute on Disabilities, www.wid.org — An internationally recognized public policy center organized by and for people with disabilities.

ORGANIZATIONS

National Organization on Disability, www.nod.org; 910 16th St., NW, Ste. 600, Washington, D.C. 20006; News, advocacy organization for persons of all ages with disabilities.

National Rehabilitation Information Center, www.naric.com/ 4200 Forbes Boulevard, Suite 202, Lanham, MD 20706 — Funded by the National Institute on Disability and Rehabilitation Research (NIDRR) to serve those interested in disability and rehabilitation.

Disabled Business Persons Association, www.disabledbusiness.com/ 9625 Black Mountain Rd., Ste. 207, San Diego, CA 92126-4564 — Nonprofit organization.

Worldwide Association of Disabled Entrepreneurs, Inc. (WADE), www.ably yours.freeyellow.com/index.html; membership fee.

RESOURCES

Unless otherwise noted, please send a long (business-size), self-addressed, stamped envelope (LSASE) if you contact any of these listings through the mail.

ASSOCIATIONS:
MOTHERS, WORK-AT-HOME MOMS, PARENTS

Home-Based Working Moms (HBWM), www.hbwm.com; www.workathomekit.com/ (Work-at-Home "kit"); P.O. Box 500164, Austin, TX 78750. For moms (and dads) working from home. Offers newsletter, networking information, and more.

Mother's Home Business Network, www.homeworkingmom.com; P.O. Box 423; East Meadow, NY 11554. Home business guidance; newsletter and resource guide.

ASSOCIATIONS: HOME BUSINESS/SMALL BUSINESS

American Association of Home Based Businesses, www.aahbb.org; P.O. Box 10023, Rockville, MD 20849. "A national, nonprofit association dedicated to the support and advocacy of home-based businesses." Does not sell or endorse any business opportunities.

Home Office Association of American, www.hoaa.com; P.O. Box 51, Sagaponack, NY 11962-0051; (212) 588-9097. A national organization "dedicated to serving home-based and small business professionals." Includes newsletter, group savings on health insurance, and other membership benefits; $49 U.S./$79 Canada.

Small Office Home Office Association International (SOHOA), www.SOHOA.com; 1765 Business Center Drive, Suite 100 Reston, VA 20190-5326. "Specialize in providing products and services to our members—the small office and home office professionals—that will help them run a more effective and successful business."

SOHO America, Inc., www.soho.org; P.O. Box 941, Hurst, Texas 76053-094. Offers online resource and virtual community for owners of small businesses, home-based businesses, telecommuters and other work-from-home persons. Free membership.

ASSOCIATIONS:
BUSINESS OWNERSHIP (MEN AND WOMEN)

The U.S. Chamber of Commerce, www.uschamber.com; 1615 H Street, NW, Washington, D.C. 20062-2000; (202) 659-6000. One of the largest business ownership organizations in the U.S. Search their Web site for local chambers near you (also a directory of chambers by state), or look in your local telephone directory for a listing.

National Association for the Self-Employed, www.nase.org; 2121 Precinct Line Rd., Hurst, TX 76054; (800) 232-6273. Offers health insurance and other benefits to members.

ASSOCIATIONS: TRADE

For listings, check the reference sections of public and college libraries for the current editions of these directories.

Encyclopedia of Associations, current edition (Detroit, MI: Gale Research), www.gale.com.

National Trade and Professional Associations of the United States, published annually by Columbia Books, Inc., 1212 New York Ave. NW, Suite 303, Washington, D.C. 20005.

(*Note:* Trade associations in your industry may or may not have startup business information, but they do provide members with networking opportunities [trade shows, conventions], current publications [newsletters, journals, guides], marketing information, assorted benefits, legislative advocacy in behalf of the industry, future outlooks and trends for your industry, and more. Research to see which ones best suit your home business needs.)

ASSOCIATIONS: SPECIAL INTEREST

Women's Business Enterprise National Council (WBENC), www.wbenc.org; 1120 Connecticut Avenue, NW, Suite 950, Washington, D.C. 20036. This nonprofit organization works with U.S. women's business organizations to provide access to a national standard of certification and provides information on certified women's businesses to purchasing managers through an Internet database: WBENCLink.

ASSOCIATIONS, BUSINESS OWNERSHIP (WOMEN'S)

American Women's Economic Development Corp. (AWED), www.awed.org; 216 E. 45th Street, 10th Floor, New York, NY 10017. Committed to helping women start and grow their own businesses. Based in New York City but also works with organizations, both in the U.S. and internationally, that want to develop programs for women entrepreneurs based on the AWED models.

National Association of Women Business Owners (NAWBO), www.nawbo.org; 1411 K St. N.W., Ste. 1350 Washington, D.C. 20005. National organization exclusively for women business owners with chapters in many major U.S. cities.

The National Association for Female Executives (NAFE), www.nafe.com/; P.O. Box 469031, Escondido, CA 92046-9925; (800) 643-NAFE.

U.S. Women's Chamber of Commerce, www.uswomenschamber.com; 2415 E. Camelback Road, Ste. 940; Phoenix, AZ 85016; (888) 96-WOMEN; promotes leadership, economic growth, leadership training, and other related member benefits and programs. e-mail: info@uswomenschamber.com

Women Incorporated (WI), www.womeninc.org/; 8522 National Blvd., Suite 107, Culver City, CA 90232. "A national nonprofit organization designed to improve the business environment for women through access to capital, credit, business discounts and products, and financial services."

BUSINESS, NONPROFIT FOUNDATIONS

The Center for Women's Business Research, www.womensbusinessresearch .org, 1411 K St. NW, Ste. 1350; Washington, D.C. 20005. Founded originally as the National Foundation for Women Business Owners; provides original research to document the economic and social contributions of women-owned firms.

Count-Me-In (for Women's Economic Independence), www.count-me-in.org. An Internet-based microloan fund for aspiring women entrepreneurs (see Financing).

Edward Lowe Foundation, www.lowe.org; 51990 Decatur Rd., Cassiopolis, MI 49031. Founded by Edward Lowe, inventor of "Kitty Litter." Offers online publications and informative and helpful articles for entrepreneurs through "Business Builders" and "Find Your Edge: 1,415 Ideas to Help Grow Your Company."

Kauffman Foundation, www.entreworld.org; Kauffman Center for Entrepreneurial Leadership, at the Ewing Marion Kauffman Foundation, 4801 Rockhill Rd., Kansas City, MO 64110. The Kauffman Foundation's "A

World of Resources for Entrepreneurs," featuring their listing of best resources for small-business owners.

The Women's Alliance, 374 Northeast 171st St., Ste. 62, Miami, FL 33160. A national organization of independent community-based members who provide professional attire, career skills training and related services to low-income women seeking employment.

BOOKS

Best Home Businesses for the 21st Century: The Inside Information You Need to Know to Select a Home-Based Business That's Right for You, 3rd ed., by Paul and Sarah Edwards (New York, The Putnam Publishing Group, 1999).

C-E-O & MOM: Same Time, Same Place by Rochelle B. Balch (Glendale, AZ: RB Balch Associates, Inc., 1997).

The Complete Idiot's Guide to Starting a Home-Based Business by Barbara Weltman (Indianapolis, IN: Alpha Books, 1997).

Homemade Money: How to Select, Start, Manage, Market and Multiply the Profits of a Business at Home, 5th ed., by Barbara Brabec (Cincinnati, OH: F & W Publications, 1997).

Women's Home-Based Business Book of Answers: 78 Important Questions Answered by Top Women Business Leaders by Maria T. Bailey (Roseville, CA: Prima Communications, 2001).

The Work-at-Home Mom's Guide to Home Business: Stay at Home and Make Money with Wahm.com by Cheryle Demas (Naples, FL: Hazen Pub. Inc., 2000).

BOOKS AND GUIDES THROUGH THE MAIL

The New Careers Center, *Whole Work Catalog,* 1515-23rd St., P.O. Box 339-CT, Boulder, CO 80306. Books on specific businesses and careers.

Small Business Bookstore, www.smallbizbooks.com; (800) 421-2300. *Entrepreneur Magazine's* (Entrepreneur Media) selection of specific business startup guides and software. Call for guide information or visit the Web site.

ONLINE BOOKSTORES

Amazon.com, www.amazon.com.

Barnes & Noble, www.barnesandnoble.com.

Borders Books, www.borders.com.

INTERNET SITES

Mothers, Women's Business, Work-at-Home, Telecommuting Information

www.BizyMoms.com — Founded by author Liz Folger; offers home business ideas, e-books, chats.

www.BlueSuitMom.com — Founded by Maria Bailey; tips and advice for the working mother.

www.GenerationMom.com — Founded by Amy von Kaenel; career and work-at-home information.

Business@Home, www.gohome.com —- Provides home business information with About.com.

DigitalWomen, www.digital-women.com — "Digital Women was founded to create a place for women from all over the world to come and gather resources, business advice and tips, marketing tips, sales techniques and any other business tools they need to aid them in their success."

EWorkingWomen, www.EWorkingWomen.com — Created for women in business and for those who just want to find jobs online. It was founded by Georganne Fiumara, also the founder of the Mother's Home Business Network, www.homeworkingmom.com; work-at-home ideas and jobs.

www.HerPlanet.com — Dottie Gruhler's site. A network of sites geared toward women's issues and their lives; including a business.

The Women's Network, *iVillage,* www.iVillage.com/work/index.html — This is a comprehensive informational site for women including profiles of successful women business owners, weekly chats with *Mompreneurs* Patricia Kobe and Ellen H. Parlapiano, plus articles and message boards for home businesses.

www.MomsNetwork.com — Founded by Cyndi Webb and offers tools, resources, and networking to support moms working at home.

Myria "The Magazine for Mothers," www.Myria.com — Includes eighty discussion boards and features including home business articles to "enlighten, inform, and encourage moms everywhere."

The Telecommuting Jobs Page, www.tjobs.com. Lists positions at companies looking for home-based workers. (Check for references before signing any contracts.)

The Online Magazine for Work at Home Moms, edited by Cheryl Demas, www.WAHM.com.

www.WomensForum.com — One of the leading online communities with women's partner sites.

www.WomensEnews.org — Women's current social and business news.

www.WorkingSolo.com — Web site of Terri Lonier, author of *Working Solo* and other helpful small business books.

Women's Business

IBM Women's Business Center, www.ibm.com/smallbusiness/women — Resources and special offers for women entrepreneurs; online courses; and additional information.

GOVERNMENT

Federal Government Portal, FirstGov: www.firstgov.gov/.

Federal: Women-Related

The National Women's Business Council, www.nwbc.gov; 409 3rd St., S.W., Ste. 210, Washington, D.C. 20024; (202) 205-3850. A federal government advisory panel created to serve as an independent source of advice and counsel to the president and Congress on issues of importance to women entrepreneurs.

Office of Women's Business Ownership, www.sba.gov/womeninbusiness/; (202) 205-6673.

U.S. Department of Labor, www.dol.gov/wb/; Women's Bureau, JFK Federal Bldg, Rm E-270, Boston, MA 02203.

Federal: General

U.S. Small Business Administration, www.sba.gov/; 409 Third St., SW, Sixth Floor, Washington, D.C. 20416.

Business Information Centers (BICs), (800) 827-5722. Operated by the SBA offices located in some U.S. cites, which offer state-of-the-art technology, informational resources, and on-site counseling.

Service Corps of Retired Executives (SCORE), www.score.org; (800) 634-0245. A national organization sponsored by the SBA of volunteer business executives who provide free business counseling and seminars.

U.S. Patent and Trademark Office, www.uspto.gov; Crystal Plaza 3, Rm 2C02, Washington, D.C. 20231; (703) 308-4357.

U.S. Copyright Office, www.loc.gov/copyright/.

The U.S. Census Bureau, www.census.gov — Has CenStats, a fee-based subscription service on the Internet that can help you find the demographics
of certain populations and areas, which will help you in market research.
For more information, call (301) 457-4100.

Consumer Product Safety Commission (CPSC) Publications Request, Washington, D.C. 20207. The CPSC offers guidelines for product safety requirements.

The U.S. Department of Agriculture (USDA), www.usda.gov/, 12th St. and Independence Ave. SW.

Washington, D.C. 20250. The USDA offers publications on selling to the
USDA. Its county extension offices (one in every county in the U.S.) also
offers publications and programs on entrepreneurship. Contact the office
in your county for more information.

The U.S. Department of Commerce (DOC), www.doc.gov; Office of Business
Liaison, 14th St. and Constitution Ave., NW Room 5898C, Washington,
D.C. 20230. Provides listings of business opportunities available in the
federal government and refers businesses to different programs and services in the DOC and other federal agencies.

U.S. Environmental Protection Agency (EPA), www.epa.gov; Ariel Rios Bldg.,
1200 Pennsylvania Ave. NW, Washington, D.C. 20460; (202) 260-2090;
The EPA offers more than 100 publications designed to help small businesses understand how they can comply with EPA regulations.

U.S. Food and Drug Administration (FDA) Center for Food Safety and Applied
Nutrition, www.fda.gov, 5600 Fishers Lane, Rockville, MD 20857-0001.
The FDA offers information on packaging and labeling requirements for
food and food-related products.

U.S. Postal Service, www.usps.com. — Calculate postage rates online; small
business tools.

U.S. Business Advisor, www.business.gov. — Provides business with one-stop
access to federal government information, services, and transactions.

DIRECTORIES

Telephone

National Toll-Free & Internet Yellow Pages: "Shopper's Guide," www.inter-
nettollfree.com.

National Toll-Free & Internet Yellow Pages: Businesses Buyer's Guide,
www.internettollfree.com.

HOME STUDY: CORRESPONDENCE

Distance Education and Training Council (DETC), www.detc.org; 1601 18th St. NW, Washington, D.C. 20009-2529. Write for a brochure of schools offering home study courses or search the Web site.

Graduate School USDA (U.S. Department of Agriculture), www.grad.usda .gov/, Ag Box 9911, Room 1112, South Agriculture Bldg., 14th St. & Independence Ave. SW, Washington, D.C. 20250-9911. Correspondence courses on accounting, auditing, editing, library technology, and others. Write for a copy of their current course offerings or visit the Web site.

Government Publications of Interest to Small Business

These are available from the Government Printing Office (GPO), which sells them through GPO bookstores located in over twenty-four major cities and listed in the Yellow Pages under the "bookstore" heading. You can request a "Subject Bibliography" by writing to the GPO, Superintendent of Documents, Washington, D.C. 20402-9328, or GPO, P.O. Box 3719754, Pittsburgh, PA 15250-7954.

The Consumer Information Catalog, P.O. Box 100, Pueblo, CO 81002. This is a catalog of free and low-cost federal publication, including the *Resource Directory for Small Business Management,* which lists home and small business publications. Write for a catalog or visit the Web site at www.pueblo.gsa.gov.

MAGAZINES: BUSINESS, HOME BUSINESS, WOMEN'S

Look for the print magazines and others on home and small business topics at your local newsstand or independent or chain bookstore (such as Barnes & Noble, Borders Books, Walden Books).

Business

Entrepreneur Magazine, www.entrepreneur.com.

Small Business Success, www.SmallBizPartners.com — Annual publication distributed free by Pacific Bell Directory in partnership with a team of corporations, Southwestern Bell Yellow Pages, and the SBA. Partners for Small Business Excellence; Editorial Offices: Pacific Bell Directory, Communication Dept. CWS13, 101 Spear St., Rm 429, San Francisco, CA 94105; (800) 848-8000. Site features excellent business-related articles and resources published in the annual magazine.

Opportunity World, oppworld@aol.com; 28 Vesey St., #257, New York, NY 10007-2701.

Spare Time Magazine, www.spare-time.com; Kipen Pblg. Corp., 2400 S. Commerce Drive, Milwaukee, WI 53151.

Home Business

Home Business Magazine, www.homebusinessmag.com; United Marketing and Research, Company, Inc., 9061 Five Harbors Dr., Huntington Beach, CA 92646. Articles and information for home-based entrepreneurs and others who work from home.

Home Business Journal, www.HOMEBusinessJournal.net; 9584 Main St., Holland Patent, NY 13354. "Serving the needs of home-based entrepreneurs . . ."

HomeBusinessReport, www.homebusinessreport.com (See Canadian Resources in the Appendices.)

Women

Enterprising Women Magazine, 1135 Kildare Farm Rd., Ste. 200, Cary, NC 27511; e-mail: ewomenmagazine@aol.com — Excellent articles and information for women business owners.

Working Mother, www.workingwoman.com/; Working Mother, P.O. Box 5240, Harlan, IA 51593-2740. U.S.: 1 year (10 issues) for $9.97; Canada, $21.97. (*Working Woman* magazine is now part of the *Working Mother* publication.)

PRODUCTS

Computer Hardware

Apple Computer, Inc. www.apple.com.

Dell, www.dell.com/dell4biz; P.O. Box 224588, Dallas, TX 75222-4588.

IBM, Inc. www.ibm.com.

Gateway www.gateway.com.

Office Supplies

Office Depot, www.officedepot.com — Order office supplies; also a comprehensive "Small Business Center," with business tools and news.

Kinko's, www.kinkos.com — You can electronically transmit documents from your home office to Kinko's.

Staples, www.staples.com — office supplies, furniture, business services.

Business Forms, Checks, Labels, Tags

NEBS, Inc., www.nebs.com; 500 Main St., Groton, MA 01471; (800) 225-9540; business forms, products, services.

RapidForms, www.rapidforms.com; 301 Grove Rd., Thorofare, NJ 08086-9499; (800) 257-83354; checks, envelopes, forms, cards, promotional products.

Containers, Boxes, Bags, Packing Tissue

Cornell Paper & Box Co., Inc., Robbins Container Corp.,www.cornellrobbins.com/ 222 Conover St., Brooklyn, NY 11231; (888) 251-1297.

Office Supplies

PENNY-WISE Office Products, www.penny-wise.com; 6911 Laurel Bowie Rd., Suite 209, Bowie, MD 20715.

Quill Office Products, www.quillcorp.com; Quill Corp., 100 Schelter Rd., Lincolnshire, IL 60069-3621.

VIKING Office Products, www.vikingop.com; 950 W. 190th St., Torrance, CA 90502; (800) 421-1222.

Papers (Desktop Publishing, Certificates, Business Stationery, Etc.)

Paper Showcase, www.papershowcase.com, P.O. Box 8465, Mankato, MN 56002-8465.

Premier Papers, Inc., P.O. Box 64785, St. Paul, MN 55164.

Computers, Software, and Related Equipment

CDW Computer Centers, Inc., www.cdw.com; 200 N. Milwaukee Ave., Vernon Hills, IL 60061; Print, online: 1720 Oak St., P.O. Box 3014, Lakewood, NJ 08701-5926.

Nationwide Supplier of Computer Products, www.cyberguys.com — Catalog (print, online) 1-800-892-1010.

Global Computer Supplies, www.globalcomputer.com; 11 Harbor Park Dr., Dept. ZA, Port Washington, NY 11050. Print, online.

MicroWAREHOUSE, www.warehouse.com — Computers, scanners, much more.

RADIO AND TV

Small Business School, www.sb2000.com — PBS TV series on small business issues. Crown Financial Ministries, www.crown.org; 601 Broad St. SE,

Gainesville, GA 30501-3729. Has various radio shows around the country on finances including small business topics. Visit the Web site for locating a station near to you.

For Vendors

Home Shopping Network, www.hsn.com; One HSN Dr., St. Petersburg, FL 33729. Write for information for selling your products.

QVC/Vendor Relations, www.qvc.com; 1385 Enterprise Dr. West Chester, PA 19380. Write for information for selling your products.

Videos

"Home-Based Business: A Winning Blueprint," SBA Publications, P.O. Box 46521, Denver, CO 80201.

VIRTUAL EDUCATION

Dell's "Educate U," www.dell.com — Online university offering 900 subjects.

MBA, www.getmymba.com — Fully accredited online program offered by Jones Intl. University.

NAWBO's "Internet-Supplied Training," www.nawbo.org — Available through Tutorial.com from IBM.)

MISCELLANEOUS SOURCES

Company Information: Contracting Number

Dun & Bradstreet, www.dnb.com/, One Diamond Hill Rd., Murray Hill, NJ 07974; (866) 719-7158. Can provide background reports on businesses (contact for fees); and a free D-U-N-S number, which is part of D & B's Data Universal Numbering System that allows you, among other things, to gain a federal contract by registering with the government's Central Contractor Register (CCR). Also sells "Resource Toolkit" for business owners, which includes merchant status to accept credit cards, business forms and agreements, business publications, Website trial offer, and more.

APPENDICES

State-by-State Information: Web Sites

(*Note:* These U.S. States' Web sites are good places to help you find information about starting businesses in the respective states, about state agencies and contact names that handle industry licensing and regulations, and about contract information. Visit your local state representative's and state senator's office to find additional information for small and women-owned businesses. Introduce yourself to your legislators and staff and inform them about your business. They could provide you with some good business leads, as well as assist you through any bureaucratic mazes or "roadblocks.")

State	Capital	Zip Code	Web Site Address
Alabama	Montgomery	36132	http://www.state.al.us/
Alaska	Juneau	99801	http://www.state.ak.us/
Arizona	Phoenix	85007	http://www.az.gov/ webapp/portal/
Arkansas	Little Rock	72201	http://www.state.ar.us/
California	Sacramento	95814	http://www.ca.gov/
Colorado	Denver	80203	http://www.state.co.us/
Connecticut	Hartford	06106	http://www.state.ct.us/
Delaware	Dover	19901	http://delaware.gov/
Florida	Tallahassee	32399	http://www.firn.edu/
Georgia	Atlanta	30334	http://www.state.ga.us/
Hawaii	Honolulu	96813	http://gov.state.hi.us/
Idaho	Boise	83720	http://www.state.id.us/
Illinois	Springfield	62706	http://www100.state.il.us/
Indiana	Indianapolis	46204	http://www.state.in.us/

Iowa	Des Moines	50319	http://www.state.ia.us/
Kansas	Topeka	66612	http://www.accesskansas.org/
Kentucky	Frankfort	40601	http://www.kydirect.net/
Louisiana	Baton Rouge	70821	http://www.state.la.us/
Maine	Augusta	04333	http://www.state.me.us/
Maryland	Annapolis	21401	http://www.state.md.us/
Massachusetts	Boston	01103	http://www.mass.gov/portal/index.jsp
Michigan	Lansing	48909	http://www.michigan.gov/
Minnesota	St. Paul	55155	http://www.state.mn.us/
Mississippi	Jackson	39201	http://www.ms.gov/
Missouri	Jefferson City	65010	http://www.state.mo.us/
Montana	Helena	59620	http://www.mt.gov/css/default.asp
Nebraska	Lincoln	68509	http://www.state.ne.us/
Nevada	Carson City	89701	http://silver.state.nv.us/
New Hampshire	Concord	03301	http://www.state.nh.us/
New Jersey	Trenton	08625	http://www.state.nj.us/
New Mexico	Sante Fe	87504	http://www.state.nm.us/
New York	Albany	12207	http://www.state.ny.us/
North Carolina	Raleigh	27602	http://www.ncgov.com/
North Dakota	Bismarck	58501	http://discovernd.com/
Ohio	Columbus	43215	http://www.state.oh.us/
Oklahoma	Oklahoma City	73105	http://www.oklaosf.state.ok.us/
Oregon	Salem	97301	http://www.oregon.gov/
Pennsylvania	Harrisburg	17126	http://www.state.pa.us/PAPower/; and its site for doing business in PA: www.paopen4business.state.pa.us

Rhode Island	Providence	02903	http://www.state.ri.us/
South Carolina	Columbia	29211	http://www.myscgov.com
South Dakota	Pierre	57501	http://www.state.sd.us/
Tennessee	Nashville	37201	http://www.state.tn.us/
Texas	Austin	78701	http://www.texas.gov/
Utah	Salt Lake City	84114	http://www.utah.gov/
Vermont	Montpelier	05609	http://www.state.vt.us/
Virginia	Richmond	23219	http://www.state.va.us/
Washington	Olympia	98504	http://access.wa.gov/
West Virginia	Charleston	25305	http://www.state.wv.us/
Wisconsin	Madison	53702	http://www.wisconsin.gov/state/home
Wyoming	Cheyenne	82001	http://www.state.wy.us/

Canadian Resources

For a database of companies and examination of the Canadian government's business strategies in industries and trade statistics, see Courtesy of Industry Canada's Strategis Web site: www.strategis.ic .gc.ca/SSG/er00017e.html (associations).

ASSOCIATIONS

Canadian Women's Business Network
3995 MacIssac Drive
Nanaimo, British Columbia
Canada V9T 3V5
Web site: www.cdnbizwomen.com

**Women Business Owners of Canada/
Femmes Proprietaires du Canada, Inc.**
20 York Mills Road, Suite 100
York Mills, Ontario
Canada M2P 2C2
Web site: www.wboc.ca

Women Entrepreneurs of Canada
Toronto Chapter & Head Office
169 Eastern Avenue, Toronto ON M5L 1H7
Web site: www.wec.ca/

BOOKS

Building a Dream: A Canadian Guide to Starting Your Own Business, 4th ed.,
by Walter S. Good (Whitby, Ontario: McGraw-Hill Ryerson, Ltd., 2000).

Internet Law and Business Handbook by Dianne Brinson and Mark F. Radcliffe
(Menlo Park, CA; Ladera Press, 2000); Web site: www.laderapress.com.
Includes information about Canadian e-commerce laws.

BUSINESS SERVICES

Canada/British Columbia Business Services
601 West Cordova Street
Vancouver, British Columbia
Canada V6B 1G1
(604) 775 5525
Web site: www.smallbusinessbc.ca/

"The mandate of the Canada/British Columbia Business Services is to serve as
the primary source of timely and accurate business-related information and referrals on federal and provincial government programs, services and regulations, without charge."

GOVERNMENT

Canada Business Service Centres
Web site: www.cbsc.org/ — Provides contact information for each province
and territory.

The Canada Business Service Centres (CBSCs) provide a wide range of information on government services, programs, and regulations, and answer questions about starting a new business or improving an existing one.

INTERNET SITES

Strategis
Web site: www.strategis.ic.gc.ca/
Strategis is produced by Industry Canada, a department of the federal govern-
ment; a valuable resource of information for consumers and businesses; in-

cludes information and guides on starting, financing a business, exporting, and other pertinent issues of having a business in Canada.

Canada.com
Web site: www.canada.com
Canadian information and news portal, including a business directory.

CanadaOne Web site: www.canadaone.com/
An online magazine for Canadian small businesses that features a business directory, resources, articles, and more related information.

PERIODICALS

Home Business Report
2625a Alliance Street
Abbotsford, British Columbia
Canada V2S 4G5
Web site: www.homebusinessreport.com/
E-mail: HBRCanada@aol.com

Profit *magazine* (print)
PROFIT Subscriber Services
8th Floor — 777 Bay St.
Toronto, ON
Canada M5W 1A7
(416) 596-5523
Web site: www.profitguide.com/
Business information and resources for Canadian entrepreneurs.

Glossary

Accounting period – Is a regular period of time, such as a quarter or year, for which a financial statement is produced for a business.

Accounts payable – The money owed by your business for goods and services you received.

Accounts receivable – The money owed you by customers for your good and services.

Accrual basis – The financial record keeping in which income is recorded when it is earned and expenses recorded when incurred.

Advertising – To inform people in your marketing community of the features and advantages of your service or product.

Amortization – The reduction of debt through installment payments.

Appreciation – An increase in the value of property.

Assets – All the items of value (tangible or intangible) owned by a person or corporation.

Audit – Is a formal review and confirmation of financial accounts and records.

Balance sheet – A financial description showing the assets, liabilities, and a business owner's net worth in a business as of a given date.

Bandwidth – The speed at which information is transferred over networks of the Internet.

Barter – The exchanging of goods or business services without the use of money.

Baud – The speed at which computer modems can transmit data. Baud speed is registered in BPS or bits per second.

Bid pricing – To estimate all the expenses in finishing a project, then adding your profit margin to arrive at the total cost to complete the project as specified in contract terms.

Boilerplate – Legal language, often labeled the "fine print," that states the details in a business contract or agreement.

Break-even point – The dollar amount your business must make so that your sales income equals your total costs. From this point, you can determine the prices you must charge for your product or services so that your business will make a profit.

Brokering – Marketing other people's talents or products and taking a fee. Examples: literary, sports, and talent agenting.

Browser – Software programs such as Netscape or Microsoft Internet Explorer that enable you to read and navigate the HTML Internet documents so you can "search" or "browse" for information.

Business interruption insurance – Insurance that covers a business's continuing expenses, such as taxes and payroll, as well as loss of net profit.

Business opportunity – A business venture sold by a company or entrepreneur who wishes to expand her company or sell her idea to others who want to start a business. A business opportunity usually is a "package" complete with manual, business forms, and sometimes the equipment. Customer support may or may not be included. Be sure to research any opportunity before you invest any money to make sure it is legitimate and not a scam. Ask for references.

Business plan – A written description and strategic plan that includes a definition of the business's products and/or services, financial strategies, organization, summation of overhead, startup and operating costs, potential markets, and the people involved in making the business operate and succeed.

C & F – A commercial designation that means the stated value of a shipment of goods; includes all costs and freight involved in shipping the goods to their destination.

Capital – The worth of a person's assets; or a business's net worth—the assets minus the liabilities.

Cash flow – The amount of money coming into your business from its sales, and the expenditure of money going out to pay your businesses expenses. *Projected cash flows* are calculated on a regular basis to ensure the business has an adequate amount of money coming in to meet its expenses and to show a profit after it pays those expenses.

Certified lender – These are banks certified by the SBA to participate in the SBA's guaranteed loan program. The banks agree to the SBA's conditions, and in return the SBA agrees to process any guaranteed loan application within three business days. SBA district offices can provide you with lists of certified banks in your area.

COD – Stands for collect (or cash) on delivery. It means payment must be made on goods when they are received or delivered.

Cold-calling – This is a form of contacting potential customers by calling (or visiting), unannounced, to inform them of your business products and services.

Collateral security – What a borrower gives to a lender to guarantee a loan. Examples are property, vehicles, equipment, securities, and other items of value.

Consulting – Working on a variety of projects simultaneously, often for different clients, and on separate premises from the client companies. Examples: project management and organizational consulting.

Consumables – Items used up or "consumed" when equipment operates, such as cartridges for photocopiers or printers.

Contingency fee – A person is paid only if she successfully completes the assigned job.

Contracting – Taking on work within an organization for a period of time as an independent contractor or subcontractor without receiving employee benefits. Examples: computer programming, editing, graphic design.

Corporation – The legal business structure that recognizes the owner(s) as a separate entity. There are several forms such as C-Corporations, S-Corporations, Nonprofit Corporations. (See also sole proprietorship, partnership, and LLC.)

Cost – The total of the fixed and variable expenses (costs to you) to manufacturer or offer your product or service.

Credit – The power or ability to obtain goods in exchange for a pledge to pay later.

Current liabilities – A business's debts that are due and payable within the next twelve months.

DBA – "Doing Business As," the fictitious name under which the business owner(s) will operate.

Debt financing – Borrowing money that is to be repaid over a period of time, usually with interest (short- or long-term).

Deficit – A business's net loss due to expenditures exceeding income, or the excess of liabilities over assets.

Demographics – Statistics that provide information about a group of people such as their ages, gender, income level, occupation, nationality, race, and education levels. The U.S. Department of Labor (www.dol.gov) and the U.S. Census Bureau (www.census.gov) are two of our federal government's largest provider of these statistics.

Depreciation – This is a deduction than can be written off the value of property (for example, office equipment; but not land because it is not expendable) over a period of time. Check with your accountant for the latest updates on home business tax deductions.

Direct costs – Costs that can be traced and designated directly to a specific product, such as the cost of wax in decorative candles.

Direct loans – Financial assistance provided through the lending of federal monies for a specified period of time, with a reasonable expectation of repayment. These loans may or may not require interest payments.

Direct marketing – Mailing of promotional materials, face-to-face selling, and other sales methods a business uses to let potential customers know about its goods and/or services it has for sale.

Distributor – A wholesaler who has purchased the rights to market one company's goods (usually not numerous companies' products as an independent sales representative would do) to customers within a given territory—though not always exclusive. You are in business for yourself and set your own hours.

Double-entry accounting – An accounting system in which the total of all left-side entries (*debits*) is balanced by an equal total of all right-side entries (*credits*). Credits or debits can be applied to any general ledger account, whether it is an expense, asset, a liability, income, or capital.

Download – Transferring files to your computer from another computer.

Due diligence – The concern that a reasonable person uses under the circumstances to avoid harm to other persons or their property.

Employer identification number (EIN) – A number assigned to a business from the IRS that is to be shown on all business tax returns, documents, and statements. Many sole proprietors and independent contractors use their social security numbers. Contact your local IRS office and consult with your accountant for more information.

Enterprise – Another term for a business or venture.

Equity financing – The money contributed to the firm by the owner(s) and investors.

Expense – Money spent for services or products.

FAQ – Stands for "frequently asked questions," which are often listed on Internet sites to help supply answers to common questions on a certain topic or subject.

Firewalls – A type of computer programming used for security so that network users can see through their own firewall into the Internet, but other Internet users cannot see through the firewall. Businesses who sell products or services over the Internet use firewalls to protect customers' private information, such as credit card numbers used for ordering.

Fiscal year – Any twelve-month calendar year used by a business or a government agency as an accounting period.

Fixed expenses – Expenses that generally do not change significantly from month to month (such as rent and taxes).

Flaming – Hate e-mails, often the result from unwanted e-mail solicitations *(spamming)* from a business owner over the Web.

Franchise – A business operated with a standardized format and recognized products and services. With a business contract, you pay the owner of the franchise (franchisor) for the right to sell the franchise's product or service within a certain area.

Franchisee – You, the licensee, is the person who pays a royalty and often a franchise fee for the right to sell and distribute the franchisor's products and use its trade name or trademark.

Franchisor – The owner of a franchise, also called the licensor, who sells his or her trade name and business system to franchisees.

Freelancer – A person who works independently and is paid fees for his or her services. They may work at home or at their customers' locations. Freelancers include writers, graphic designers, consultants, job trainers, desktop publishers, software developers, and other professionals.

Fulfillment – The operation of receiving orders and shipping and tracking goods sold through direct marketing.

General ledger – The primary records of a business's expenses, income, assets, and liabilities of a business.

General partnerships – Partners share equally in risks, rewards, and the rights of control in the business. Partnerships can be formal with written agreements or informal with no agreements. Only general partnerships, however, are generally eligible for bank loans.

Gross income – Usually pertains to a business's income before deductions. With your home office, gross income is your business's income minus the expenses that do not relate to your home use. Contact your accountant or local IRS office for "business use of your home" deductions.

Gross profit – The result of subtracting the cost of services/goods sold from sales.

Guarantor – Often referred to as the "cosigner," this is a person who agrees to pay a loan if the borrower cannot pay (defaults).

Home page – The page your Internet browser loads at startup and also the first Web site document that is shown when you visit a new Web site or follow a link.

HTML – Stands for Hypertext Markup Language, which is the standard format for creating documents and pages on the Internet, the World Wide Web.

Hyperlink – Often just shortened to "Link," this is a listing of one Web site's URL on another site's page, usually to provide related information, which a user can click on to move immediately, possibly to an entirely different Web site.

Income – Money you have received for your products or services. It can also refer to investment returns.

Income statement – The financial statement showing your business's profit or loss within a specified period of time.

Internet – A cooperatively run and globally distributed collection of computer networks that was started about twenty years ago as a government-funded project to set up communications in the event of a nationwide nuclear attack. The Internet has since been adopted by businesses, organizations, and individuals worldwide to promote commerce and exchange information. The Internet exchanges information via a common set of rules for exchanging date and is referred to as the "information super highway."

Internet service provider (ISP) – A company that provides access to the Internet.

JPEG – A Web graphics format used to display photographs and artwork on the Web (was developed by the Joint Photographic Experts Group).

Lead time – The amount of preparation time a business owner estimates it will take to implement a new product or service (research, market testing, and so on).

Liability – In relation to accounting, liability means a commitment to another party and the amounts to be paid to others.

Lien – The legal right to hold or sell property of another for purposes of getting payment for money owned.

LLC (Limited liability corporation) – A form of legal structure that limits the business owner's risk to her personal assets; costs less to form and maintain than corporations.

Line of credit – When a lender agrees to permit a borrower to draw a pre-specified amount on an as-needed basis from an account.

Liquid assets – Assets that can be readily changed into cash.

Liquidation – Selling a business's assets to pay off debts.

Market potential – The principles of determining market share and market potential are the same for all geographic areas. First, determine a customer profile (who) and the geographic size of the market (how many). This is the general market potential. Knowing the number and strength of your competitors (and then estimating the share of business you will take from them) will give you the market potential specific to your enterprise.

Net profit – The result obtained when expenses are subtracted from revenues.

One-person enterprise – Working on one's own, usually at home. Examples: computer repair and servicing, bookkeeping, and crafts.

Overhead – All of a business's nonlabor expenses needed to operate.

Partnering or work sharing – Obtaining a contract as an individual or small business and sharing a portion of the work with another individual or group in a one-time effort.

Partnership (general) – An alliance of two or more persons as co-owners of a business-for-profit.

Percentage fee – Payment is made to you based on your ability to make a sale, such as is the case with real estate agents or literary agents.

Personal financial history – A record of your borrowing and repayments, plus a listing of your personal assets and liabilities (extremely important to a lender when you are applying for a business loan).

Pixel – This is the smallest element of a display that can be assigned a color. The higher the number of pixels (from Picture and Element), the better the resolution of a picture taken with a digital camera or displayed on a computer screen.

Plug-in – A feature that basically can be added to a browser, enabling you to receive the multimedia features of certain Web pages.

Price – The selling price per unit customers pay for your product or service.

Price analysis – An breakdown of how much money you need to make per hour in order to cover your overhead and operating costs, your time involved, and your desired profit margin.

Principal – The remainder of what is owed on a loan, without the interest.

Profit and loss statements – A report of a business's financial operations for a specified period, usually a full year. The *bottom line* reveals the net profit or loss of your business.

Pro forma – This is a financial planning statement that projects a business's future performance.

Promotion – Includes everything you do to promote sales of your service or product.

Pyramid – Illegal business scams in which a few people at the top take money from many people at the bottom of the list, who generally lose their initial (and often substantial!) investment. Many pyramids are disguised and tout themselves as legitimate *MLM (multi-level marketing)* enterprises.

Receivables – The money your customers owe to your business.

Retainer – A payment made to a business expert or consultant in either one or regular payments to insure their availability if their expertise is needed.

"Sandwich Generation" – Age group of the population that is responsible for their older parents and relatives, as well as for their children and even grandchildren.

SASE – Abbreviation for "self-addressed, stamped (first-class) envelope." An *LSASE* means a "long (business-sized) self-addressed, stamped envelope." This is often used for a return reply in request of information or a query (often used by professional freelance writers).

Scam – An illegal business opportunity that typically promises quick profits. Many today offer lucrative work-from-home schemes. Check their references or with the Better Business Bureau, Federal Trade Commission, and The National Fraud Information Center.

Seasonality – Business buying patterns affected by weather seasons (businesses affected by the outdoors) and/or holidays (such as Christmas and Mother's Day).

Segmentation – How a business targets marketing efforts to the people or businesses most likely to buy its products or services.

Small business – A venture owned by one or several persons that produces and markets a product or service, usually operating from a building, though it can be home-based, and has employees. Examples would be retail stores, restaurants, dry cleaners, and other small establishments.

Small business incubator – An association of small businesses usually housed in one building to share building facilities, staff, and other business services that a small business could not afford on its own. A number of home businesses join incubators if their business needs to expand out of its home location.

SOHO – Acronym for "small office/home office" that generally stands for a small business operating out of a home or small office suite with one to five employees. Often these SOHO enterprises are consulting firms, professional practices, and other service-type of businesses.

Sole proprietorship – The simplest legal form of business ownership, in which a single owner has sole control and responsibility over her business. One's own name or under a fictitious name (DBA) can be used for the business. The owner is fully liable and personal assets are not protected from lawsuits.

Spam – Promoting or sending unwanted solicitations or materials to unknown users or to user groups on the Internet.

Spreadsheet – Numerical data table consisting of columns and rows related by formulae. Used by businesses for tracking customer profiles and other business data. Software for spreadsheets is often found in office suites.

Talent pooling – Forming a group of self-employed people with different talents to win a contract that no individual could handle on her own. Examples: film production and large publication projects.

Target market – Potential customers to whom you are directing your marketing activities.

Tax number – Also called sales tax number, which is given to a business by your state revenue department, enabling you to purchase goods and products wholesale without paying sales tax. You also need this number to go to wholesale shows and also exhibit your goods there. Contact your local state legislator's office for the address of your state government's office.

Telecommuter – An employee who works for a company at her own home one or more days a week. Using technology and communications equipment (telecommunications) to complete the assigned work is said to be telecommuting. The telecommuter usually meets periodically at the location of her employer for meetings and consultations.

Upload – Transmitting a file from your computer to another.

URL (uniform resource locator) – The address notation that points to a particular document or site on the World Wide Web.

Usenet – The system that disburses a multitude of newsgroups all over the Internet.

Variable costs – Costs that change as a result of the production output of your goods and/or services (shipping, materials, labor).

Venture capital – Financing invested in new or existing firms that exhibit the potential for extensive growth.

Way bill – The document sent along with shipped products that explains the shipment's costs and route.

Working capital – Money that is available for your business's daily operations.

World Wide Web – The Web is a collection of millions of computers on the Internet that contain information and multimedia (sound, graphics, animation, etc.) that has been put in a single format—called HTML (Hypertext Markup Language).

INDEX